Honorius

"Chris Doyle takes up an unenviable task in reviewing the life and reign of the much-despised emperor Honorius. His study presents a very good and much fairer evaluation of this controversial ruler, bringing him out from under the shadow of his general Stilicho and his sister Galla Placidia, and showing how he survived and preserved the western Roman Empire for nearly 30 years against long odds."

Richard Billows, *Columbia University, USA*

Honorius explores the personal life and tumultuous times of one of the last emperors of the Roman West. From his accession to the throne aged ten to his death at thirty-eight, Honorius' reign was blighted by a myriad of crises: military rebellions, political conspiracies, barbarian invasions, and sectarian controversies. The notorious sack of the city of Rome occurred on Honorius' watch, and much of the western empire was given over to anarchy and violence.

This book should interest undergraduates, research students, and professional scholars. Given the enduring appeal of the fall of Rome and the collapse of western Roman civilization, the wider public should also find much of interest.

Chris Doyle currently lectures in Ancient and Medieval History at the National University of Ireland, Galway, Republic of Ireland. He is interested in the art and religion of the late antique period, and has published on stylistic developments in late Roman coinage. He is presently working on two books: a study of rebellion and dissent during the Christianization of the Roman world; and a biography based on his grandmother's experiences as a frontline nurse with the British army in North Africa, Italy, and Greece during the Second World War.

Roman Imperial Biographies

For more information on this series, please visit: www.routledge.com/classicalstudies/series/SE0265

Honorius

The Fight for the Roman West
AD 395–423

Chris Doyle

Routledge
Taylor & Francis Group

LONDON AND NEW YORK

First published 2019
by Routledge
2 Park Square, Milton Park, Abingdon, Oxon OX14 4RN

and by Routledge
711 Third Avenue, New York, NY 10017

Routledge is an imprint of the Taylor & Francis Group, an informa business

British Library Cataloguing-in-Publication Data
A catalogue record for this book is available from the British Library

Library of Congress Cataloging-in-Publication Data
A catalog record for this book has been requested

ISBN: 978-1-138-19088-7 (hbk)
ISBN: 978-1-315-64079-2 (ebk)

Typeset in Times New Roman
by Out of House Publishing

MIX
Paper from
responsible sources
FSC   FSC® C013985
www.fsc.org

Printed in the United Kingdom
by Henry Ling Limited

In memory of my grandparents
Chris and May

"Do you really believe," he said, "that this imperial robe has been put on me with my approval? Do you think that if it were possible for me to run away I would refuse to escape? Of course not! They persuaded me to take this course in the first place, and now I am in their power, hemmed in on all sides."

Michael Psellus, Chronographia

Contents

Illustrations

Figures

(All coin images are courtesy of the *Classical Numismatics Group, Inc.* www.cngcoins.com)

Maps

Acknowledgements

An off-the-cuff conversation with Richard Burgess at Ottawa in late 2013 sowed the seed for this book. At the time, I was researching rebellion and propaganda of the Honorian era for my doctoral thesis. It had struck me that Honorius was truly the great survivor of his day. How was this possible if he was, as so many have claimed, such a terrible ruler? After all, he was the western Augustus for thirty years, during which time many powerful individuals tried to manipulate him for their own enrichment. All these people came and went, yet Honorius remained. I reasoned that there had to have been more substance to Honorius than is usually credited. Furthermore, much of the modern opinion of this late Roman emperor is formed by a modern cultural narrative, more so than by a common ancient consensus. In the meantime, Meaghan McEvoy's excellent study of late Roman child-emperors with a section on Honorius came out. It inspired me to follow his story further to see where it might lead. What follows, therefore, is my interpretation of one of the Rome's least admired rulers.

A great many people have helped me in different ways along the way, but any errors in this book are entirely mine. As Oliver Goldsmith's preface to *The Vicar of Wakefield* declares, 'there are a hundred faults in this Thing, and a hundred things might be said to prove them beauties. But it is needless. A book may be amusing with numerous errors, or it may be very dull without a single absurdity.'

So, without further ado, and in no particular order, I offer warm thanks to the following people for their support and advice. My editors at Routledge, Elizabeth Risch and Amy Davis-Poynter, for their exceptional patience throughout this project, and Nicola Howcroft and Kim Richardson at Out of House Publishing.

Mark Humphries (Swansea) and David Gwynn (Royal Holloway) for their early reviews and thoughtful response to my initial proposal. My academic colleagues in the late antique and early medieval research community: Enrico Dal Lago for our many chats about Roman history and modern Italian cinema; Dáibhí O Cróinín, Michael Clarke, Jacopo Bisagni, Pádraic Moran, Geraldine Curtin, Hans Lejdegård, Catherine Ware, John F. Drinkwater, Richard W. Burgess, Janette Peters, Bente Kiilerich, Michael Kulikowski, Antti

Lampinen, Charles Odahl, Victoria Clarke, Adrastos Omissi, Edwin Hustwit, Steve Joyce, Theresa Urbainczyk, Gavin Kelly, and Anique Hamelink. Special thanks to Joanna Story for sharing her research on what lies beneath Saint Peter's Basilica, and for her suggestion to use the Maria burial artefact as a frontispiece image.

For their help with material resources: Melanie Neil at the Chrysler Museum; Loredana Faletti at the Catedral de Aosta; Olga Novoseltseva at the State Hermitage Museum, Saint Petersburg; La Segreteria, Fondazione Gaiani, Museo e Tesoro del Duomo di Monza; Barbara Van Kets and Frederique Kartouby at the Louvre Museum, Paris; and much appreciation is extended to the Classical Numismatic Group for letting me use their wonderful coin images.

My friends Miles Kennedy, philosopher and teacher, for our many discussions about money, mutiny, and murder; and Peter Casby, artist extraordinaire and archaeologist, for our coffee chats over the nature of political rule and sacred trees! Eamonn O' Donoghue, that ever inspirational restorer of the past; Jane Stark's keen artist's eye; Andrew Sargent, Tudor historian, for his editing advice on Gildo; and to Patrick, Shannon, and Lizzy Belmont for their encouragement, pasta-making sessions, and Japanese whisky!

My deepest gratitude is for my family, Therese, Luke, and Seán, who have had to share their home with a long dead Roman emperor for what must have often seemed an eternity. Thank you for your love and laughter.

Abbreviations

Journals and reference works

ABzF	*Acta Byzantina Fennica*
AC	*L'Antiquité Classique*
ACO	*Acta Conciliorum Oecumenicorum*
AÉ	*Année Épigraphique*
AEspA	*Archivo Español de Arqueología*
AfrRom	*L'Africa Romana*
AHR	*American Historical Review*
AJA	*American Journal of Archaeology*
AJP	*American Journal of Philology*
ANF	Ante-Nicene Fathers
ANS	*American Numismatic Society*
AnTard	*Antiquité Tardive*, Revue Internationale d'Histoire et d'Archéologie, IVe–VIIIe siècle
Art Bull	*The Art Bulletin*
BAR-IS	*British Archaeological Reports, International Series*
BICS	*Bulletin of the Institute of Classical Studies of the University of London*
CA	*Classical Antiquity*
CAH	*The Cambridge Ancient* History (13): *The Late Empire, AD337–425*. Edited by A. Cameron and P. Garnsey
CCSL	*Corpus Christianorum Series Latina*
CJ	*The Classical Journal*
CLRE	*Consuls of the Later Roman Empire*. 1987. Edited by R. S. Bagnall, A. Cameron, S. R. Schwartz, and K. A. Worp
CPh	*Classical Philology*
CPL	*Clavis Patrum Latinorum*. 1995. Edited by E. Dekkers
CQ	*Classical Quarterly*
CSEL	*Corpus Scriptorum Ecclesiasticorum Latinorum*

DIR	*De Imperatoribus Romanis, An Online Encyclopedia of Roman Emperors*
DJN	*Deutsches Jahrbuch für Numismatik*
DOCat	*Dumbarton Oaks Collection*
DOP	*Dumbarton Oaks Papers*
EHR	*English Historical Review*
FCHLRE	*Fragmentary Classicising Historians of the Later Roman Empire.* 2 volumes. 1981–3. Edited and translated by Roger C. Blockley
GRBS	*Greek, Roman, and Byzantine Studies*
H&T	*History and Theory*
Hist.	*Historia, Zeitschrift für Alte Geschichte*
HSPh	*Harvard Studies in Classical Philology*
ICS	*Illinois Classical Studies*
IHR	*International History Review*
JbAC	*Jahrbuch für Antike und Christentum*
JbPrKs	*Jahrbuch der Königlich Preussischen Kunstsammlungen*
JDAI	*Jahrbuch des Deutschen Archäologischen Instituts*
JECH	*Journal of Early Christian History*
JECS	*Journal of Early Christian Studies*
JIH	*Journal of Interdisciplinary History*
JLA	*Journal of Late Antiquity*
JLS	*Journal of Libyan Studies*
JRS	*Journal of Roman Studies*
JThS	*Journal of Theological Studies*
LAA	*Late Antique Archaeology*
LCL	*Loeb Classical Library*
LRE	*The Later Roman Empire.* 2 volumes
MAAR	*Memoirs of the American Academy in Rome*
MAN	*Journal of the Royal Anthropological Institute of Great Britain and Ireland*
MEFRA	*Mélanges de l'Ecole Française de Rome: Antiquité*
MGH (AA)	*Monumenta Germaniae Historica: Auctores Antiquissimi*
MGH (SRM)	*Monumenta Germaniae Historica: Scriptores Rerum Merovingicarum*
NC	*Numismatic Chronicle*
NPNF	Nicene and Post-Nicene Fathers
PBSR	*Papers of the British School at Rome*
PG	*Patrologia Graeca/Collected writings of the Church Fathers in Greek*
Philologus	*Philologus. Zeitschrift für antike Literatur und ihre Rezeption*

PL	*Patrologia Latina*/Collected writings of the Early Church Fathers in Latin
PLRE	*The Prosopography of the Later Roman Empire.* 3 volumes. Edited by A. H. M. Jones, J. R. Martindale, and J. Morris
PO	*Patrologia Orientalis*/*Collected writings of the Early Church Fathers from the East*
RN	*Revue Numismatique*
SNR	*Schweizerische Numismatische Rundschau*/*Revue Suisse de Numismatique*
TAPA	*Transactions of the American Philological Association*
TM	*Travaux et Mémoires*
TTH	*Translated Texts for Historians*
VC	*Vigiliae Christianae*
ZPE	*Zeitschrift für Papyrologie und Epigraphik*

Primary literary sources

Agnellus	Agnellus of Ravenna, *The Book of Pontiffs of the Church of Ravenna*
AM	Theophanes the Confessor, *Chronicle*/*Chronographia*
Amb.	Ambrose of Milan
De ob. Theod.	*Sancti Ambrosii oratio de obitu Theodosii*/*Funeral oration for Theodosius*
Epp.	*Epistulae et acta*/*Letters and Acts*
Amm. Marc. *Hist.*	Ammianus Marcellinus, *Historia Rerum Gestarum*/*Historical Events*
Ann. Rav.	*Annals of Ravenna*
Appian, *BC*	Appian, *Bella civilia*/*The Civil Wars*
Apoph. Patr.	*Apophthegmata Patrum*/*Sayings of the Desert Fathers*
Aug.	Augustine of Hippo
C. lit. Pet.	*Contra litteras Petiliani*/*Letters against Petilian*
De civ. Dei.	*De civitate Dei*/*On the City of God*
Epp.	*Epistulae*
Contra. ep. Parm.	*Contra epistulam Parmeniani*/*Against the letters of Parmenian*
Aus.	Ausonius
De Sp. S.	Basil of Caesarea, *De Spiritu Sancto*/*On the Holy Spirit*
Chron. Gall. 452	*Chronica Gallica*
Chron. Marcell.	Chronicle of Marcellinus
Chron. Min.	*Chronica Minora*
Chron. Pasch.	*Chronicon Paschale*

Chrys.	John Chrysostom
Ad vid. iun.	*Ad viduam iuniorem/Letter to a Young Widow*
Hom de. Stat	*Homilies on the Statues*
Cl.	*Claudius Claudianus*
Prob.	*Panegyricus dictus Probino et Olybrio consulibus*
Ruf.	*In Rufinum* I, II
Gild.	*De bello Gildonico* I
Eutr.	*In Eutropium* I, II
Fesc.	*Fescennina de nuptiis Honorii Augusti* I–IV
Nupt.	*Epithalamium de nuptiis Honorii Augusti*
III Cons.	*Panegyricus de tertio consulatu Honorii Augusti*
IV Cons.	*Panegyricus de quarto consulatu Honorii Augusti*
Theod.	*Panegyricus dictus Manlio Theodoro consuli*
Stil.	*De consulatu Stiliconis* I, II, III
VI Cons.	*Panegyricus de sexto consulatu Honorii Augusti*
Get.	*De bello Pollentino sive Getico*
c. m.	*carmina minora* I–LIV
Cons. Const.	*Consularia Constantinopolitana*
Cons. Ital.	*Consularia Italica*
De prov. Dei.	*Carmen de providentia Dei*
Elvira. Can.	*Canons of Elvira*
Ep. Sev.	*Epistula Severi*
Epit. de Caes.	*Epitome de Caesaribus*
Eunap. *fr.*	Eunapius of Sardis, *Historiarum fragmenta/History after Dexippus*
Gen.	Gennadius, *Lives of Illustrious Men*
Gesta Coll. Carth.	*Gesta Collationis Carthaginensis habitae inter Catholicos et Donatistas anno 411/Acts of the Council of Carthage, 411*
Greg. Nyss.	Gregory of Nyssa
In Flacc.	*Oratio funebris in Flaccillam imperatricem/Funeral Oration for the Empress Flaccilla*
In Pulch.	*Oratio consolatoria in Pulcheriam/Consolation for Pulcheria*
HR	Paulus Diaconus, *Historia Romana*
Hyd. *Chron.*	Hydatius, *Chronicle*
Jer. *Ep.*	Jerome, *Epistulae*
Jord. *Rom. Get.*	Jordanes, *Romana et Getica*
Lactant. *De mort. pers.*	Lactantius, *De mortibus persecutorum, On the Deaths of the Persecutors*
Lib.	Libanius, *Selected Works*
LP	*Liber Pontificalis*
Lydus. *De Mag.*	John the Lydian, *De Magistratibus Republicae Romanae Libri Tres*
MS	Chronicle of Michael the Syrian

Not. dig. [*occ.*] [*or.*]	*Notitia dignitatum in partibus Orientis et Occidentis*/List of offices for the Eastern and Western parts
Olymp. *fr.*	Olympiodorus of Thebes, *Historiarum fragmenta*
Orientius. *Comm.*	Orientius. *Commonitorium* I, II
Oros.	Orosius, *Historia adversum paganos libri VII*/Seven books of history against the Pagans
Pall. *Dial.*	Palladius, *Dialogue on the Life of St. John Chrysostom*
Pan. Lat.	*Panegyrici Latini*/Latin Panegyrics
Paulin. *Amb.*	Paulinus of Milan, *Sancti Ambrosii Mediolanensis episcopi*/Life of St. Ambrose, Bishop of Milan
Philost. *HE.*	Philostorgius, *Historia Ecclesiastica*
Plut. *Alex.*	Plutarch, *Life of Alexander*
Proc. *BV.*	Procopius, *De bello Vandalico*/Vandalic War
Prosp. Tiro.	*Prosperi Tironis epitoma chronicon*/Chronicle of Prosper Tiro
Prudent.	Prudentius
Apoth.	*Apotheosis*
Contra Symm.	*Contra Symmachum* I, II
Ruf. *HE*	Rufinus, *Historia Ecclesiastica*
Rut. Nam.	Rutilius Namatianus, *De reditu suo*/On his return
Sev. Ant.	Severus of Antioch, *Hymns*
SHA	Scriptores Historiae Augustae
Aur.	*Aurelian*
Dom.	*Domitian*
Mar. Ant.	*Marcus Antonius*
Sid. Ap.	Sidonius Apollinaris
Soc. *HE*	Socrates Scholasticus, *Historia Ecclesiastica*
Soz. *HE*	Sozomen, *Historia Ecclesiastica*
Sym.	Quintus Aurelius Symmachus
Syn. *De Reg.*	Synesius, *De Regno*/On Kingship
Tac. *Agr.*	Tacitus, *Agricola*
Them. *Or.*	Themistius, *Orationes*
Theod. *HE*	Theodoret of Cyrus, *Historia Ecclesiastica*
Veg.	Vegetius, *Epitoma rei militaris*/On Military Matters
Zon.	Zonaras, *Epitome Historiarum*
Zos.	Zosimus, *New History*

Epigraphic sources

CIG	*Corpus Inscriptionum Graecarum*
CIL	*Corpus Inscriptionum Latinarum*
ICUR	*Inscriptiones Christianae Urbis Romae*
IEph	*Inscriptiones Ephesi*

IG	*Inscriptiones Graecae*
ILAfr.	*Inscriptions Latines d'Afrique*
ILS	*Inscriptiones Latinae Selectae*
LSA	*Last Statues of Antiquity*

Legal sources

Cod. Iust.	*Codex Iustinianus/Code of Justinian*
Dig.	*Digesta/Digest*
Inst.	*Institutiones*
Nov.	*Novellae/Novels*
CTh.	*Codex Theodosianus/The Theodosian Code*
Nov. Theod.	*Novellae Theodosianae*
Sirm.	*Constitutiones Sirmondianae/Sirmondian Constitutions*

Numismatic sources

Bendall	Bendall, Simon. *Byzantine Weights*
CNG	*Classical Numismatic Group, Inc.*
Cohen	Cohen, Henry. *Description historique des monnaies frappées sous l'Empire romain*
DOC	*Dumbarton Oaks Collection*
LRBC	*Late Roman Bronze Coinage*
MFA	*Museum of Fine Arts, Boston, Massachusetts*
PAS	*Portable Antiquities Scheme*
Reinhart, *Münzen*	Reinhart, Wilhelm. *Die Münzen des tolosanischen Reiches der Westgoten*
RIC	*Roman Imperial Coinage.* 10 volumes
RNS	*Royal Numismatic Society of London*
RSC	*Roman Silver Coins.* 5 volumes

Chronology

Maps

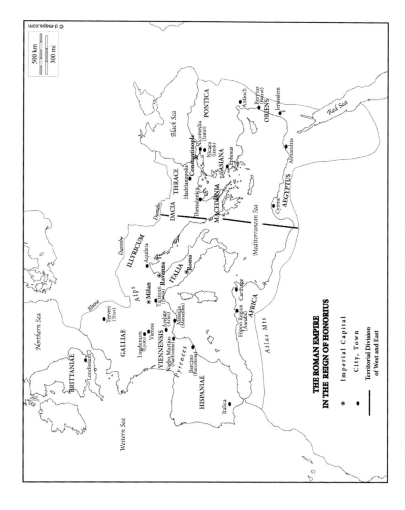

Map 1. The Roman Empire in the Reign of Honorius

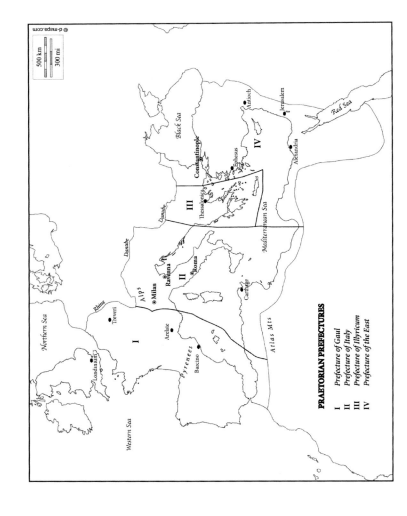

500 km

300 mi

PRAETORIAN PREFECTURES

I   *Prefecture of Gaul*
II   *Prefecture of Italy*
III   *Prefecture of Illyricum*
IV   *Prefecture of the East*

Map 2. Praetorian Prefectures

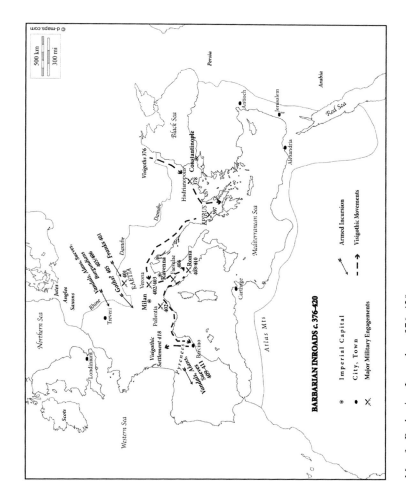

500 km
300 mi

Northern Sea

Jutes

Angles
Saxons

Treveri

Rhine

Vandals, Alans, Sueves
405/406

Goths? 405 *Franks 401*

401

RAETIA

Danube

Milan

Verona

402/403

Ravenna

Faesulae
406

Pollentia

402

Barcino

Visigothic
Settlement 418

Pyrenees

Vandals, Alans,
Sueves
409-411

Alps

Rome
408-410

Carthage

Atlas Mts

Western Sea

Londinium

Scots

Danube

Visigoths 376

Hadrianopolis
378

Constantinople

EPIRUS
397

Black Sea

Mediterranean Sea

Antioch

Jerusalem

Alexandria

Red Sea

Persia

Arabia

BARBARIAN INROADS c. 376–420

⊛ Imperial Capital

● City, Town

✕ Major Military Engagements

→ Armed Incursion

--→ Visigothic Movements

Map 3. Barbarian Inroads *c.* 376–420

1 Opinion and source

> Rumor is of all pests the swiftest ... she begins as a small and timorous crea-
> ture, but then she grows till she towers into the air ...
>
> Virgil, *Aeneid* 4.173–5

Modern opinion

Ever since the English historian Edward Gibbon wrote off Honorius
Augustus as an 'unworthy' occupant of the imperial throne, subsequent
generations of scholars have tended to pass over the emperor either in silence
or with a cold eye (Gibbon 1781, 466, 510). Of course, earlier scholars had
written on Honorius, among them the seventeenth-century French historian
Jean-Sebastien Tillemont, whose *Histoire des empereurs* Gibbon borrowed
much from.

> Seldom do those who conduct business under a young Prince take the
> trouble to prepare him for command, because few prefer their duty and
> their honor to the principles of ambition. Woe in many ways to states that
> have children for Princes
>
> (Tillemont 1732, 211)

Tillemont was one of a long line of French scholars, thinkers, and artists –
from the seventeenth to the nineteenth centuries – for whom the devoutly
Catholic emperor Honorius was frequently a target for ridicule. The great
Enlightenment figure Voltaire, whose disdain for the Church's influence on
state matters strongly influenced his personal view of history, heaped scorn
upon Honorius' religiosity. In the Revolutionary Age, French historians
saw in Honorius all that was wrong with their own monarchial system.
Following on from the end of the ancien régime, amid the nationalist fervor
of Republican France, Honorius was recast as an erstwhile foreign oppressor
of the Gallic people (Blasen 2012). By the end of the nineteenth century,
school textbooks like Victor Duruy's *Histoire du Moyen Age* (1861) reinforced
the idea of a decadent Honorius nonchalantly presiding over the destruction

of the Western Roman Empire. In England, Honorius' reputation fared just as badly. Wilkie Collins's popular historical novel *Antonina, or The Fall of Rome* featured a prematurely aged Honorius lost in a dreamlike state; 'an instrument fitted for the uses of every ambitious villain who could succeed in gaining his ear.' In short, an 'imperial trifler' (Collins 1850, 12).

Honorius on canvas

Artists have played their part in perpetuating the image of Honorius as a weak emperor, unsuited for rule. An oil painting by the French artist Jean-Paul Laurens (1838–1921), *Le Bas-Empire, Honorius* (Figure 1.1), garnered significant attention during its exhibition at the 1880 Salon in Paris's Académie des Beaux-Arts. Laurens's realistic style was already well-received both in France and abroad. A proud believer in the principles of the Third French Republic, Laurens was a professed anti-ecclesiastic, with a deep disdain for hereditary monarchial rule. Many of his paintings have a historical focus, and reflect his secular and political views.

　　Le Bas-Empire, Honorius was negatively received during its premier at the 1880 Salon, though not for its artistic quality. One critic dismissed the painting's subject as a 'silly idiot' with the most 'droopy, stupid expression.' I do not agree. If anything, Laurens's Honorius is a study in vulnerability, something which contemporary reviewers perhaps overlooked or ignored. *Le Bas-Empire, Honorius* depicts a child in an adult role; a boy whose dangling feet are unable to reach the base of his large throne. It is a scene where the symbols of state – a *parazonium* (ceremonial sword), *Victoriola* (a globe surmounted by the goddess Victory) – are disproportionate in size to the emperor's small figure. The painting suggests the overbearing responsibility of governance on such a young sovereign. As for the critique of his painting at the Salon, Laurens might well have been personally affronted – his own son, Paul Albert, was the life model for Honorius. Criticism of Laurens's *Le Bas-Empire, Honorius* did not end there, however. In 1986, just over a hundred years after its premiere, the Parrish Art Museum in Southampton, New York held an exhibition of nineteenth-century paintings from the Parisian salons entitled *In Support of Liberty*. The late John Russell, then the New York Times's senior art critic, reviewed the Parrish exhibition. Russell's imagination ran wild, though how he drew the following conclusions is anyone's guess.

> As for the evocation of the boy-emperor Honorius, it is the epitome of the Roman Empire in decline. Laurens in his historical paintings never stinted on voluptuous detail, and we realize at once that this is a boy-monster, as well as a boy-emperor. Where evil inclinations are concerned, this Honorius ranks level with Oscar Wilde's *Salome*.
>
> (Russell 1986)

Another artist, the English painter John William Waterhouse (1849–1917), made Honorius his compositional focus in *The Favorites of the Emperor*

Figure 1.1 Le Bas-Empire, Honorius. Oil on canvas by Jean-Paul Laurens, 1880. 153.7
    × 108 cm.

Honorius. Waterhouse's art was generally historically themed, but this particular painting was directly influenced by Laurens's *Le Bas-Empire*, *Honorius*, and also by Wilkie Collins's novel *Antonina* (Hobson 1980). As it happened, Waterhouse illustrated Collins's book, which included an early sketch of his later Honorius painting. First exhibited in 1883, *The Favorites of the Emperor Honorius* depicts a lackluster young emperor, secluded from the outside world behind heavy drapes, seated upon his throne, feeding grain to fowl, while stooped courtiers look on. Whether the artist intended to or not, *The Favorites of the Emperor Honorius* conveys a quiet melancholy that evokes the viewer's pathos for the emperor's personal situation.

The celluloid Honorius

Honorius has appeared intermittently in both cinema and television. One such outing was *La Vendetta dei Barbari*, or *The Revenge of the Barbarians*, a semi-historical film by the Italian director Giuseppe Vari (1960). The film was one of a series of *pepla* (sword and sandal) films, which were popular in Italian cinema from the late 1950s to the mid-1960s. The Honorius of *La Vendetta* was played by Mario Scaccia, a well-known theatrical actor of his day. Scaccia's Honorius is a capricious individual whose poetry recitation and lyre-playing are very reminiscent of Peter Ustinov's famous turn as Nero in *Quo Vadis* (1951). Entertaining as *La Vendetta* is, the film's portrayal of Honorius adds another unfavorable element to the longstanding, unsympathetic tradition. Interestingly, however, the central villain of the film is not the emperor, but his sister (Galla) Placidia, played with gusto by Daniela Rocca. A more recent screen version of the Honorius story is the BBC docudrama *Rome: Rise and Fall of an Empire* (2006). In this adaptation, Honorius is a pathetic, one-dimensional caricature, with a singularly bad hairstyle.

The labels of dismissal

Since Gibbon's day, the corpus of terms which historians have used to define and dismiss Honorius as an embarrassment to the annals of imperial Rome has grown considerably. Indeed, most of these terms would be rightly deemed inappropriate and insensitive by present standards. In effect, what has happened to Honorius is an academic form of *damnatio memoriae* (memory condemnation) – a Roman custom reserved for enemies of the state. Thus, Honorius has been obliterated from any meaningful place in history because he was – according to modern interpretations – 'imbecilic,' 'stupid,' 'slow,' 'dim-witted,' 'retarded,' 'dull,' 'weak,' 'fearful,' 'sluggish,' 'insignificant,' 'pusillanimous,' 'inglorious,' 'docile,' 'pliable,' 'soft,' 'gentle,' 'treacherous,' 'vacillating,' 'simple,' or 'sleepy'. Not the most inspiring words for the opening pages of a book about Honorius, perhaps, but I draw attention to them nevertheless. Such simplistic terms are not useful if we want to understand the life of one of Rome's least well-known emperors; a man whose reign coincided with one of the most crucial periods in all Roman history.

Honorius is generally referred to as one of Rome's worst rulers, but there were plenty of so-called 'bad' emperors; and they have received far more literary attention over the centuries than Honorius. Generations of readers have obtained much entertainment from the infamous stories about Caligula, Nero, Domitian, Commodus, and Elagabalus, for example. Why do they receive all the attention? Their appeal lies in their excesses, their licentious lives, murderous pursuits, and their often dramatic last moments. This is understandable: people tend to prefer a good story – the bloodier and seedier the better. Perhaps if Honorius had been more like Nero and less pious – as ecclesiastic primary sources claimed – he would have attracted more cinematic attention than he has to date.

The blame game

So, why is Honorius such an apparently universal figure of scorn? It is precisely because it was on his watch that the Roman West was torn apart by foreign invasion and civil war. The western empire lost huge swathes of territory, and suffered the ignominy of the eternal city itself being sacked by barbarians – people whom the Romans considered inferior, uncivilized savages. However, all the blame should not be placed solely on Honorius. Nor was it at the time. Any negative reflection regarding Honorius came directly from pagan writers who tended to criticize most of Rome's Christian emperors. Stewart Irvin Oost once remarked that 'a characteristic feature of the history of the fifth century is the habit of making some individual responsible for the successive disasters which befell the Roman Empire' (Oost 1968, 75–6). Oost's words are as pertinent now as they were then. Enter the name Honorius in a basic internet search, and the results will invariably squarely lay the blame for Rome's destruction at his feet. Honorius is the perfect whipping boy for historical critique. We do the same scapegoating of our own modern leaders. Think of how much time is given over to debating which particular individual is personally culpable for the ills of a society – a plainly ridiculous and counterproductive pastime.

It is necessary to insert a caveat here. I am not suggesting that it was solely Honorius who guided the state through dark times. But, when all seemed lost, when the Roman West was engulfed in a bloody storm, the imperial center did hold fast. Diminished though Honorius' government undoubtedly was, from a relentless series of crises, it still managed to prevail. Honorius was not a field commander like his father, Theodosius I, though he could have become one, had not his father's premature death in 395 left him extremely unready, and had his so-called protector, Stilicho, really intended him to rule independently. Theodosius had already begun training his youngest son in the arts of war and governance. Unfortunately, Honorius has been measured against the imposing achievements of his father, even though most of the crises Honorius endured were the result of his father's policies. It proved impossible to escape such a legacy. In his tragedy *L'Illustre Olympie ou le Saint Alexis* (1645), the French playwright Desfontaines reminds us of Honorius' struggle to stand on his own merit; 'Je suis Honorius, non Theodose'; 'I am Honorius and not Theodosius' (1.1).

Deconstructing Honorius

The purpose of this book is to trace Honorius' maturing from childhood to manhood; exploring the story of an orphaned boy who grew up while performing the duties of the loneliest job that there could possibly be in the Roman Empire. It examines the life – and by extension the times – of a boy at the helm of vast power, adrift in a dangerous environment without the guidance of his father, or his brother Arcadius, far removed in Constantinople. What must it have been like for Honorius to constantly suspect the true intentions of those closest to him, aware that others plotted to overthrow and kill him? Did he ever really trust anyone at his own court? How did such experiences affect him over time? Did he learn from those experiences in a constructive way, or did he simply retreat into seclusion as traditional opinion contends?

With his father gone, the young Honorius had no choice but to assume full imperial office. If he had not done so, he would likely have been assassinated – the typical fate for many children elevated to the throne. Honorius may not have been the first Roman child emperor, but he was the first such ruler to survive into adulthood. From Honorius' reign onward, child emperors became more prevalent, though these were largely figureheads who rarely – if ever – went on military campaigns. Common though it was, the late Roman phenomenon of child emperor rule has been neglected by scholarship. A recent study by Meaghan McEvoy, *Child Emperor Rule in the Late Roman West, AD 367–455*, has stimulated significant interest in the subject, however, and has a full section dedicated to the Honorian period (2013, 135–220).

After Theodosius' death, Honorius' development was stymied, chiefly by Stilicho, his father's trusted *magister militum* (commander of the army), along with Serena, Stilicho's wife and Honorius' cousin. Stilicho is supposed to have claimed guardianship over the ten-year-old Honorius immediately following Theodosius' death. Serena effectively assumed a mother's role for Honorius. In the beginning, Stilicho might have felt that he was acting in his young charge's best interests, but Stilicho continued to exert influence over Honorius well into manhood. Whether this was for Stilicho's own personal gain or other reasons is a matter of debate (Matthews 1975, 253–83; O' Flynn 1983; MacGeorge 2002, 7–8). Claudian, Honorius' propagandist, was keen to stress Stilicho's guiding hand in the young emperor's early life. Ultimately, though, Honorius might well have grown to resent his surrogate parents, especially when we read how Stilicho was more a father to the young emperor than Theodosius ever was.

Now the purple lays aside its pride and disdains not to have judgment passed upon itself. Such were the principles of rule taught by Stilicho to his son-in-law, Honorius; thus he guided his youth with the reins of prudence, and with precepts such as these directed his tender years, a truer father to the emperor than Theodosius, his stay in war, his adviser in peace. Thanks to him dishonor is banished and our age blossoms with Rome's ancient virtues; thanks to him power, long degraded and all but transferred, no longer, forgetful of itself, is exiled in lands of servitude but, returned to its rightful home, restores to Italy its victorious destiny, enjoys the promised auspices of its foundation and gives back its scattered limbs to the head of the empire.

(Cl. *Stil*. III.114–29)

Honorius was no shrewd politician like Augustus; he had no personal military accomplishments to match Trajan; nor was he a philosopher king in the manner of Marcus Aurelius. Yet, neither was Honorius the 'boy-monster' of popular lore. In fact, Honorius, remained in power as long as many of his forerunners – actually longer than most. How was this achieved? Did Honorius feign docility, as Claudius (41–54) once did in order to escape the notice of his maniacal nephew, the emperor Caligula? How much credit can be assigned to Honorius himself for his longevity? We know that he relied heavily on others for much of his reign, but then again, nearly all of Rome's emperors had assistance in administering the state. Practical emperors depended upon advisors to provide them with good counsel. It was a foolish – usually short-lived – emperor who assumed he did not need help to run the empire. The central difference between Honorius and his predecessors was he was a ten-year-old child when he ascended the throne in 395 – most of them were not. Ruling under Stilicho's supervision made sense therefore. An emperor so young needed a guardian, or 'regent' (Cameron 1970, 38–40). But, for the entirety of his reign? Surely not.

Ancient views

Notwithstanding the largely negative and unsympathetic opinions held by many modern historians towards Honorius, there is actually very little criticism of him among ancient, contemporary, sources. It was a fearless – or foolish – individual who insulted a reigning emperor, as Eunapius indicates.

If anyone else has the courage to write down these things, I salute him for his bravery and judge him a brave man for his endurance. It was proper that those who both made their accounts as accurate as they could, considering the times when and the persons about whom they were writing, and proposed to write in safety should incline their narrative to favor and disfavor.

(Eunap. *fr*. 66.1)

As mentioned, the dissenting voices are by and large pagan – specifically Eunapius, Olympiodorus – both contemporaneous with Honorius' reign – and Zosimus, whose *New History* was composed decades after Honorius' death. Yet, their criticism of Honorius, and his brother Arcadius for that matter, pale in comparison to those voiced in the modern era.

Actually, there is a lot of favorable primary source material for Honorius – panegyric, imperial laws, inscriptions, coinage, art, sculpture, and so on. Understandably so, as these media forms were the state's official voice. Ecclesiastic authors were as equally upbeat as the state propaganda in their praise of Honorius; it was his religious piety that did it for them. Extrapolating some form of truth from the Christian idealization of Honorius is therefore problematic, but occasionally there were some clerics that questioned the behavior of their emperors. In his *De regno* (*On Kingship*), Synesius, the bishop of Cyrene (modern Shahhat, Libya), admonished Honorius' brother Arcadius. Synesius warned Arcadius against the vice of extravagance, and of becoming isolated from his subjects. *De regno* also attacked the chicanery of the imperial court. Despite Synesius' castigation of the government, he was not, however, insane. *De regno* was a rhetorical exercise. It was never destined to be heard, especially not by the emperor (Heather 1988; cf. Kaldellis 2017; Barnes 1986). For the most part, late fourth- and early fifth-century churchmen were complimentary about their sovereigns, in particular those who patronized the Church.

The keeper of chickens

It took nearly a century after Honorius' death for a truly negative literary tradition about him to emerge. Around the mid-sixth century, the eastern Roman historian Procopius of Caesarea implies that Honorius might not have been well-regarded in Rome, with an anecdote about the emperor's pre-occupation with his pet chickens instead of that of his citizens. Bearing in mind that Procopius wrote his histories from the long reach of time, where did he obtain stories like this from? Procopius traveled through Italy in the 530s when he served on the high command of the eastern emperor Justinian I during his military campaigns there against the Ostrogoths. The historian probably sought out interesting material to put in his histories, which was not extant in eastern sources or official records. In the Italy of Procopius' day, the story of Honorius and the chickens was very likely a well-known urban myth. Here, then, we find the inspiration for Gibbons, Waterhouse, and company – Procopius has much to answer for! As is common with unconfirmed urban myths, the more they are repeated, the more accepted they become. A recent example of a well-debunked urban myth concerns a story which circulated during the 2016 American presidential campaign, and which has since resurfaced in the public eye (Fisk 2017). The story concerned General John J. Pershing's alleged mistreatment of Muslim prisoners during the Philippine-American War of 1899–1902. Though there is no proof of Pershing's actions, some continue to disseminate it as fact. Should we accept similarly unfounded statements from the ancients?

> At that time, they say that the emperor Honorius in Ravenna received the message from one of the eunuchs, evidently a keeper of the poultry, that Rome had perished. And he cried out and said, "And yet it has just eaten from my hands!" For he had a very large cock, Roma by name; and the eunuch comprehending his words said that it was the city of Rome which had perished at the hands of Alaric, and the emperor with a sigh of relief answered quickly: "But I thought that my fowl Rome had perished." So great, they say, was the folly with which this emperor was possessed.
>
> (Proc. *BV*. 3.2.25–6)

The key phrase in this excerpt is 'they say,' and is twice repeated in order to lend greater plausibility to the story. Actually, Procopius employs the phrase almost one hundred times throughout his entire body of work. This was – and still is – a technique which enabled authors and commentators to avoid having to name their sources, if indeed there were any. Thus, opinions were expressed as fact. To be fair to Procopius, however, he was neither the first nor the last ancient writer to use unsubstantiated gossip in order to tell a good story. His Honorius yarn has carried well down the ages. The influence that this, admittedly amusing, though uncorroborated story has had upon subsequent generations demonstrates how difficult it is to change deep-rooted perceptions about historical figures. As the renowned Scottish Byzantinist Robert Browning once said, 'we are all prisoners of our predecessors' ideas' (1976, 1).

Source problems

No single, complete historical account exists for the Honorian period. In order to construct a coherent narrative, we are reliant upon multiple primary sources: literature, coinage, inscriptions, laws, art, architecture, and archaeology. Even with all of this material to choose from, it is, as Keith Hopkins once pointed out, difficult to 'deduce feelings from artefacts' (1978, 215). In addition, the written record is generally so biased that it gives a one-sided version of events. It is therefore a challenge to find the 'real' Honorius. How can one get close to the man himself? Even ancient historians were frustrated in similar pursuits, as Eunapius realized when he tried to uncover details about the personal life of the emperor Gratian (367–83). Eunapius' efforts were stymied by a veil of bureaucratic secrecy, hence he concluded that it was nearly impossible to get past the wall of official propaganda. The same sort of restrictions applies to many late Roman emperors, including Honorius.

> Despite a diligent enquiry I was unable to make a full investigation and gain information on the individual actions of the emperor Gratian and

the qualities he showed therein, since these things were extremely guarded secrets in the palace. The reports passed on by individuals contained many and various discrepancies and did not reveal the simple truth, but rather concealed it like some forbidden treasure.

(Eunap. *fr.* 50)

As Eunapius' experience shows, an emperor's true nature was largely inaccessible to anyone outside imperial government's inner circle. Such matters were kept from the public, who were fed just enough information about their emperor as was deemed necessary by the élite. This poses a significant question. If ancient writers like Eunapius could be deterred by such deflection strategies, then what hope is there for the modern enquirer? Though we have the advantage of access to more information – literary and material – than our antique predecessors, we must tread cautiously in assessing the reliability of our primary evidence.

As noted, modern opinion about Honorius is near unanimously contentious. Yet, there are some relatively optimistic views – though these are few. Arnold Hugh Martin Jones, a leading twentieth-century classicist, complimented Honorius and Arcadius as 'personally decent, respectable men.' It was a backhanded comment. In the same breath Jones described the two emperors as 'weak and sluggish' (*LRE* I, 173). A slightly more favorable evaluation came from the well-respected Italian historian Vito Antonio Sirago, who pointed out that Honorius successfully weathered a storm of military and political chaos. Honorius was the great survivor of his age, therefore. Sirago maintained that, once major political and military upheaval drew to a close in the West – about 415 or so – Honorius became a symbol of legality for Roman citizens, a beacon of hope for many (1961, 43–4; 243). More recently, the late antique archaeologist and art historian Hendrik W. Dey has assigned Honorius greater credit than previously given by scholars for the restoration of Rome's defensive walls. Dey suggests that Honorius wanted to remake Rome as an 'analogue of the heavenly city of Jerusalem,' a concept that would fit well with what is known about Honorius' strong Christian beliefs (2011, 142). Honorius began renovations of Rome's Aurelian Walls as early as 401, thus showing that he was conscious of the threat posed by an increasingly aggressive barbarian presence – in this case the Visigoths, inching ever closer to Italy. The emperor therefore made practical preparations for urban defense – and not just in Rome. This does not support the popular parody of an emperor paralyzed by indecision, and disconnected from his people's welfare. Instead, it indicates Honorius' understanding of reality; that the western empire was simply not strong enough to withstand military assault and that it was better to fortify and consolidate strength as much as possible.

Primary literary and material sources

This book draws from a wide spectrum of primary literary and material evidence. Therefore, for brevity, only the main sources are outlined below. The evidence is both Christian and non-Christian, or 'pagan,' in its perspective. For simplicity, the label pagan is applied hereafter, with the acknowledgement of that term's limitations in describing the diverse sweep of polytheist beliefs and practices (Jones 2014, 6ff.). First then, the literary sources.

Claudian (*c.* 370–*c.* 404)

Possibly from Alexandria, Egypt, according to the late Alan Cameron (1970, 2–3), the poet Claudian arrived in Rome about 394, just as the usurpation of Eugenius against Honorius' father Theodosius I came to a climactic and shocking end. Maurice Platnauer, translator of the most commonly used English-language version of Claudian, was more circumspect on Claudian's origins (Platnauer 1922, (1) xii–xiv). It has recently been suggested that Claudian was in fact a westerner educated in Egypt, and who had been on the side of the usurper Eugenius (392–4) prior to joining with the Theodosian house (Christiansen and Christiansen 2009, 138–42; cf. Mulligan 2007). At some point shortly after Theodosius' death on January 17, 395, Claudian entered Honorius' service as a court panegyrist.

From about 395 to about 404, Claudian served as Honorius' court panegyrist. While there, he produced a substantial body of work in just under a decade. Claudian's poems embellished the achievements of Honorius and his household, in particular those of Stilicho, the emperor's *magister militum*. Stilicho, through deliberate manipulation of Honorius, is traditionally felt to have been the de facto power behind the imperial throne, until, that is, his dramatic demise in 408 (Cameron 1969; O' Flynn 1983). When Stilicho was consul in 400, Claudian wrote three panegyrics in his honor. Much of the poet's other works are interspersed with praise of Stilicho. All this, while Claudian was ostensibly the emperor's spokesman. Around 404, Claudian's literary output abruptly breaks off. His last known work is a panegyric about Honorius' sixth consulate. This sudden disappearance has led some to speculate that the poet must have died in 404; while a plausible explanation, it is not the only theory (Barnes 2005; Cameron 1970; cf. Fletcher 2009). The English landscape painter Jacob George Strutt (1790–1864) translated some of Claudian. Strutt remarked that the poet spent his last years in 'poverty and disgrace,' but gave no supporting evidence for this claim (Strutt 1814, v). Suffice to say, we simply do not know what became of Claudian, the so-called 'last great Classical poet' (Hodgkin 1875, 52).

Claudian recited his works for an élite court audience that included the emperor, his government, the senatorial aristocracy, senior ecclesiastical figures, and others (Gillett 2012). An important function of court panegyrists was to act as an intermediary between the emperor and the upper echelons of society, a 'focus of the symbolic communications between the emperor and the Roman aristocracy' (Gillett 2013, 91). Through excessively flattering portrayals of their emperor, Roman élites were reminded of the power and glory of the imperial throne. In some ways, Roman imperial panegyrists are akin to modern governmental press secretaries, whose pronouncements, no matter how apparently absurd or fraudulent, contrive to present an official version of policy to the public. Roman panegyrics were, however, not intended for mass consumption – they were the preserve of the upper class. The general population received the imperial message through the widespread circulation of tried and tested media – coinage, public inscriptions, art – and, in a way, through the writings of churchmen eager to associate biblical virtue with the figure of the emperor.

Claudian's extant works comprise eight panegyrics, two invectives, three epics, and a collection of shorter poems (Barnes 2005, 543). He is therefore a central authority for the first decade of Honorius' reign. Yet to think of Claudian as primarily an historical source is not accurate since he was foremost a trained poet. (Ware 2012; cf. Crees 1908). Nevertheless, due to the disjointed nature of late Roman historical evidence, Claudian's richly descriptive verse preserves important information about the society and events of Honorius' early regal period. We should be cautious with what Claudian reveals to us, though. He was a partisan of Honorius and his administration – especially so of Stilicho. Furthermore, since Claudian's work only covers the timeframe 395–*c.* 404, his use as a source for the entirety of the Honorian era is limited.

Eunapius of Sardis (*c.* 346–*c.* 414)

A sophist rhetorician and committed pagan from Sardis, Asia Minor, Eunapius wrote two significant works: a biographical treatise, *Lives of the Philosophers and Sophists*, and a narrative, *Universal History*, concerning the years *c.* 270–404. Eunapius' *Lives* is complete, but only a very small portion of the second edition of his *History* survives, preserved by the ninth-century Byzantine historian Photius in his *Bibliotheca* (Sacks 1986). Photius retained what he considered to be Eunapius' most interesting elements. Problematic is the fact that Photius included his own analysis side by side with Eunapius' fragments, in lieu of actual transcripts from the rhetorician in many instances. Photius' reshaping of Eunapius' *History* has therefore also shaped later understanding of the latter's work. There is a certain amount of anti-Christian sentiment expressed in the *History*, though this is not the overriding focus. Eunapius was interested in how and why, in his opinion, his world was changing for the worse.

Eunapius was contemptuous of Christian emperors, notably Theodosius I, whom the historian held personally responsible for the ruination of the state. Eunapius repeatedly criticized the emperor's heavy-handed measures against paganism, and apparently pro-barbarian policies in the East (Eunap. *fr.* 46–7, 48.3). Eunapius also expressed concerned about the rising power of barbarian generals and senior officials at the imperial court. For instance, Valentinian II's *magister militum*, Arbogastes, murdered many members of the imperial consistorium, and threatened and subsequently murdered the emperor, before elevating his own nominee as western emperor (Eunap. *fr.*

58; cf. Oros. VII.35.1). Eunapius repeats the point about dangerous barbarian generals in relation to Arcadius and Honorius' joint succession in 395. In the historian's view, the two brothers were titular rulers only, the 'real and absolute power lay with Rufinus in the East and Stilicho in the West,' whose deviousness and greed was boundless. Eunapius added blame for this abuse of power on the emperors' 'soft and feeble spirits' (Eunap. *fr.* 62). Granted, much of Eunapius' account concerns the East, but he does provide some information about similar circumstances taking place in the West as well.

Olympiodorus of Thebes (*c.* 380–*c.* 425)

A professional poet, Olympiodorus was an Egyptian from Thebes. He recorded events for the period 407–25. Written in Greek, and interspersed with Latin terms, Olympiodorus' work dealt primarily with western events. His *History* was intended to illuminate eastern readers on the chaotic events in the West. Though evidently a pagan, Olympiodorus does not resort to as much anti-Christian vitriol as Eunapius. Olympiodorus was a seasoned traveler who often referred to the places he had visited. A 'professional diplomat' according to Cameron, Olympiodorus must have had access to official documents on which he based his central narrative, which would suggest a rank and status of some significance (2011, 643). Liebeschuetz thinks that because of the level of detail in Olympiodorus' text, the historian must have had strong personal connections with the top tiers of western society; and that it was from them that he obtained much of his anecdotal information (2003, 202).

Olympiodorus is generally amenable towards Stilicho, particularly for his military gains against barbarian invaders. Olympiodorus' view was at odds with a good deal of his literary contemporaries; possibly the western sources with whom the historian consulted spoke favorably of Stilicho. This implies that Stilicho was not universally considered a pariah, as some authors would have us believe (Oros. 7.38.1–6; Rut. Nam. 2.41–60). Olympiodorus also felt that Stilicho's execution in 408 was a dreadful miscarriage of justice (Olymp. *fr.* 5.3).

Unfortunately, Olympiodorus' work – originally a twenty-two book tome – is only partially summarized in Photius' *Bibliotheca*, quite likely because of the latter's contempt for the earlier historian's writing style (Treadgold 2004). On the plus side, however, there are other parts of Olympiodorus' *History* found within the late fifth-century historian Zosimus' *New History*, and also in Sozomen's *Historia ecclesiastica*. Zosimus, though a clumsy historian and habitual plagiarist, is helpful nevertheless. Books 5 and 6 of Zosimus' *New History* provide us with what are probably directly quoted pieces of Olympiodorus, an unintended consequence of literary piracy. Since Sirago's and Matthews's studies on Olympiodorus appeared in 1970, scholarly interest in the Egyptian historian has grown. Some of the best research to date includes Baldwin (1980), FCHLRE, Gillett (1993), Rohrbacher (2002), Liebeschuetz (2003), and Treadgold (2004).

Orosius (*c.* 375–*c.* 418)

It is not at all clear where Orosius came from, and while he has frequently been described as a Spanish presbyter, and called Paulus Orosius, both of these would appear to be misnomers. Much more important is the historical detail offered by his work *Seven Books of History against the Pagans* (*Historia adversum paganos libri VII*). It is a biblical interpretation of world history starting with the Flood, but it is not until the seventh and final book – the thirty-sixth chapter to be precise – where we first encounter Honorius and his brother Arcadius as ruling emperors. The remaining eight chapters are intensely packed with events covering the years 395–418. Ultimately, Orosius sought to prove that there was a divine plan at play from creation to his own time. Biblical exegesis was his means of legitimizing his work, and he was particularly good at using scripture to make his point. As Rohrbacher states, 'history writing was a form of rhetoric, or persuasive speech. The ancient historian had to convince the reader that his history was worth reading' (2002, 150).

For some, Orosius is a lesser version of Augustine. Orosius' prose is not as complex or as philosophically enquiring as Augustine's, but, despite its deeply Christian moralizing tone, this should not detract from his importance in terms of the historical detail it does offer.

Orosius admired Honorius, his family, and Catholic Christian emperors in general. The historian condemned those who had plotted against Honorius, who Orosius considered a devout ruler set upon the throne by God. Orosius saw individuals like the *comes Africae* Gildo or Stilicho as traitors, pagans, and conniving barbarians typical of their race (Oros. 7.36.2–12; 7.38.1–6).

The barbarian protagonists of the Honorian age come away in a better light than most other contemporaries. Orosius saw the Visigoth Alaric, and other non-Romans, as instruments of God's retribution upon a (in Orosius' eyes) sinful Roman populace. Some scholars consider Orosius a less than credible historical source, a 'tendentious hack who tried to shoe-horn world and especially Roman history into a pre-conceived theological interpretation' (Burgess 2004).

Augustine of Hippo (*c.* 354–430)

There is not enough space in this book to adequately account for Augustine's life and work. In brief, therefore, Augustine, or Aurelianus Augustinus, was from Thagaste (modern Souk Ahras, Algeria). Initially he had been interested in Manichaeism, a gnostic sect of Persian origin that was introduced into the Roman Empire in the third century. Manichaeism spread throughout the empire, and was subsequently ruled heretical by the Catholic Church in the late fourth century. In 384, Augustine moved to Rome, and then to Milan, where he taught rhetoric at the imperial court. While in Milan, Augustine came under the influence of the city's bishop, Ambrose, who, in 386, baptized the young North African, along with his infant son Adeodatus, into the Christian faith. Augustine wrote about his conversion to Christianity in book 10 of the *Confessiones*, one of his most famous works. The *Confessiones* is a personal account of Augustine's life from childhood to the death of his mother Monica in 387. In 388, Augustine returned to North Africa with Adeodatus, who died shortly after their arrival. Following this, Augustine renounced most of his possessions and property, and by 395 had been appointed bishop of Hippo Rhegius (modern Annaba, Algeria). There he remained until the Vandals besieged the city in 430, during which he died.

The other most well-known work by Augustine is *De civitate Dei* (The City of God), a twenty-two-volume set which survived intact through the ages, in sharp contrast to the works of pagan authors like Olympiodorus above. *De civitate Dei* was very influential on the Church's evolution in the centuries after Rome's disintegration – the so-called medieval era.

Augustine was at the forefront of the Roman Catholic Church's rise to supremacy. He railed against pagans, especially through *De civitate Dei*, and contested the ideologies of heretical groups like the Manichees, Donatists, and Pelagians. Augustine is therefore very important for understanding the nature of late Roman theological conflict – so pervasive in the age of Honorius. Indeed, Honorius supported Augustine's North African Catholic mission, and found the bishop's doctrinal arguments instructive for his own religious policies.

Socrates Scholasticus of Constantinople (*c.* 380–*c.* 440)

Other than his writing, we know little about Socrates other than that he was born and bred at Constantinople. It has been suggested that his surname is either a medieval addition or possibly infers his profession as an advocate (Urbainczyk 1997, 13–14; Rohrbacher 2002, 108). Socrates' *Ecclesiastical History* consists of seven books, the last four of which are an important source of information for the Honorian period, right up to the emperor's death in 423. Though Socrates does not give much detail about Honorius' personal life, he nevertheless relates a great deal about Church politics of the age, a subject which was of considerable interest to the emperor.

Sozomen (*c.* 400–*c.* 450)

Salamanes Hermeias Sozomenos is thought to have come from Bethelia (modern Beit Lahiya, Gaza). Much of Sozomen's *Ecclesiastical History* is concerned with monasticism, heresies, and dogmatic disputes. Sozomen also appears to have used Socrates as a guide, but includes new material on Honorius, who, in Socrates' view, was a pious, god-fearing ruler.

Like Socrates, Sozomen is of particular importance for the later period of Honorius' reign after about 410, when our other main authors end. Socrates' work is in nine books, but does not reach Honorius' birth until chapter 14 of the seventh book. Socrates had no love for Stilicho, who he accused of malice towards the brother emperors, and the whole Roman world in general (Soz. *HE*. 8.25). A detailed account about the Visigothic sack of Rome, and of the various usurpers pitted against Honorius, is given in the ninth book. In Socrates' view, these usurpers were destroyed solely by Honorius' deep piety, and God's reciprocal love for the emperor. The same went for the emperor's sister Placidia, who was in Socrates' opinion as devout as her brother. Like Orosius and other ecclesiastical writers, Socrates' emphasis was to project the Christian faith as the backbone of strong imperial governance:

> ... to insure the stability of imperial power, it is sufficient for an emperor to serve God with reverence, which was the course pursued by Honorius.
>
> (Soz. *HE*. 9.16)

Zosimus (late fifth/early sixth century)

Zosimus' origins are unknown. Photius tells us that Zosimus held the rank of *comes*, and was an advocate, or attorney, in the treasury department at Constantinople, under the emperor Anastasius (491–518). A dedicated pagan, Zosimus denounced Christianity wherever he found the opportunity. Though much of his *New History* appears to be plagiarized from the works of Dexippus, Eunapius, and Olympiodorus, this is a boon for the modern historian in terms of the material it preserves from these earlier historians. Caution must be used with Zosimus, however, for there are numerous errors – a 'catalogue of blunders' – throughout the *New History* (Thompson 1982, 447). Unfortunately, Zosimus' text ends abruptly midway through the sixth book of his *New History*, just prior to the Visigothic capture and sack of Rome in August 410. As a consequence, Zosimus can provide us with no further evidence for the remaining thirteen years of Honorius' reign.

Imperial law

Two legal compilations, the *Codex Theodosianus* (Theodosian Code) and *Codex Justinianus* (Code of Justinian), offer valuable insight into the religious, social, and bureaucratic apparatus of late imperial governments. The fifth-century *Codex Theodosianus* consists of imperial laws issued between 312 and 468. Theodosius II, in 429, tasked a panel of legal scholars with collecting as many state laws as possible from the Christian period, with the aim of codifying their results into one collection. By 438, after much time spent collecting and revising, the panel had gathered and edited over two and a half thousand imperial *constitutiones* (laws/decisions) from central and provincial archives, as well as from private libraries. There were different categories of *constitutiones*, of which the main types were: decrees (*decreta*), judicial decisions made by the emperor, the judiciary, or municipal councils; rescripts (*rescripta*), the emperor's responses to requests for advice from public officials, or to private citizens' petitions or prayers; and edicts (*edicta*), general legislative enactments which were binding on all the emperor's subjects (Pharr 1952, 577ff.).

The result of the panel's efforts was the *Codex Theodosianus*. It was officially launched in the presence of the emperor and the senate at Constantinople to great applause in 438. In its present form, the *Codex Theodosianus* contains later *constitutiones*, bringing it up to the year 468, during the reign of the western emperor Anthemius (467–72). The legal panel omitted certain laws for a number of reasons, some practical, others ideological. In the 430s, some archives and libraries were simply out of bounds to the imperial commission due to safety concerns. Britain, for example, had slipped from imperial juris-diction in about 411, and was fast becoming a battleground between Romans, Angles, Saxons, Jutes, and Scots. The island province was too dangerous to travel to. Getting across Europe was equally perilous, considering the numerous barbarian armies operating inside Roman borders at the time – Visigoths, Vandals, Alans, Suebi, and others. Theodosius' legal panel also excluded the legislation of usurpers as illegal acts – the same thing applied to a usurper's coinage, sculpture, and other propaganda. Laws of a non-Catholic/Nicene nature were generally ignored, for instance, those made by Rome's last pagan emperor, Julian the Apostate (361–3). Sometimes laws only survived in fragmented form, for which references were inserted into the *Codex*.

To date, the only English-language translation of the *Codex Theodosianus* is from the combined efforts of Clyde Pharr, Theresa Sherrer Davidson, and Mary Brown Pharr (1952). The story behind these scholars' incredible achievement is in itself worthy of merit (Hall 2012, 1–42). While ancient texts are always under revision by new generations of scholars, it has to be said, however, that it would be very hard to outdo the work that Pharr, Davidson, and Pharr accomplished. In the decades since then, there has been a growing interest in late Roman law. Two books in particular are essential companions for understanding the complexities of the late Roman legislative: Tony Honoré's *Law in the Crisis of Empire* (1998), and John F. Matthews's *Laying Down the Law* (2000). Other important and influential scholarship on the subject includes Jill Harries's *Law and Empire in Late Antiquity*, an examination of the effectiveness – or ineffect-iveness – of implementing imperial law (1999). Elizabeth A. Meyer's *Legitimacy and Law in the Roman World: Tabulae in Roman Belief and Practice* is a wide historical sweep of ancient Greek and Roman law from the first century BC to the sixth century AD (2004). Meyer's chief focus is the physical materials – wax tablets (*tabulae*) – on which laws were recorded, and to what extent the actual materials validated the laws they described. Caroline Humfress's *Orthodoxy and the Courts in Late Antiquity* analyzes the merging of secular imperial law with Christian ideology, from the early fourth to the early sixth century (2007). Among other themes, Humfress examines the growth of epis-copal power in the late Roman world, and the persecution of heretics through theologically influenced state laws. On the other hand, David Hunt advises against overdependence on the *Codex Theodosianus* as primary evidence for the Christianization of the Roman world (Hunt 1993, 143–58). Still, it is hard not to see at least a partial absorption of Christian thinking into imperial law during the late empire. More recently, Noel Lenski's 'Imperial Legislation and the Donatist Controversy: From Constantine to Honorius' traces how state law became a significant tool in the war on heresy orchestrated by the Catholic Church – and Catholic emperors – in this case the North African Donatists (2016, 167–219). In the wake of the Gildonic War in North Africa in 398, Honorius passed punitive legislation against Donatism. In 405, Honorius officially declared Donatism a heresy, with the requisite penalties.

> We provide, by the authority of this decree, that adversaries of the Catholic faith shall be rooted out ... those who are called Donatists are said to have progressed so far in wickedness that with criminal lawlessness ... they have infected with the profane repetition men who have been cleansed once for all by the gift of divinity ... thus it happened that a heresy was born from a schism ... offenders shall be punished by the confiscation of all their property, and they shall suffer the penalty of poverty ... flogged with leaden whips (and exiled) ...
>
> (*CTh.* 16.6.4; 16.6.5. Feb 12, 405)

The other great legal compilation of antiquity is that which was commissioned by Justinian (527–65). In 528, nearly one hundred years after Theodosius II commissioned his codification of imperial law, Justinian followed suit. He ordered a complete overhaul of the Roman legal system as part of his personal interest in reviving Roman learning and prestige. Justinian's revised legal code was also a reaction to the less sophisticated legislature that some of the new barbarian rulers in the West were enacting.

Commonly called the Code of Justinian (*Codex Justinianus*), its more accurate title is the *Corpus iuris civilis* (*Body of Civil Law*). This compilation has twelve books, divided into four sections, though the original 529 edition had only three. The first section, the *Codex Justinianus*, contains *constitutiones* from the *Codex Theodosianus*, and from private collections. The *Codex Justinianus* has an earlier starting point than the *Codex Theodosianus*, incorporating legal documentation from the time of Hadrian (117–38). The second section, the *Digesta* (*Digest*), includes Justinian's own *constitutiones*, as well as material from past Roman jurists, such as Papinian (*c.* 142–212) and Ulpian (*c.* 170–*c.* 228). The third section, the *Institutiones* (*Institutions*), was primarily a textbook meant for the law schools of the Roman East, which included those of Constantinople and Berytus (Beirut). The latter, a famed establishment, was unfortunately destroyed by an earthquake in 551, not long after the publication of the *Codex Justinianus*. The fourth and final section, the *Novellae* (*novels/new legislation*), was mostly in Greek and therefore intended for the predominantly Greek-speaking eastern provinces; the first three sections were in the Latin language. The *Novellae* is an assortment of contemporary laws, and was an addition to the second edition of the *Codex Justinianus* in 534. And, while Christianity certainly had an influence on the original three sections of the *Codex Justinianus*, in the *Novellae*, Christian ideology plays a central role in shaping the state's legal discourse.

One area in particular, that of punishment, stands out from the entire corpus of late Roman imperial legislation. It is hardly a generalization to say that, in the late imperial legal system, the imposition of penalties became a growth sector. In addition to fiscal and physical punishments, there is a massive array of misdemeanors – many of which seem fairly innocuous – for which capital punishment was a common method of dispensing justice. What is more, a good proportion of such crimes involve infractions against Christians. Besides their historical research value, both the *Codex Theodosianus* and *Codex Justinianus* form the very foundations of modern western law. Some very good studies involving the *Codex Justinianus* include an edited volume on the treatment of Jews in medieval law, and a work on Roman women's legal status of women (Linder 1997; Grubbs 2002). In contrast to the level of scholarly interest in the *Codex Theodosianus*, however, its later counterpart distinctly lacks attention. Consequently, there is at present no comprehensive anglophone study of the *Codex Justinianus*.

In the late empire, when there were two or more co-ruling legitimate emperors, it was standard practice that imperial legislation should bear their names and titles. Apart from the obvious omission of a usurper's name, to omit a legitimate colleague's name from laws would have been disrespectful, and potentially dangerous, even when political disunity existed between the western and eastern courts. In the case of Arcadius and Honorius, whose administrations continually plotted against one another, it was possible to project some semblance of unity to the Roman world through laws that bore both their names. Coinage worked in a similar – though not consistent – fashion. It should be noted, however, that although late Roman legal pronouncements were issued in the names of concurrent legitimate emperors, this did not necessarily mean, for example, that a law decreed in the East had authority in the West, and vice versa (Honoré, 1998, 148; 128–32).

Material evidence

What did Honorius look like? A moot question, since his official portraits are idealized, as are those of other emperors. In text also, Honorius is described in a manner that is difficult to ascertain the accuracy of. For instance, writing about Honorius' marriage to Maria in 398, Claudian describes an emperor who was even more handsome than Adonis or Achilles (Cl. *Fesc.* I.1–9). But then of course he would – that was his job, after all. In the panegyric for Honorius' sixth consulship in 404, Claudian again commented upon the emperor's vigor and good looks. The poet presented Honorius as the man other men wanted to be. For women, the emperor was a sex symbol.

> Young men rejoice in an emperor as young as themselves … and then the women marveled ceaselessly at the unmatched bloom upon his cheeks, at

his hair crowned with the diadem, at limbs that reflected the green light from his jewel-studded consular robe, at his strong shoulders and at his neck which, soaring through oriental emeralds, could match in beauty that of Lyaeus; and the innocent maiden, the blush of simple modesty burning on her cheek, lets her eyes rove over every detail …

(Cl. *VI Cons.* 547, 560–5)

It is impossible to deduce what Honorius really looked like from Claudian, who was never going to describe his patron as anything else but elegant and attractive. We must turn to other media – coinage, sculpture, art – to try and get a better picture of Honorius' appearance. But, these too are problematic.

The public image

Very little sculpture of Honorius exists. The scarcity of late imperial sculpture is a widespread phenomenon for which there are a myriad of reasons – ritual destruction and mutilation, burning of marble statues for lime, melting down of bronze pieces, or declining trends (Varner 2004; Kalas 2015; Kristensen and Stirling 2016; Panayides 2016). Honorius' image is ubiquitous on coinage but, as is the case with the written accounts, it is uncertain how closely his official portraits actually resemble him. However, as the first-century biographer Plutarch points out in his *Life of Alexander*, the artist's job was to capture the likeness of their subject as closely as they could, especially in the case of important clients; whereas, Plutarch mused, the task of writers like himself was to capture their subject's very soul.

Portrait-painters are more exact in the lines and features of the face, in which the character is seen, than in the other parts of the body, so I must be allowed to give more particular attention to the marks and indications of the souls of men.

(Plut. *Alex.* 1.3)

When creating an official imperial image, a commissioned artist made a preparatory drawing, which was then used as a template for all official images, whether for coinage, busts, diptychs, or paintings. This technique has not changed much at all over time. The official images of modern leaders are created in a similar fashion – for use on currency, postage stamps, or paintings. In antiquity, depending on the skill of the craftsmen in the imperial mints, sculptural workshops, and art studios, an emperor's image could vary slightly, but his most distinctive, recognizable features were retained. Eunapius offers a good description of the design process involved in creating official portraits of Roman emperors:

A parallel is offered by the portrait painter who seeks to capture the sitter before him. The likeness of the face is captured through some of its minor characteristics – a deep furrow on the brow, prominent sideburns, or some similar insignificant detail of the features, which, if overlooked, causes the portrait to fail, but if rendered accurately, is the sole reason why the likeness has been caught.

(Eunap. *fr.* 50)

Occasionally, literature gives us more information than official portraiture does about an emperor's physical appearance. Perhaps then, as Plutarch contended, the written word relates a more realistic picture than that presented to the public through official portraits. For instance, Arcadius' likeness on coins is blemish-free, and purposeful, but his contemporary, the heretical Christian Philostorgius, describes him quite differently. A note of caution, though, in accepting literary treatments as unbiased.

Arcadius, by contrast, was short, slight of build, weakly, and dark in complexion. And his dullness of mind was evident in his speech and the way his eyes closed as they drooped sleepily downward beneath their drowsy lids.

(Philost. *HE.* 11.3)

Coinage

Coinage was a vital conduit for the transmission of government propaganda to the Roman population. Coins had mobility, in contrast to static media like inscriptions. Because of its portability, coinage was a highly effective channel for the dissemination of the imperial message to every corner of the Roman world, no matter how geographically distant that might be from the administrative center. Through their coinage output, emperors publicized their virtues and achievements, disclosing only particular elements of their private lives that they wanted to reveal. Whatever the occasion – imperial accession, military victories, domestic policies, births, marriages, or deaths – all these were observed in the monetary record. Coins also recorded an emperor's development. This is especially useful for tracing Honorius' maturing process, from his childhood through to his late thirties.

Furthermore, maintaining an adequate coin supply was critical in order to pay the state's guardians – the army, and the immense bureaucracy that administered it. Failure to do so could sometimes lead to discontent and mutiny.

Numismatic study

The term numismatics refers to the study of coins and medals, and other monetary aspects. Apart from the fiscal value of our contemporary currency, most of us probably have little interest in the creative process involved in modern monetary designs, or the ideological motives at play behind them. Our money is mass-produced by machine, and comes in base metal, paper, and plastic form. Likewise, Roman money was mass-produced – though by hand – and was made from gold, silver, bronze, or brass. It too was widely circulated, and was of course important for everyday life, as it is today. Over hundreds of years, millions of coins must have been struck in mints that were strategically situated across the empire.

A vast number of Roman coins survives, offering classicists, cultural and art historians, coin/numismatic specialists, and archaeologists a superb primary material resource for analysis. Many European museums have online numismatic databases that allow public access to their collections. For example, Bologna's Museo Civico Archeologico hosts an excellent online database which is linked to its enormous coin collection. In Britain, the Portable Antiquities Scheme (PAS), a government-funded project which encourages members of the public to hand in new coin finds, has resulted in an exponential increase in new numismatic material from all over the United Kingdom. Depending on their rarity, coins can fetch considerable prices on the antiquities market. On a much darker note, however, as the recent and ongoing conflicts in Iraq, Libya, and Syria have proved, there has been a marked rise in the appearance of coins and other antiquities – both real and counterfeit – on the illegal market (Shaheen and Black 2015).

Coins as propaganda

Coins projected a precise image that ruling administrations wanted to publicly convey (Brennan et al. 2007). The symbols, images, and texts that were stamped on imperial Roman money held clear meaning for their specific target audience, the public. While money was important for the running of the Roman economy, it held another value. Coinage was the greatest newsfeed of its time. It worked as a communication network that repeated specific messages to the masses, much like contemporary political, commercial, and social advertising does. Roman coin designs were used to construct and project images of imperial power. Coins were also continuous reminders to the populace of the emperor's supreme power, and his association with cult and religion, which, in the empire of Honorius' day, had become Christianity. The success of the new religion was facilitated in no small part by numismatic propaganda. Through the medium of coinage, the nascent Catholic Church expressed its ideology, and in turn, imperial iconography began to reflect Christian values.

Coin symbols and legends

Of vital importance were the inscriptions and symbols used on imperial coins. These included titulature, imperial regalia (diadem/ornate headband, scepter), military paraphernalia (armor, helmet, weapons, and the *labarum*/standard), and religious associations (pagan deities, *Chi-Rho*, and the *manus Dei*/hand of god). Equally crucial was a coin's legend (inscription), of which there were many different types. The following coin legends are some of the most common from the late empire: *Spes Reipublicae* (Hope of the State), *Victoria Augustorum* (Victory of the Augusti/Emperors), *Restitutor Reipublicae* (Restorer of the State), *Virtus Exercitum* (Valor of the Army), *Salus Reipublicae* (Health of the State), *Concordia Augustorum* (Concord of the Emperors), *Gloria Romanorum* (Glory of the Romans), *Virtus Romanorum* (Valor of the Romans), *Pius Felix* (Dutiful and Fortunate), *Adventus Augusti* (Approach of the Emperor), and *Roma Aeterna* (Eternal Rome).

Gesture

Physical gesture, or body language, was a design feature of Roman coins ever since their first use in the fourth century BC (Brilliant 1963). The use of gesture on coins was a necessary form of communication in a society where literacy was perhaps not always widespread. Typical gestures involved the emperor raising his right hand in greeting or command, advancing on horseback, subjugating enemies, holding secular and religious symbols of power, performing sacrifices, and so on.

Abbreviations

Naturally, it was impractical to try to fit a large amount of text on small pieces of metal in a coherent manner, therefore abbreviations were substituted. For instance, where there was one ruling Augustus, the legend AVG was used. To indicate more than one emperor, the number of Gs was increased. For example, for three Augusti, the legend was spelt AVGGG. There is only one known case of four emperors (AVGGGG) being referred to on a coin, which was issued by the usurper Constantine III (407–11). This particular coin is illustrated in chapter 7 (Figure 7.2).

Numismatic scholarship

Ancient numismatic study is a vibrant, always growing, research area. The *Roman Imperial Coinage* (*RIC*) series, in ten parts, remains a valuable resource, with several volumes currently under revision to reflect new scholarship in the field (Mattingly et al. 1923–94). Philip Grierson's *Numismatics* (1975) is still a standard work on the subject. Some of the most important research of recent years on Roman coinage is: *Imperial Rome and Christian Triumph* (Elsner 1998); 'Coins and Messages: Audience Targeting on Coins of Different Denominations' (Hekster 2003); *The End of Roman Gold Coinage and the Disintegration of a Monetary Area* (Carlà 2010); *Chronicles, Consuls, and Coins* (Burgess 2011); *Coining Images of Power: Patterns in the Representation of Roman Emperors on Imperial Coinage, A.D. 193–284* (Manders 2012); *Constantine, Divine Emperor of the Christian Golden*

Age (Bardill 2012); *Rethinking Roman Britain: Coinage and Archaeology* (Walton 2012).

The field of numismatics is ever changing and evolving. It tends to be online numismatic research databases and collections, auction houses, and journals which provide the most up-to-date resources. These include the Classical Numismatic Group Inc. (https://cngcoins.com/); Portable Antiquities Scheme (www.finds.org.uk); The British Museum Collection; the American Numismatic Society (http://numismatics.org/); as well as numismatic journals such as the German *Deutsches Jahrbuch für Numismatik*; the British *Numismatic Chronicle*; and the French *Revue Numismatique*.

Epigraphy

Epigraphy is the study and interpretation of ancient inscriptions. In the Roman Empire, official public inscriptions were similar in function to coinage, for they expressed the state's position through names, titles, honors, commemorations, victories, and so on. However, the main difference between the two media forms – inscriptions and coins – was that the former were static, whereas the latter were geographically mobile. Though inscriptions were made of stone, metal, and wood, they fall into the categories of both material and textual sources.

A good place to begin the study of inscriptions is the *Manual to Latin Epigraphy* (Cooley 2012) and the *Oxford Handbook of Roman Epigraphy* (Bruun and Edmonson 2014). Most of the standard epigraphic databases are available online. As is the case for coinage, online epigraphic databases offer a quicker, more effective way to add new discoveries to the existing corpus of inscriptions, in Latin, Greek, and other ancient languages. Those which have been referenced for this book are: *Corpus Inscriptionum Graecarum* (*CIG*); *Corpus Inscriptionum Latinarum* (*CIL*); *Inscriptiones Christianae Urbis Romae* (*ICUR*); *Inscriptiones Ephesi* (*IEph*); *Inscriptiones Graecae* (*IG*); *Inscriptions Latines d'Afrique* (*ILAfr.*); *Inscriptiones Latinae Selectae* (*ILS*); *Last Statues of Antiquity* (*LSA*).

Epigraphic scholarship specifically relevant to Honorius' timeframe includes Charlotte Roueché's *Written Display in the Late Antique and Byzantine City* (2007, 235–54) and Gregor Kalas's *The Restoration of the Roman Forum in Late Antiquity* (2015).

Other useful epigraphic works are the *Illustrated Introduction to Latin Epigraphy* (Gordon 1983), a student textbook that has inscriptions from the sixth century BC to the sixth century AD; *The Latin Inscriptions of Rome* (Lansford 2009), a diverse collection that contains some late fourth- and early fifth-century inscriptions. A recent edited volume with a very broad historical and geographical sweep, *Viewing Inscriptions in the Late Antique and Medieval World* (Eastmond 2015), is a fascinating examination of the role of inscriptions through the ages, and across diverse cultures.

A note on the title Flavius

By the mid-fourth century, the name Flavius, originally a family name (*gentilicium*), had assumed a 'social marker status' among upper-level civil and military officials (Keenan 1973; Cameron 1988). In Honorius' lifetime, the use of Flavius had become 'as common as dirt ... the hallmark of the newly important' (*CLRE*, 40). The *gentilicium* Flavius is not found on any of Honorius and Arcadius' coins or laws, where they are instead styled *Our Lords* (*Dominorum Nostrorum/Domini Nostri*). Even Honorius' propagandist Claudian uses Flavius only once in all of his works, in that instance for the consul Manlius Theodorus, a man originally of low birth.

Neither was Flavius common among the established Roman aristocracy, but the term was widely used by the new ascendancy in the late empire. Perhaps this was a subtle class distinction among the élites themselves – a sort of hierarchy within a hierarchy. Emperors were, however, styled as Flavii on public inscriptions, though why this and not other imperial media is uncertain. It may have depended on who erected such inscriptions. Coinage and law were the preserve of the imperial office itself, whereas inscriptions could be set up by local councils, senates, and private individuals.

Alan Cameron accused the *Prosopography of the Later Roman Empire* of overuse of the title Flavius. He felt that this has distorted the term's meaning. Hence, in the late empire, Flavius seems likely to have been a formal prefix, akin to the modern 'Sir' or 'Mister.' Another way to think about the title Flavius is to compare it to the bestowal of knighthoods, and other such honorific titles, to non-aristocrats by the contemporary British monarchy. For my part, Flavius is not generally applied as a name marker throughout this book.

References

Baldwin, Barry. 1980. "Olympiodorus of Thebes." *AC* 49: 212–31.

Bardill, Jonathan. 2012. *Constantine, Divine Emperor of the Christian Golden Age*. Cambridge and New York: Cambridge University Press.

Barnes, Michael H. 2005. "Claudian." In *A Companion to Ancient Epic*. Edited by John M. Foley: 538–49. Malden, MA and Oxford: Blackwell.

Barnes, T. D. 1986. "Synesius in Constantinople." *GRBS* (27): 93–112.

Blasen, Philippe Henri. 2012. "Images de l'empereur en France au XIXe siècle." *Acta Musei Napocensis* 47–48.1: 241–63.

Born, Lester K. 1934. "The Perfect Prince According to the Latin Panegyrists." *AJP* 55.1: 20–35.

Brennan, Peter, Turner, Michael, and Wright, Nicholas L. 2007. *Faces of Power: Imperial Portraiture on Roman Coins*. Sydney: Nicholson Museum.

Brilliant, Richard. 1963. *Gesture and Rank in Roman Art: The Use of Gestures to Denote Status in Roman Sculpture and Coinage*. Connecticut Academy of Arts and Sciences 14. New Haven, CT: The Academy.

Browning, Robert. 1976. *The Emperor Julian*. London: Weidenfeld and Nicolson.

Bruun, Christer, and Edmonson, Jonathan (eds). 2014. The *Oxford Handbook of Roman Epigraphy*. Oxford: Oxford University Press.

Burgess, Richard W. 1998. *The Chronicle of Hydatius and the Consularia Constantinopolitana: Two Contemporary Accounts of the Final Years of the Roman Empire*. Oxford Classical Monographs. Oxford: Clarendon Press.

Burgess, Richard W. 2004. Review of *Greek and Roman Historiography in Late Antiquity: Fourth to Sixth Century AD*. 2003. Edited by Gabriele Marasco. Leiden: Brill. In *Bryn Mawr Classical Review* 2004.03.49.

Burgess, Richard W. 2011. *Chronicles, Consuls, and Coins: Historiography and History in the Later Roman Empire*. Variorum Collected Studies 984. London: Ashgate.

Burgess, Richard W., and Kulikowski, Michael. 2013. *Mosaics of Time: The Latin Chronicle Traditions from the First Century BC to the Sixth Century AD*, Volume 1: *A Historical Introduction to the Chronicle Genre from its Origins to the High Middle Ages*. Studies in the Early Middles Ages 33. Turnhout: Brepols.

Burnett, Andrew. 1991. *Interpreting the Past: Coins*. London: British Museum Press.

Cameron, Alan. 1969. "Theodosius the Great and the Regency of Stilico." *HSCP* 73: 247–80.

Cameron, Alan. 1970. *Poetry and Propaganda at the Court of Honorius*. Oxford: Oxford University Press.

Cameron, Alan. 1988. "Flavius: A Nicety of Protocol." *Latomus* 47: 26–33.

Cameron, Alan. 2011. *The Last Pagans of Rome*. Oxford: Oxford University Press.

Carlà, Filippo. 2010. "The End of Roman Gold Coinage and the Disintegration of a Monetary Area." *Annali dell'Istituto Italiano di Numismatica* 56: 103–72.

Christiansen, Peder G. 1971. "Claudian and Eternal Rome." *AC* 40.2: 670–74.

Christiansen, Peder G, and Christiansen, David. 2009. "Claudian: The Last Great Pagan Poet." *AC* 78: 133–44.

Christiansen, Peder G, and Sebesta, Judith Lynn. 1985. "Claudian's Phoenix: Themes of Imperium." *AC* 54: 204–24.

Collins, Wilkie. 1850. *Antonina, or The fall of Rome: A Romance of the Fifth Century*. London: Richard Bentley.

Cooley, Alison E. 2012. *The Cambridge Manual of Latin Epigraphy*. Cambridge: Cambridge University Press.

Crees, James H. E. (1908) 2013. *Claudian as an Historical Authority*. Cambridge Historical Essays 17. Cambridge: Cambridge University Press. Reprint. London: Forgotten Books.

Croke, Brian. 2001. "Chronicles, Annals and Consular Annals in Late Antiquity." *Chiron* 31: 291–331.

Desfontaines, Nicolas-Marc. 1645. *L'Illustre Olympie ou le Saint Alexis: tragedie*. Paris: Pierre Lamy.

Dey, Hendrik W. 2011. *The Aurelian Wall and the Refashioning of Imperial Rome, AD 271–855*. Cambridge: Cambridge University Press.

Eastmond, Antony (ed.). 2015. *Viewing Inscriptions in the Late Antique and Medieval World*. Cambridge: Cambridge University Press.

Elsner, Jas. 1998. *Imperial Rome and Christian Triumph: The Art of the Roman Empire, AD 100–450*. Oxford: Oxford University Press.

Fisk, Robert. 2017. "Trump's Claim that a General Dipped Bullets in Pig's Blood Is Fake News: But the US Massacre of Moro Muslims Isn't." *The Independent*. August 18, 2017. www.independent.co.uk/voices/donald-trump-barcelona-attack-twitter-tweet-pigs-blood-general-fake-news-duterte-philippines-a7899826.html.

Fletcher, David T. 2009. "Whatever Happened to Claudian Claudianus? A Pedagogigcal Proposition." *CJ* 104.3: 259–73.

Gibbon, Edward. (1781). 1906. *The History of the Decline and Fall of the Roman Empire*, Volume 2. Edited by J. B. Bury, with an introduction by W. E. H. Lecky. New York: Fred de Fau and Co.

Gillett, Andrew. 1993. "The Date and Circumstances of Olympiodorus of Thebes." *Traditio* 48: 1–29.

Gillett, Andrew. 2012. "Epic Panegyric and Political Communication in the Fifth-Century West." In *Two Romes: Rome and Constantinople in Late Antiquity*. Oxford Studies in Late Antiquity. Edited by Lucy Grig and Gavin Kelly: 264–90. Oxford: Oxford University Press.

Gillett, Andrew. 2013. *Envoys and Political Communication in the Late Antique West, 411–533*. Cambridge: Cambridge University Press.

Gordon, Arthur E. 1983. *Illustrated Introduction to Latin Epigraphy*. Los Angeles, CA: University of California Press.

Grierson, Philip. 1975. *Numismatics*. Oxford: Oxford University Press.

Grubbs, Judith Evans. 2002. *Women and Law in the Roman Empire: A Sourcebook on Marriage, Divorce and Widowhood*. London and New York: Routledge.

Hall, Linda Jones. 2012. "Clyde Pharr, the Women of Vanderbilt, and the Wyoming Judge: The Story behind the Translation of the the the Theodosian Code in Mid-Century America." *Roman Legal Tradition* 8: 1–42.

Hannestad, Niels. 1988. *Roman Art and Imperial Policy*. Aarhus: Aarhus University Press.

Harries, Jill. 1999. *Law and Empire in Late Antiquity*. Cambridge: Cambridge University Press.

Heather, Peter. 1988. "The Anti-Scythian Tirade of Synesius." *Phoenix* 42.2: 152–72.

Hekster, Oliver. 2003. "Coins and Messages: Audience Targeting on Coins of Different Denominations?" In *Representation and Perception of Roman Imperial Power*. Edited by Luuk de Blois: 20–35. Amsterdam: Gieben.

Hobson, Anthony. 1980. *The Art and Life of J. W. Waterhouse RA 1849–1917*. London: Studio Vista.

Hodgkin, Thomas. 1875. *Claudian: The Last of the Roman Poets*. London: Newcastle-upon-Tyne.

Honoré, Tony. 1998. *Law in the Crisis of Empire, AD 379–455: The Theodosian Dynasty and its Quaestors*. New York: Oxford University Press.

Hopkins, Keith. 1978. *Conquerors and Slaves*, Volume 1. Sociological Studies in Roman History. Cambridge: Cambridge University Press.

Humfress, Caroline. 2007 (a). *Orthodoxy and the Courts in Late Antiquity*. Oxford: Oxford University Press.

Humfress, Caroline. 2007 (b). "Cracking the *Codex*: Late Roman Legal Practice in Context." *BICS* 49: 251–64.

Humfress, Caroline. 2007 (c). "Law and Justice in the Later Roman Empire." In *A. H. M. Jones and the Later Roman Empire*. Edited by David M. Gwynn: 121–42. Leiden and Boston, MA: Brill.

Hunt, David. 1993. "Christianizing the Roman Empire: The Evidence of the Code." In *The Theodosian Code: Studies in the Imperial Law of Late Antiquity*. Edited by Jill Harries and Ian Wood: 143–58. London: Bloomsbury.

Johnson, Scott Fitzgerald (ed.). 2012. *The Oxford Handbook of Late Antiquity*. Oxford: Oxford University Press.

Jones, Christopher P. 2014. *Between Pagan and Christian*. Cambridge, MA: Harvard University Press.

Kalas, Gregor. 2015. *The Restoration of the Roman Forum in Late Antiquity: Transforming Public Space*. Austin, TX: The University of Texas Press.

Kaldellis, Anthony. 2017. "How Perilous Was it to Write Political History in Late Antiquity?" *Studies in Late Antiquity* 1.1: 38–64.

Keenan, James G. 1973. "The Names Flavius and Aurelius as Status Designations in Later Roman Egypt." *ZPE* 1: 33–63.

Kelly, Gavin. 2016. "Claudian's Last Panegyric and Imperial Visits to Rome." *CQ* 66.1: 336–57.

Kristensen, Troels Myrup, and Stirling, Lea Margaret (eds). 2016. *The Afterlife of Greek and Roman Sculpture: Late Antique Responses and Practices*. Ann Arbor, MI: University of Michigan Press.

Lansford, Tyler. 2009. *The Latin Inscriptions of Rome: A Walking Guide*. Baltimore, MD: The Johns Hopkins University Press.

Lenski, Noel. 2016. "Imperial Legislation and the Donatist Controversy: From Constantine to Honorius." In *The Donatist Schism: Controversy and Contexts*. Edited by Richard Miles: 167–219. Liverpool: Liverpool University Press.

Liebeschuetz, Wolf. 2003. "Pagan Historiography and the Decline of the Empire." In *Greek and Roman Historiography in Late Antiquity: Fourth to Sixth Century*. Edited by Gabriele Marasco: 177–218. Leiden: Brill.

Linder, Amnon (ed.). 1997. *The Jews in the Legal Sources of the Early Middle Ages*. Detroit, MI: Wayne State University Press; Jerusalem: Israel Academy of Sciences and Humanities.

Maas, Michael. 2010. *Readings in Late Antiquity: A Sourcebook*. 2nd edition. London: Routledge.

MacGeorge, Penny. 2002. *Late Roman Warlords*. Oxford Classical Monographs. Oxford: Oxford University Press.

Manders, Erika. 2012. *Coining Images of Power: Patterns in the Representation of Roman Emperors on Imperial Coinage, AD 193–284*. Impact of Empire 15. Leiden: Brill.

Matthews, John F. 1970. "Olympiodorus of Thebes and the History of the West, AD 407–425." *JRS* 60: 79–97.

Matthews, John F. 1975. *Western Aristocracies and Imperial Court, AD 364–425*. Oxford: Clarendon Press.

Matthews, John F. 2000. *Laying Down the Law: A Study of the Theodosian Code*. New Haven, CT: Yale University Press.

Mattingly, Harold, et al. (eds). 1923–94. *The Roman Imperial Coinage*, 10 volumes. London: Spink.

McEvoy, Meaghan. 2013. *Child Emperor Rule in the Late Roman West, AD 367–455*. Oxford: Oxford University Press.

Meyer, Elizabeth A. 2004. *Legitimacy and Law in the Roman World: Tabulae in Roman Belief and Practice*. Cambridge: Cambridge University Press.

Muhlberger, Steven. 1990. *The Fifth-Century Chroniclers: Prosper, Hydatius, and the Gallic Chronicler of 452*. Leeds: Francis Cairns.

Mulligan, Bret. 2007. "The Poet from Egypt? Reconsidering Claudian's Eastern Origin." *Philologus* 151: 285–310.

O' Flynn, John Michael. 1983. *Generalissimos of the Western Roman Empire*. Alberta: University of Alberta Press.

Oost, Stewart Irvin. 1968. *Galla Placidia Augusta: A Biographical Essay.* Chicago, IL and London: The University of Chicago Press.

Panayides, Panayiotis. 2016. *The Fate of Statues: A Contextualized Study of Sculpture in Late Antique Cyprus.* 2 volumes. Unpublished doctoral thesis. Durham University.

Pharr, Clyde, Davidson, Theresa Sherrer, and Brown Pharr, Mary. 1952. *The Theodosian Code and Novels and the Sirmondian Constitutions.* Princeton: Princeton University Press.

Platnauer, Maurice. Trans. 1922. *Claudius Claudianus,* Volume 1. London and New York: Harvard University Press.

Quasten, Johannes. 1966. *Patrology: The Golden Age of Greek Patristic Literature from the Council of Nicaea to the Council of Chalcedon,* Volume 3. 3rd edition. Utrecht, Antwerp: Spectrum.

Rohrbacher, David. 2002. *The Historians of Late Antiquity.* London: Routledge.

Roueché, Charlotte. 2007. "Written Display in the Late Antique and Byzantine City." *Proceeding of the 21st International Congress of Byzantine Studies 2006*: 235–54.

Roueché, Charlotte. 2009. "Digitising Inscribed Texts." In *Text Editing, Print and the Digital World.* Edited by Kathryn Sutherland and Marilyn Deegan: 159–68. London: Routledge.

Russell, John. 1986. "Liberty Echoes 1883 Show." *The New York Times.* July 11. www.nytimes.com/1986/07/11/arts/art-liberty-echoes-1883-show.html?page wanted=all&mcubz=1.

Sacks, Kenneth S. 1986. "The Meaning of Eunapius' History." *H&T* 25.1: 52–67.

Shaheen, Kareem, and Black, Ian. 2015. "Beheaded Syrian Scholar Refused to Lead ISIS Terrorists to Hidden Palmyra Antiquities." *Levant Research Institute.*

Sirago, Vito Antonio. 1961. *Galla Placidia e la trasformazione politica dell'Occidente.* Louvain: Publications Université de Louvain.

Sirago, Vito Antonio. 1970. "Olimpiodoro di Tebe e la sua opera storica." In *Richerche storiche ed economiche in memoria di Corrado Barbagallo.* Edited by Luigi de Rosa: 3–25. Naples: Edizioni Scientifiche Italiane.

Strutt, Jacob George. 1814. *The Rape of Proserpine: With Other Poems from Claudian.* London: A. J. Valpy.

Thompson, E. A. 1982. "Zosimus 6. 10. 2 and the Letters of Honorius." *CQ* 32.2: 445–62.

Tillemont, Louis-Sebastien. 1732. *Histoire des empereurs: qui comprend depuis Valentinien I jusqu'à Honoré,* Volume 5. Brussels: Eugene Henry Fricx.

Treadgold, Warren. 2004. "The Diplomatic Career and Historical Work of Olympiodorus of Thebes." *IHR* 26.4: 709–33.

Urbainczyk, Teresa. 1997. *Socrates of Constantinople: Historian of Church and State.* Ann Arbor, MI. University of Michigan Press.

Varner, Eric. 2004. *Mutilation and Transformation: Damnatio Memoriae and Roman Imperial Portraiture.* Leiden: Brill.

Walton, Philippa J. 2012. *Rethinking Roman Britain: Coinage and Archaeology.* Collection Moneta 137. Wetteren: Moneta.

Ware, Catherine. 2012. *Claudian and the Roman Epic Tradition.* Cambridge: Cambridge University Press.

Wasdin, Katherine. 2014. "Honorius Triumphant: Poetry and Politics in Claudian's Wedding Poems." *CP* 109.1: 48–65.

2   The stage is set

All the earlier emperors seem to have been very pleased to accept the honor and to use this title [Pontifex Maximus], even Constantine who, when he came to the throne, was perverted religiously and embraced the Christian faith, and all his successors including Valentinian and Valens. When, however, the pontifices as usual brought the robes to Gratian, he rejected their offer, considering it impious for a Christian to wear such a thing.

Zosimus, *New History*, 4.36.4–5

Religious revolution

As the fourth century dawned, and the last great state persecution of Christians was underway, an ecclesiastical synod convened at Elvira (Illiberis), a southern Spanish town somewhere in the region of modern Granada. The Council of Elvira drew up a list of eighty-one canons to address such issues as clerical celibacy, sexual morality, attendance at mass, funerary procedure, idolatry, fasting, and sacramental protocol. One rule even forbade Christian women to marry hairdressers and men with long hair (*Elvira. Can.* 67), a clause based on Saint Paul's dislike of what he considered male effeminacy (1 Corinthians 11.14). Misogynistic in character, the Council of Elvira was also deeply intolerant of other religions – a sign of things to come. Christians were still an illegal, persecuted group when the Elvira session sat, but within a few years the sect gained legality via imperial edicts. First in 311, from the eastern Augustus Galerius, a former persecutor of Christianity, then from the co-Augusti Constantine I (West) and Licinius II (East) in 313.

… wherefore it will be the duty of the Christians, in consequence of this our toleration, to pray to their God for our welfare, and for that of the public, and for their own; that the commonwealth may continue safe in every quarter, and that they themselves may live securely in their habitations.

(*Edict of Galerius*, Lactant. *De mort. pers.* 34. ANF-07: 729)

Christians and all others should have liberty to follow that mode of religion which to each of them appeared best ... open and free exercise of their respective religions is granted to all others, as well as to the Christians. For it befits the well-ordered state and the tranquility of Our times that each individual be allowed, according to his own choice, to worship the Divinity, and We mean not to detract anything from the honor due to any religion or its followers ...

(*Edict of Constantine and Licinius*,
Lactant. *De mort. pers.* 48. ANF-07: 745–6)

Within a short time of declaring universal religious toleration, Constantine began discriminating against those to whom he had promised freedom of worship. His religious policies provided a template for his successors. Constantine's laws and support for the Catholic Church exacerbated existing tensions, paving the way for decades – centuries even – of sectarian violence between Christians, Jews, pagans, and other groups. At the Council of Nicaea in 325, which Constantine facilitated, a Christian dogma was formulated – the Nicene Creed (Lubhéid 1982). Inspired by the canons of Elvira, it was not fully endorsed as official Christian doctrine until 381.

We believe in one God, the Father Almighty, maker of all things visible and invisible, and in one Lord Jesus Christ, the Son of God, the only-begotten of his Father, of the substance of the Father, God of God, Light of Light, very God of very God, begotten not made, being of one substance with the Father. By whom all things were made, both which be in heaven and in earth. Who for us men and for our salvation came down [from heaven] and was incarnate and was made man. He suffered and the third day he rose again, and ascended into heaven. And he shall come again to judge both the quick and the dead. And [we believe] in the Holy Ghost. And whosoever shall say that there was a time when the Son of God was not, or that before he was begotten he was not, or that he was made of things that were not, or that he is of a different substance or essence [from the Father] or that he is a creature, or subject to change or conversion, all that so say, the Catholic and Apostolic Church anathematizes them.

(*The Nicene Creed of 325*, NPNF2–14: 42)

One word in particular stands out from the Elvira and Nicaea council proceedings – heresy. The term derived from the Greek for 'freedom to choose' (*hairesis*), an ironic and cynical use of the word in light of its Christian context. From the language tempering the early church councils, it is apparent that there would be very little choice of religious expression. After Constantine, heresy was an extensively used label in imperial legal jargon against the enemies of the Nicene order. Indeed, heresy became a 'splendid tonic – except for heretics' (Perowne 1962, 64).

Emperor Constantine Augustus to Dracilianus. It is necessary that the privileges which are bestowed for the cultivation of religion should be given only to followers of the Catholic [universal] faith. We desire that heretics (*haereticos*) be not only kept from these privileges, but be subjected to various fines.

(*CTh*. 16.5.1. Sept 1, 326)

Emperors Gratian, Valentinian, and Theodosius Augustuses. An Edict to the People of the City of Constantinople. It is Our will that all the peoples who are ruled by the administration of Our Clemency shall practice that religion which the Divine Peter the Apostle transmitted to the Romans ... We shall believe in the single Deity of the Father, Son, and the Holy Spirit, under the concept of equal majesty, and of the Holy Trinity. We command that those persons who follow this rule shall embrace the name of Catholic Christians. The rest, however, whom We judge demented and insane, shall sustain the infamy of heretical dogmas (*haeretici dogmatis*), their meeting places shall not receive the name of churches, and they shall be smitten first by divine vengeance and secondly by the retribution of Our own initiative, which We shall assume in accordance with the divine judgment.

(*CTh*. 16.1.2. Feb 28, 380)

It was a similar story for pagan Roman citizens.

Emperors Constantius and Constans Augustuses to Taurus, Praetorian Prefect. It is Our pleasure that the temples shall be immediately closed in all places and in all cities, and access to them forbidden, so as to deny to all abandoned men the opportunity to commit sin. It is also Our will that all men shall abstain from sacrifices. But if perchance any man should perpetrate such criminality, he shall be struck down with the avenging sword (*gladio ultore*). We also decree that the property of a man thus executed shall be vindicated to the fisc. The governors of the provinces shall be similarly punished if they should neglect to avenge such crimes.

(*CTh*. 16.10.4. Dec 1, 346).

Emperor Constantius Augustus and Julian Caesar. If any persons should be proved to devote their attention to sacrifices or to worship images, We command that they shall be subjected to capital punishment (*poena capitis*).

(*CTh*. 16.10.6. Feb 20, 356)

Emperors Gratian, Valentinian, and Theodosius Augustuses to Eutropius, Praetorian Prefect. Those Christians who have become pagans shall be deprived of the power and the right to make testaments, and every testament of such decedent, if there is a testament, shall be rescinded by the annulment of its foundation.

(*CTh*. 16.7.1. May 2, 381)

Emperors Gratian, Valentinian, and Theodosius Augustuses to Evagrius, Augustal Prefect and Romanus, Count of Egypt. No person shall be granted the right to perform sacrifices; no person shall go around the temples; no person shall revere the shrines. All persons shall recognize that they are excluded from profane entrance into temples by the opposition of Our law, so that if any person should attempt to do anything with reference to the gods or the sacred rites, contrary to Our prohibition, he shall learn that he will not be exempted from punishment by any special grants of imperial favor. If any judge also, during the time of his administration, should rely on the privilege of his power, and as a sacrilegious violator of the law, should enter polluted places (*polluta loca*), he shall be forced to pay into Our treasury fifteen pounds of gold, and his office staff a like sum, unless they oppose him with their combined strength.

(*CTh*. 16.10.11. June 16, 391)

Likewise, for the empire's Jewish citizens.

Emperor Constantius to Evagrius ... It shall be observed that Jews shall not hereafter unite Christian women to their villainy; if they should do so, however, they shall be subject to the peril of capital punishment (*capitali periculo*).

(*CTh*. 16.8.6. Aug 13, 339)

Emperor Constantius to Evagrius ... If the Jew should purchase a [Christian] slave and circumcise him, he shall be penalized not only with the loss of the slave, but he shall also be visited with capital punishment (*capitali sententia*).

(*CTh*. 16.9.2. Aug 13, 339)

Similar vitriol to that used in law also flavors the literary sources, some of which placed paganism and heresy together in the same vein. When Gregory of Nyssa (in modern Turkey) gave his funeral oration for Honorius' mother, Aelia Flaccilla Augusta, in September 386, he condemned the Arian heresy as essentially the same as pagan idolatry. Arian Christianity was at odds theologically with the Nicene Creed about Christ's true nature, and for a time threatened Nicene hegemony until Theodosius I's vigorous persecution of the heresy. Arianism was popular, though, especially among barbarian peoples, and anti-Arian laws continued to be passed well into the sixth century until its eventual demise. So much for the freedom of choice. Coming back to Flaccilla's funeral oration, its author, Gregory, owed his episcopal see at

Nyssa to Theodosius, and as such was compliant with his imperial patron's position on matters doctrinal.

> Hatred of idols is common to all who share the faith, but the Arian infidelity and its idolatry is an abomination. They consider the divinity to be in creation and do not believe the material from which such idols are fashioned as blasphemous, thereby considering it as suitable for worship. He who adores a creature in name of Christ is an idolater.
>
> (Greg. Nyss. *In Flacc.* 489)

In 381, Theodosius, in the manner of Constantine before him at Nicaea, summoned a synod of 150 bishops to Constantinople to formally ratify the Nicene Creed as the official doctrine of the Roman state. Once again heretics, pagans, Jews, and even the long-haired men mentioned in the canons of Elvira drew fire (NPNF2–14: 349–93). Theodosius apparently felt that yet harsher measures were in order after the Council of Constantinople. His subsequent laws criminalized religious dissent as high treason (*maiestatis*). Backed up by the threat of extreme violence, legally enforced obedience to what had become the 'imperial church' of a Catholic empire was foisted upon the population by their government (Humfress 2007, 243ff.). The writ of imperial law was extensive. From Italy to Gaul, from Britain down to Spain, across the Gibraltar Straits into North Africa, up the Levant into Asia Minor, across the Aegean to Greece, and through the Balkans up to Germania – Catholic Christianity became the official religion across the empire, and anything else was considered treason.

> Emperors Valentinian, Theodosius, and Arcadius Augustuses to Eusignius, Praetorian Prefect. We bestow the right of assembly upon those persons who believe according to the doctrines which in the times of Constantine of sainted memory were decreed as those that would endure forever ... if those persons who suppose that the right of assembly has been granted to them alone should attempt to provoke any agitation against the regulation of Our Tranquility, they shall know that, as authors of sedition and as disturbers of the peace of the Church, they shall also pay the penalty of *maiestatis* with their life and blood (*capite ac sanguine*).
>
> (*CTh.* 16.1.4. Jan 23, 386)

The Nicene Church's path to victory was therefore not clear-cut by any means. Heretical groups offered much obstruction, but there was little coordinated pagan resistance (Cameron 2011). Successive post-Constantinian administrations passed law after law aimed at shutting down pagan places of worship. This legislation had little success until the reign of Theodosius, who, in 391, banned pagan religions outright, cut their state subsidies, and closed temples everywhere (Zos. 5.38.2; Lavan 2011). Each legal revision carried ever greater menace – monetary fines, incarceration, torture, and execution. It is worth noting that penal cruelty was not confined to the late imperial judiciary, for 'at no period in their history were the Romans known for their leniency towards the condemned' (Harries 1999, 135). Nevertheless, late imperial justice is distinct from earlier periods because of the increasingly wide range of minor offenses for which persons could be punished – a veritable 'progress of cruelty' (MacMullen 1990, 209ff.).

With the noted exceptions of Julian II, the so-called apostate, and the Arian Valens, most fourth-century Augusti adopted Constantine's Nicene program, in particular Theodosius I, an enthusiastic oppressor of heterodoxy and paganism. Christian symbolism influenced the official propaganda and primary written sources of emperors, their families, and many of the élites (Elsner 1998, 138–43, 221–35; Salzman 2002). Constantine was the first to use Christian imagery on his coinage after becoming sole ruler in 324 (Odahl 1981). It was under the Theodosian dynasty, however, that the union of Christian iconography and imperial art found fullest expression, though pagan imagery continued to be used (Lampinen 2016). Old customs proved hard to suppress and pagan Classical motifs persisted, such as the personification of the goddess Victoria in coinage and art, but even she was gradually Christianized (Doyle 2015; Elsner 1995; Kiilerich 1993; Bellinger and Berlincourt 1962). Not only did the image of Victoria become more associated with biblical angels – she even changed sex. One of the earliest artistic representations of Victory/Christian angel in male form emerged in the 420s, as we will see later in a cameo of the emperors Honorius, Constantius III, and Valentinian III (Figure 9.6). Victoria continued to be represented as female on coinage and other art forms well into the fifth century, but her gender reconditioning might be due to the fact that there is only one, very ambiguous reference to female angels in the Old Testament. 'Then I looked up and behold, there were two women, with the wind in their wings! They had wings like those of a stork, and they lifted up the basket between heaven and earth' (Zech. 5.9).

Ecclesiastical writers mirrored official propaganda, viewing the emperor's religious piety as the mark of a great ruler. One example is Ambrose of Milan's lengthy exegetical funeral eulogy for Theodosius I in 395.

> What is more illustrious than the faith of an emperor whom sovereignty does not exalt, pride does not elevate, but piety bows down? Of whom Solomon admirably says: "The threatening of an unjust king is like the roaring of a lion, but as dew upon the grass, so also is his cheerfulness." Therefore, what a great thing it is to lay aside the terror of power, and prefer the sweetness of granting pardon?
>
> (Amb. *De ob. Theod.* 12)

Such was the Christian propaganda of the age. The few remaining pagan writers of late antiquity were less than kind about Theodosius. Take Eunapius and Zosimus, for example. Both of these historians adhered to the old religions, and therefore wrote from an alternative viewpoint to the likes of Gregory or Ambrose.

> In the reign of Emperor Theodosius ... our age seemed to ride upon the backs of asses.
>
> (Eunap. *fr*. 48.3)

> During the reign of Theodosius, no virtue was praiseworthy and every kind of luxury and licentiousness increased daily. Such was the ruin that occurred that the inhabitants of mighty Antioch in Syria, unable to bear the additions to the public taxes daily contrived by the collectors, rose up in rebellion, shamelessly pulled down the statues of the emperor and his consort, and made an appropriate clamor, albeit not without elegance and their usual wit.
>
> (Zos. 4.41.1)

Almost eighty years after Constantine and Licinius' declaration of freedom of worship for all, many Roman citizens were socially marginalized precisely because of their religious affiliations. Furthermore, the wholesale dissemination of Christian ideology should, in theory, have helped to advance general freedom across society – it did not. There were of course Christians of all persuasions, as well as pagans and Jews, who tried to alleviate the desperate poverty around them, but the late Roman world remained hierarchical and class-ridden. It was a society consumed by wealth inequality, burdened by generationally inherited debt and spiraling excessive taxation – and cowed by a terrifying judicial system.

To have and to have not

In broad terms, late Roman society was segregated between those with property and status (*honestiores*) and those without such assets (*humiliores*), the latter legally defined as having ignoble status (*condicio*). The gulf between the rich and the poor was staggering. Visiting Rome in the 390s, the historian Ammianus Marcellinus could not believe the hubris of the rich and squalor of the poor that he encountered there. Ammianus' observation captures the level of class disparity in the late empire.

> This magnificence and splendor of the assemblies is marred by the rude worthlessness of a few, who do not consider where they were born, but, as if licence were granted to vice, descend to sin and wantonness ... Some of these men eagerly strive for statues, thinking that by them they can be made immortal, as if they would gain a greater reward from senseless brazen images than from the consciousness of honorable and virtuous conduct ... [some] are clearly unaware that their forefathers,

through whom the greatness of Rome was so far flung, gained renown, not by riches, but by fierce wars, and not differing from the common soldiers in wealth, mode of life, or simplicity of attire, overcame all obstacles by valor ... In consequence of this state of things, the few houses that were formerly famed for devotion to serious pursuits now teem with the sports of sluggish indolence ... now the vain arrogance of some men regards everything born outside the *pomerium* [boundary] of our city as worthless ... But of the multitude of lowest condition and greatest poverty some spend the entire night in wine shops, some lurk in the shade of the awnings of the theaters ... or they quarrel with one another in their games at dice, making a disgusting sound by drawing back the breath into their resounding nostrils; or, which is the favorite among all amusements, from sunrise until evening, in sunshine and in rain, they stand open-mouthed, examining minutely the good points or the defects of charioteers and their horses. And it is most remarkable to see an innumerable crowd of plebeians, their minds filled with a kind of eagerness, hanging on the outcome of the chariot races. These and similar things prevent anything memorable or serious from being done in Rome.

(Amm. Marc. *Hist*. 14.6.7–26)

The early fifth-century historian Olympiodorus supports Ammianus' description of élite Roman wealth.

Many of the Roman households received an income of four thousand pounds of gold per year from their properties, not including grain, wine and other produce, which if sold, would have amounted to one-third of the income in gold. The income of the households at Rome of the second class was one thousand, or one thousand five hundred pounds of gold ... Before the capture of Rome [by the Visigoths in 410], Symmachus the orator, a senator of middling wealth, spent two thousand pounds when his son Symmachus celebrated his praetorship. Maximus, one of the wealthy men, spent four thousand pounds on his son's praetorship. The praetors celebrated their festivals for seven days.

(Olymp. *fr*. 41.2)

Life was without doubt harder for the freeborn lower social classes. The institution of chattel slavery still endured, but so too did a more insidious type of enslavement – bonded labor. It had been practiced since the early Republic, albeit to a lesser extent than its late imperial counterpart. This later incarnation of debt servitude emerged during the chaotic third century, when incessant wars, recurrent plague, and economic collapse brought the empire to its knees. Diocletian stemmed the decay, restoring stability and security through the imposition of a more totalitarian style of government (*PLRE* I, 253–4). Diocletian's revised system removed many civil liberties and furthermore restricted freeborn Romans to their locale and occupations – in the countryside and in urban centers. Children too were obligated to follow in their parents' occupations, thus creating hereditary debt bondage. Constantine continued Diocletian's policies, particularly with regard to the rustic workforce. The latter, whom the urban population depended on for their food supply, included small freeholders, laborers on medium-sized farms, and tenant farmers (*coloni*, sometimes *inquilini*) who worked the great land estates of the élite. These estates centered around the house of its master (*dominus*), the so-called *villa rustica* (country villa), producing cereals, oil, livestock, wine, etc. As pointed out by Olympiodorus above, estate owners made great profits from their holdings.

> Emperor Constantine Augustus to the Provincials. Any person in whose possession a *colonus* that belongs to another is found not only shall restore the aforesaid *colonus* to his birth status (*origo*) but also shall assume the capitation tax for this man for the time that he was with him. *Coloni* also who meditate flight must be bound with chains and reduced to a servile condition, so that by virtue of their condemnation to slavery, they shall be compelled to fulfill the duties that befit freemen.
>
> (*CTh*. 5.17.1. Oct 30, 332)

Coloni were bound legally and financially to their *dominus* (Lenski 2017; Wickham 2005; Banaji 2001; Mirković 1997; cf. Harper 2011; Carrié 1982). The treatment of tenants varied, depending on the character of their *dominus*, in much the same way as chattel slaves relied on the goodwill of their owners. As the fourth century progressed, and provincial security was threatened by insurrection or foreign invasion, the agricultural labor force looked to their *domini* for their livelihood and security more than to central government (Arce 1997). Still, imperial laws continued to impose restrictions on the rural population, usually in favor of estate owners. By the early part of Honorius' reign, rural workers had become defined as 'slaves of the soil' (*serui ... terrae*), with no freedom of mobility without the express permission of a *dominus* (*Cod. Iust*. 11.52.1. Jan 23, 393–Jan 17, 395).

Urban life was not much better for the working poor – male and female – collectivized as they were into guilds (*familiae*). The *familia* also referred to a slave household. In the cities and towns, as in the countryside, the lower socio-economic classes were fixed to their posts, such as those working in imperial production centers. The *fabricensis* (armorer) in the weapons factory (*fabrica*), the mint worker (*monetarius*) in the mints, the weaver (*gynaecearius*) in the clothing factories – all these and more were stuck in perpetual bondage to the state, as were their descendants.

It is not the intention of this chapter to engage with the long-running debates about whether or not the late Roman bonded worker should be considered the same as a chattel slave. These are questions about terminology; but, if slavery can be defined as living in constant dread of physical or financial punishment for oneself and one's family, then slavery is what it was for the late Roman lower social classes. What is more, the legal record, supplemented by literary sources, make it clear that fear and repression was the norm for the *humiliores*. Small wonder that bonded workers fled – or attempted to flee – their allotted environs. As with religious dissidents, the law protected the interests of the propertied class. The worker who illegally absconded from his or her miserable lot could expect brutal retribution. This applied not just to the primary escapee, but to their family as well. To add further insult to injury, captured – it must be remembered, freeborn – Romans could be branded with hot irons, or tattooed, marking them as felons for the remainder of their lives.

> Emperors Honorius and Arcadius Augustuses to Hosius, Master of Offices. Brands (*stigmata*), that is, the official State mark (*nota publica*), shall be stamped upon the arms of armorers, in imitation of the practice of branding army recruits, so that in this manner at least it may be possible to recognize skulkers. If any man should harbor such armorers or their children, he shall be vindicated without doubt to an arms factory, just as those who for the purpose of avoiding their labor have surreptitiously passed over to the enlistment oaths of any form of the public imperial service.
>
> (*CTh*. 10.22.4. Dec 15, 398)

However, as Stewart Irvin Oost pointed out, we should try not to be overly judgmental of late Roman élites, for 'it is easy to regard the late empire as a vast prison house where the rank and file were exploited for the benefit of the guards, that is, the ruling classes, but where even the latter were horrifyingly subject to the most destructive vicissitudes of circumstance and ill fortune' (1968, 6). This is not a justification for what we would consider atrocious treatment of the masses by the few, but it is worth bearing Oost's statement in mind while progressing through this book, which tells the story of one particular member of those same ruling classes.

Endless war, barbarian twilight

The late Roman Empire had long ceased any meaningful territorial expansion since Trajan's early second-century annexation of Dacia (roughly modern Romania), the last significant imperial land grab. Rome's wars became primarily defensive and often internal, fighting over dwindling resources. In the fourth century alone, there were at least twenty cases of insurrection, mostly in the West. Some were rebellions, the majority were usurpations. There was a difference between the two. Basically, usurpers claimed imperial power, issued coinage in their name and image, appointed officials, and passed laws, whereas rebels did not (Doyle 2014; Humphries 2008; Elton 1996; Wardman 1984). In the fourth century, only two usurpers had any success – Constantine I and Julian II. With very few exceptions, the rest generally ended up as decapitated heads on city walls. Civil war had a detrimental effect on the political, economic, and social fabric of the Roman state.

In addition to the seemingly perpetual civil discord, the fourth century witnessed an increase in foreign immigration and invasion. Barbarian peoples – Franks, Visigoths, Alamanni, Lombards, Burgundians, Vandals, and Huns – encroached en masse along the Roman frontiers (*limes*). The movement of foreign peoples – both peaceful and violent – across the *limes* had been a fact of life for a very long time, but nothing on the scale of what transpired from about the mid-fourth century onward. There is no single definitive explanation to explain this particular rise in barbarian migration. Various factors were involved – climate change, displacement caused by war, fear of more aggressive barbarians such as the Huns, a people the historian Jordanes described as inhuman beasts (Jord. *Get.* 24). While some barbarian groups sought plunder, others wished for a quiet existence, or for some farmland, to have what they perceived as a better standard of living than their own.

Some barbarians, even former combatants against the empire, freely submitted to the emperor's authority in a ritual act (*deditio*). Sometimes, entire barbarian tribes or nations were received in this way by the state, becoming *dediticii*, though not all barbarian *dediticii* lived within imperial borders. There were those who displayed loyalty to Rome from beyond the *limes*, while some were assigned fallow lands to farm as *coloni*. Others took up military service as *foederati* in the Roman army. The dividends for service were considerable: asylum, the possibility of citizenship for their descendants, and a food subsidy (*subsidia*). Emperors recognized the value of this manpower resource, and barbarian *foederati* played an important role in the many civil wars of the fourth and fifth centuries. In fact, *foederati* fought on the side of both legitimate emperors and usurpers. To contemporary observers like Ammianus Marcellinus, Eunapius, and Synesius, the imperial policy of employing foreign troops to fight Roman wars was utter madness. Such shortsightedness, these writers contended, could only result in the ruination of the state (Amm. Marc. *Hist.* 31.4.6; Eunap. *fr.* 42.1–77; Syn. *De Reg.* 24–5).

In 376, the eastern Augustus Valens permitted certain Visigothic tribes – the Tervingi and Greuthungi – to cross the River Danube into northern Thrace as *dediticii*. The reason they gave to Valens for their request was that the Huns pressed them from the rear. Some years prior to this, Valens had sent the army across the Danube to punish the Visigoths for having sided with a usurper against him (Eunap. *fr.* 37). Valens' army indiscriminately murdered unarmed civilians, burnt farmsteads and crops, enslaving many, and suspending the Visigoths' *subsidia* – pauperizing them. When the very same Visigoths asked to be let into the empire in 376, Valens assented, feeling that they had been well subjugated into obedience (Eunap. *fr.* 42).

Unfortunately, Roman organization of the barbarian influx was hopelessly inept. Deep-seated Roman xenophobia and bureaucratic corruption contributed to terrible mistreatment of migrant women and children. Inevitably, their menfolk revolted and ravaged northern Greece. Two years later, the crisis reached a bloody confrontation – the famous battle of Hadrianopolis (modern Edirne, Turkey). On August 9, 378, virtually the entire eastern Roman field army was annihilated. Thousands, including Valens, fell in a single, scorching hot summer's day (Kulikowski 2007, 123–43; Heather 2005, 327–56; Ferrill 1997, 56–67). From this point on, the Visigothic presence on Roman soil was permanent. Ironically, the eastern empire replenished its military through levying the Visigoths as *foederati*. However, Hadrianopolis was a major crossroads in many respects – militarily, politically, and psychologically. In Constantinople, John Chrysostom recorded the immediate reaction to the defeat.

> A great crowd of widows ... all arrayed in a dark mourning robe and spending their whole time in lamentation ... these women ... having all sent out their husbands to war in the hope of receiving them back again, instead of which it has been their lot to receive the bitter tidings of their death. Neither has any one come back to them with the bodies of their slain, or bringing anything save a message describing the manner of their death. And some there are who have not even been vouchsafed this record, or been enabled to learn how their husbands fell, as they were buried beneath a heap of slain in the thick of battle.
>
> (Chrys. *Ad vid. iun.* 5)

The ecclesiastical writer Tyrannius Rufinus was adamant that it was Valens' impious heretical religious beliefs – Arianism – which were responsible for the disaster at Hadrianopolis (Ruf. *HE.* 4.28–32). Another ecclesiastic, the Spaniard Orosius, writing early in the following century, also reproached Valens saying that it was 'the righteous judgment of God that they [the Visigoths] burnt alive the man ... for the error of heresy' (Oros. 7.33.19). Eunapius' quip about living in an age of donkeys is vindicated by the opinions of Rufinus, Orosius, and others. They were more concerned about the color of a man's religion than by the existential danger the barbarians posed to the state. Religious rifts continued unabated well beyond Honorius' reign. The overriding interest to preserve unity and strength at any cost, under a single Catholic banner, achieved the exact opposite. Criminalizing divergent religious beliefs deepened societal divisions, and diverted critical resources from more pressing matters. In an impassioned letter primarily intended for Valentinian II, the urban prefect Symmachus, a pagan aristocrat, maintained that it was the ancient 'sacred rites' which had repelled Rome's barbarian enemies in the past. To break with ancestral traditions would be detrimental to the state (Symm. *Rel.* 3.8–13).

The Theodosian dynasty

In the months after Hadrianopolis, a state of emergency prevailed in the East, and concerns mounted in the West about Visigothic troop movements in the Balkans. With the eastern throne vacant, new, capable leadership was urgently needed. The man whom the western emperor Gratian chose to be his eastern colleague was Theodosius, an experienced commander from a distinguished military Spanish family. Theodosius was appointed eastern Augustus by the young western ruler Gratian in January 379 at Sirmium (Sremska Mitrovica, Serbia), capital of the prefecture of Illyricum and Gratian's hometown.

Theodosius was the first emperor from Spain in over two hundred years. Traditionally, it is held that Theodosius came from Cauca, in central Spain (modern Coca, Segovia), but a southern Spanish origin has also been proposed by Alicia Maria Canto (Hyd. *Chron.* 379; Kulikowski 2004; Arce 2009; cf. Canto 2006). Theodosius was supposed to have been descended from the great military emperor Trajan, who was from Italica, near modern Sevilla (*Epit. de Caes.* 48.1.8–10; *Chron. Marcell.* 379.1). This could possibly be a fabrication, but it worked well for Theodosius' dynastic propaganda, for it connected him and his family to a Roman golden age, enhancing his legitimacy and prestige. Theodosius' propagandists expanded further on the Trajanic association by comparing the two emperors' physical appearance and character (*Epit. de Caes.* 48.8–14; Them. *Orr.* 16.205a, 19.229c; Oros. 7.34.2–4; cf. Cass. Dio. 68.6). Theodosius was thus cast in the mold of one of Rome's finest – exactly what the state needed in a time of crisis. By extension, therefore, all of Theodosius' children received this great legacy. Later on, Honorius' master spin doctor Claudian made sure to highlight the Spanish connection on several occasions (Cl. *Fesc.* 2; *III Cons.* 177; *IV Cons.* 127–9, 393; *Stil.* II.236–8; *Stil.* III.53).

As we have seen, Theodosius I was an ardent Catholic, though exactly how committed he was to the Christian sect prior to his accession is a subject of debate (McLynn 2005, 77–120). That notwithstanding, Theodosius' *patria* (homeland) was a bastion of Catholic Christianity, but although Spain had produced the seminal Council of Elvira, the peninsula had its fair share of heretics. One of these was Priscillianism, the name given to the ascetic teachings of Priscillian, bishop of Ávila (Burrus 1995; Ubric Rabaneda 2004). Priscillian's views gained enough disciples throughout Spain to merit a state pogrom being prosecuted against it. Nevertheless, despite intense persecution, Priscillian beliefs proved difficult to dislodge. Indeed, the heresy survived the end of the western empire by at least a century, lasting well into the period of Visigothic rule in Spain (McKenna 1938).

Prior to his elevation in 379, Theodosius was already married to Aelia Flaccilla, who was also from Spain, though her origins are obscure (Holum 1982; Salisbury 2001). At the time of Theodosius' accession, they had one son, Arcadius (*c.* 377–408). Their marriage must have occurred about 375, and Flaccilla's family likely belonged to the same élite Hispano-Roman circle as her husband's. Throughout her imperial career, Flaccilla was renowned for her passionate patronage of Catholic Christianity. Years after her death, she was affectionately remembered as a 'soul faithful to God' (*fidelis anima Deo*) by no less a figure than Bishop Ambrose of Milan (*De ob. Theod.* 40.8–9). Following the example of the Augusta Helena, mother of Constantine I, Flaccilla dedicated herself to helping the poor and sick, and for this she endeared herself to many people. Imperial coinage minted in 383 depicts Flaccilla as Augusta, though she had probably held this rank since 379 (Roueché 2002). On coinage, however, Flaccilla was the first Augusta since Helena to be styled thus, and, like Helena, Flaccilla was venerated as a saint by the Orthodox Church.

> In no way exalted by her imperial rank she was rather fired by it with greater longing for divine things. The greatness of the good gift given her made her love for Him who gave it all the greater, so she bestowed every kind of attention on the maimed and the mutilated, declining all aid from her household and her guards, herself visiting the houses where the sufferers lodged, and providing everyone with what he required. She also went about the guest chambers of the churches and ministered to the wants of the sick, herself handling pots and pans, and tasting broth, now bringing in a dish and breaking bread and offering morsels, and washing out a cup and going through all the other duties which are supposed to be proper to servants and maids. To them who strove to restrain her from doing these things with her own hands she would say, "It befits a sovereign to distribute gold; I, for the sovereign power that has been given me, am giving my own service to the Giver."
>
> (Theod. *HE*. 18)

The Spanish ascendancy at Constantinople

Theodosius brought a large contingent of westerners, mostly Spaniards, with him to Constantinople. The emperor was also prudent enough to involve members of the eastern establishment in his administration. However, it was the western cohort that formed the heart of Theodosius' government, many of whom were linked to the emperor by either blood or marriage. All of the Spanish contingent were Catholic Christians, though pagans did indeed serve in the eastern court. Among Theodosius' Spanish compatriots were his uncle Eucherius – given charge of the imperial treasury, and later made consul; Paternus, later the proconsul of Africa; and Nebridius, Flaccilla's brother-in-law. It was not only male Spaniards who went east with Theodosius and Flaccilla. Female members from both sides of their families accompanied them to Constantinople, including the emperor's niece Serena, whom he later adopted as his daughter (Holum 1982, 6–47).

Theodosius enjoyed substantial Spanish support among western power circles as well. This group included Pope Damasus (366–84), an advocate of Theodosius' policies against religious dissent. Another Theodosian stalwart in the West was Antonius – praetorian prefect for Italy, and later consul in 382, and related by marriage to the emperor.

Other high-profile westerners at Constantinople included Nummius Aemilianus Dexter, son of the bishop of Barcino (Barcelona), and Rufinus, a Gallo-Roman from Elusa (Eauze, southwestern France). Rufinus became a pivotal figure in the government of both Theodosius and Arcadius. However, one of the most prominent figures of Theodosius' early administration was Maternus Cynegius from Carranque, central Spain, who may possibly have been related to the emperor (Matthews 1967). Becoming eastern praetorian prefect (*praefectus praetorio Orientis*) in 384, Cynegius launched a violent campaign against paganism throughout the Roman East. Cynegius' war on dissent was extremely destructive. His actions stirred up hostility in the region and led to public unrest, which in turn caused problems for the emperor. Pagans despised Cynegius. To them he was a 'profane wretch, an enemy of the gods' (Lib. *Or.* 30.46). When Cynegius died from illness in 388, his body reposed for a year in the Church of the Holy Apostles at Constantinople. In 389, his wife Achantia brought her husband's remains back to his ancestral home in Spain. We are told that Achantia, a deeply devout Spanish Catholic, walked alongside the cortege for the entire return journey to Spain from Constantinople (*Cons. Const.* s.a. 388; *CLRE* 55).

Theodosius was wise to surround himself with people whom he could trust. Not long before his accession, his father, the celebrated general Theodosius the Elder, had fallen foul of Valentinian I and was executed in 375. To avoid a similar end, Theodosius the younger either retired or was exiled to Spain, but his sojourn was temporary. After the Hadrianopolis debacle, the western emperor Gratian recalled Theodosius to active military service against the Visigoths in the Balkans. Shortly afterwards, in January 379, Gratian elevated Theodosius to the eastern throne. Yet, however prestigious or cordial this promotion appeared, Theodosius had grounds to be wary. Gratian's father, Valentinian I, was ultimately responsible for Theodosius the Elder's execution. Therefore, Theodosius brought a large company of people he trusted with him to Constantinople, but, as John Matthews noted, the new emperor did not take 'merely a few relatives and intimates; an entire clan moved with him to dominate the court life of Theodosian Constantinople' (Matthews 1975, 111).

What the composition of Theodosius' new administration demonstrates is the immense value he placed upon kinship, homeland, and religion. This trait was passed on to Honorius, informing his entire life. So, when ecclesiastic writers like Orosius espoused Honorius' piety and love of family; or when the poet Prudentius declared that 'we had a young warrior, mighty in Christ, to lead our army and our power' (Prudent. *Contra Symm.* II.709–10; Harries 1984); or even when imperial propaganda wrapped Honorius' image in layers of Christian iconography – these were not empty platitudes. They were the very essence of the Theodosian dynasty.

The selling of a compromise

In October 382, a Visigothic delegation to Sirmium signed an accord with the empire. Present at the negotiations were Theodosius, the *magister militum* Saturninus, a survivor of the battle of Hadrianopolis, and quite likely the western emperor Gratian. The new deal gave the Visigoths free-holdings, as

Figure 2.1 Commemorative silver medallion of Theodosius I. Rome mint, uncertain date after 382.
Obv. Theodosius pearl-diademed, draped and cuirassed. Legend: DN-THEODO-SIVS-PF-AVG (*Dominus Noster Theodosius Pius Felix Augustus*/Our Lord Theodosius, pious and fortunate emperor). Rev. Theodosius, in armor and cloak, standing, *labarum* in his right hand, a globe in his left. A barbarian prisoner genuflects on one knee, facing the emperor. Legend: TRIVMFATOR-GENT-BARB (*Triumfator Gentium Barbarum*/Victor over barbarian peoples). Exergue: R (Roma)-T (*officina* mark).
Source: *RIC* IX 52a.

well as positions with the Roman army as *foederati* (*Cons. Const.* s.a. 382; Heather 1991, 166–75). Theodosius' administration presented the peace treaty as a victory to a nervous populace, using customary media – coinage, such as the commemorative *Triumfator* series (Figure 2.1), inscriptions, public art, and statuary – to reassure public confidence. In reality, though, it was a hollow victory, since armed barbarians were still present within Rome's borders.

A few months after the Visigothic treaty, the philosopher Themistius, speechmaker supreme to the emperor, extolled his patron's peace achievements in Constantinople's senate house.

> Grant that it was possible to destroy [the barbarians] with ease, and to do everything that might be possible for us and not experience any harm in return ... Would it be better to fill Thrace with bodies or farmers? To show it full of graves or of men? To walk through wild or cultivated fields? To number the slain or the ploughmen ... to cohabit with those whom we have subdued? I hear from those who come from those lands, that they [the Visigoths] have now made the iron of their swords and armors into mattocks and sickles, and that they greet Ares at a distance, and rather worship Demeter and Dionysius ...
>
> (Them. *Or.* 16.211a–b)

Themistius' earlier orations for Theodosius had been far less concerned with making peace with the Visigoths. Then, he had urged the use of overwhelming force against them. Before the treaty of 382, Theodosius had tried valiantly to crush Visigothic power several times, but with no successful conclusion. The imperial army had not recovered from the massive loss of manpower it had sustained at Hadrianopolis. Furthermore, the massacre of thousands of Roman troops caused an increase in draft-dodging – already an issue for military recruitment. Who would have wanted to fight against such impossible odds? Soldiers' pay was good, in comparison to most other professions, with donatives distributed at specific points annually – on the occasion of imperial accession, births, weddings and the like (Treadgold 2014, 303–17). Despite the financial incentives, after Hadrianopolis many soldiers' sons – legally bound to follow their fathers' profession – tried to evade military service. Theodosius had to repeatedly issue stringent laws in an attempt stop the phenomenon (*CTh*. 7.22.9. May 14, 380; 7.22.10. July 8, 380; 7.22.11. Sept 8, 380). A favored route for evading military life were the many Christian monastic communities springing up all over the empire, most especially in the eastern provinces. Young men and women who, in another time, would have been the soldiers, administrators, and – most importantly – tax payers, completely abandoned the secular world. Some emperors were proactive against such shirkers. Valens, for instance, raided monastic settlements in Egypt, arresting thousands of monks for the army draft (Lenski 2004). It turned out, however, that press-ganged monks made for bad soldiers (Zos. 5.23.4–5).

Theodosius' problems were exacerbated as other barbarian tribal groups, taking advantage of Rome's weakened security after Hadrianopolis, began invading across the *limes*, deep into the empire. When Themistius later paid tribute to the emperor in front of the senate after the treaty, he conveniently skipped over Theodosius' shortcomings (*Them. Or.* 16. 207a–d). No matter how much triumphalism the state propaganda machine spun, the simple truth was that Rome's military morale was dangerously low. The Theodosian compromise with the Visigoths created a ripple effect that echoed far into the future. Theodosius' barbarian policies were inherited by his sons and their successors. They would have to face the new reality as best they could. The Visigoths, for their part, continued to press the empire for land to settle on until finally reaching an accord (*foedus*) with Honorius in 418 for an area in Aquitania Secunda, in Gaul.

The usurper from Spain

Not everything Spanish held good fortune for Theodosius. In the summer of 383, the *comes Britanniae*, Magnus Maximus, a Spaniard and possibly a relative of Theodosius, was proclaimed emperor by the field troops stationed on the island. Maximus reopened the London mint – closed by Constantine I since 325 – and declared his imperial ambitions by striking his own coinage.

When he had enough money to pay his forces, and to fund a campaign on the continent, Maximus crossed the sea to Gaul. He defeated Gratian's forces near Lutetia (Paris), and very soon afterwards, had eliminated the legitimate emperor through duplicitousness. Maximus' *magister equitum* (cavalry commander), Andragathius, tricked Gratian into believing he was to meet his wife at a secure location at Lugdunum (Lyon). Thinking all was well, Gratian arrived at the meeting point whereupon Andragathius revealed himself and stabbed the young emperor to death (*Cons. Const.* s.a. 383; *Epit. de Caes.* 47.7; Soc. *HE.* 5.11; Zos. 4.35.5–6). A deputation, led by Bishop Ambrose, was sent by Theodosius to obtain Gratian's body for burial but was refused by Maximus, perhaps to antagonize things further. War should have swiftly followed, but as he was preoccupied by the Visigothic question, Theodosius decided to temporarily accept Maximus as his western colleague. In the meantime, a happier event was announced. On September 9, 384, Theodosius and Flaccilla's second son was born – Honorius.

References

Arce, Javier. 1997. "*Otium et negotium*: The Great Estates, 4th–7th Centuries." In *The Transformation of the Roman World, AD 400–900*. Edited by Leslie Webster and Michelle Brown: 19–32. London: British Museum Press.

Arce, Javier. 2009. *El último siglo de la España romana, 284–409*, 2nd rev. ed. Madrid: Alianza.

Banaji, Jairus. 2001. *Agrarian Change in Late Antiquity: Gold, Labour, and Aristocratic Dominance*. Oxford: Oxford University Press.

Bardill, Jonathan. 2012. *Constantine, Divine Emperor of the Christian Golden Age*. Cambridge and New York: Cambridge University Press.

Bellinger, A. R., and Berlincourt, M. A. 1962. "Victory as a Coin Type." *ANS* 149: 1–68.

Brown, Peter. 2012. *Through the Eye of a Needle: Wealth, the Fall of Rome, and the Making of Christianity in the West, 350–550 AD*. Princeton, NJ: Princeton University Press.

Burrus, Virginia. 1995. *The Making of a Heretic: Gender, Authority, and the Priscillianist Controversy*. Berkeley, CA: University of California Press.

Cameron, Alan. 2011. *The Last Pagans of Rome*. Oxford and New York: Oxford University Press.

Canto, Alicia Maria. 2006. "Sobre el origen bético de Teodosio I el Grande, y su improbable nacimiento en 'Cauca' de' Gallaecia." *Latomus* 65.2: 388–421.

Carrié, Jean-Michel. 1982. "Le 'colonat du Bas-Empire': un mythe historiographique?" *Opus* 1: 351–70.

Doyle, Christopher. 2014. *The Endgame of Treason: Rebellion and Usurpation in the Late Roman Empire, AD 395–411*. Unpublished thesis. Galway: National University of Ireland Galway. https://aran.library.nuigalway.ie/handle/10379/4631.

Doyle, Christopher. 2015. "Declaring Victory, Concealing Defeat? Continuity and Change in Imperial Coinage of the Roman West, c.383–408." In *Shifting Genres in Late Antiquity*. Edited by Geoffrey Greatrex and Hugh Elton with the assistance of Lucas McMahon: 157–71. Farnham: Ashgate.

Elsner, Jas. 1995. *Art and the Roman Viewer: The Transformation of Art from the Pagan World to Christianity*. Cambridge: Cambridge University Press.

Elsner, Jas. 1998. *Imperial Rome and Christian Triumph: The Art of the Roman Empire, AD 100–450*. Oxford: Oxford University Press.

Elton, Hugh. 1996. *Warfare in Roman Europe, AD 350–425*. Oxford: Oxford University Press.

Errington, Robert Malcolm. 2007. *Roman Imperial Policy from Julian to Theodosius*. Cambridge: Cambridge University Press.

Ferrill, Arther. 1997. *The Fall of the Roman Empire: The Military Explanation*. London: Thames and Hudson.

Galvão-Sobrinho, Carlos R. 2013. *Doctrine and Power: Theological Controversy and Christian Leadership in the Later Roman Empire*. Transformation of the Classical Heritage. Berkley, CA: University of California Press.

Goffart, W. 2006. *Barbarian Tides: The Migration Age and the Later Roman Empire*. Philadelphia, PA: University of Pennsylvania Press.

Halsall, Guy. 2007. *Barbarian Migrations and the Roman West, 376–568*. Cambridge Medieval Textbooks. Cambridge: Cambridge University Press.

Harper, Kyle. 2011. *Slavery in the Late Roman World, AD 275–425*. Cambridge and New York: Cambridge University Press.

Harries, Jill. 1984. "Prudentius and Theodosius." *Latomus* 43.1: 69–84.

Harries, Jill. 1999. *Law and Empire in Late Antiquity*. Cambridge: Cambridge University Press.

Heather, Peter. 2005. *The Fall of the Roman Empire: A New History of Rome and the Barbarians*. Oxford: Oxford University Press.

Heather, Peter. 1991. *Goths and Romans, 332–489*. Oxford: Clarendon Press.

Herrin, Judith. 1987. *The Formation of Christendom*. London: Fontana Press.

Holum, Kenneth G. 1982. *Theodosian Empresses: Women and Imperial Dominion in Late Antiquity*. Berkeley, CA: University of California Press.

Humfress, Caroline. 2007. *Orthodoxy and the Courts in Late Antiquity*. Oxford: Oxford University Press.

Humphries, Mark. 2008. "From Usurper to Emperor: The Politics of Legitimation in the Age of Constantine I." *JLA* 1: 85–100.

Kiilerich, Bente. 1993. *Late Fourth Century Classicism in the Plastic Arts: Studies in the So-Called Theodosian Renaissance*. Odense: Odense University Press.

Kulikowski, Michael. 2004. *Late Roman Spain and its Cities*. Baltimore, MD: Johns Hopkins University Press.

Kulikowski, Michael. 2007. *Rome's Gothic Wars: From the Third Century to Alaric*. Cambridge: Cambridge University Press.

Lampinen, Antti. 2016. "A Helping Hand from the Divine: Notes on the Triumphalist Iconography of the Theodosian Dynasty." *ABzF* 4: 1–18.

Lavan, Luke. 2011. "The End of the Temples: Towards a New Narrative?" In *The Archaeology of Late Antique 'Paganism'*. Edited by Luke Lavan and Michael Mulryan: xv–lxv. *LAA* 7. Leiden: Brill.

Lenski, Noel. 2002. *Failure of Empire: Valens and the Roman State in the Fourth Century AD*. Berkeley, CA: University of California Press.

Lenski, Noel. 2004. "Valens and the Monks: Cudgeling and Conscription as a Means of Social Control." *DOP* 58: 93–117.

Lenski, Noel. 2017. "Peasant and Slave in Late Antique North Africa." In *Late Antiquity in Contemporary Debate*. Edited by Rita Lizzi Testa: 113–55. Newcastle: Cambridge Scholars Publishing.

Lubhéid, Colm. 1982. *The Council of Nicaea*. Galway: Galway University Press.

MacMullen, Ramsay. 1990. "Judicial Savagery in the Roman Empire." In *Changes in the Roman Empire: Essays in the Ordinary*. Edited by Ramsay MacMullen: 204–17. Princeton, NJ: Princeton University Press.

Matthews, John F. 1967. "A Pious Supporter of Theodosius I: Maternus Cynegius and His Family." *JThS* 18.2: 438–46.

Matthews, John F. 1975. *Western Aristocracies and Imperial Court, AD 364–425*. Oxford: Clarendon Press.

McKenna, Stephen. 1938. *Paganism and Pagan Survivals in Spain up to the Fall of the Visigothic Kingdom*. Washington, D.C.: Catholic University of America Press.

McLynn, Neil. 2005. "*Genere Hispanus*: Theodosius, Spain and Nicene Orthodoxy." In *Hispania in Late Antiquity: Current Perspectives*. The Medieval and Early Modern Iberian World 24. Edited and translated by Kim Bowes and Michael Kulikowski: 77–120. Leiden and Boston: Brill.

Mirković, Miroslava. 1997. "The Later Roman Colonate and Freedom." *TAPA* 87.2: 1–144.

Odahl, Charles M. 1981. "The Use of Apocalyptic Imagery in Constantine's Christian Propaganda." *Centerpoint* 4: 9–19.

Oost, Stewart Irvin. 1968. *Galla Placidia Augusta: A Biographical Essay*. Chicago, IL and London: The University of Chicago Press.

Perowne, Stewart. 1962. *Caesars and Saints: The Evolution of the Christian State, 180–313 AD*. London: Hodder and Stoughton.

Potter, David S. 2004. *The Roman Empire at Bay AD 180–395*. Routledge History of the Ancient World. London and New York: Routledge.

Rostovtzeff, Mikhail. (1926). 1957. *The Social and Economic History of the Roman Empire*. 2nd edition. Revised by P. M. Fraser. Oxford: Clarendon Press.

Roueché, Charlotte. 2002. "The Image of Victory: New Evidence from Ephesus." *TM* 14: 527–46.

Salisbury, Joyce. 2001. *Encylopedia of Women in the Ancient World*. Santa Barbara, CA: ABC Clio.

Salzman, Michele Renee. 2002. *The Making of a Christian Aristocracy*. Cambridge, MA: Harvard University Press.

Treadgold, Warren. 2014. "Paying the Army in the Theodosian Period." In *Production and Prosperity in the Theodosian Period*. Interdisciplinary Studies in Ancient Culture and Religion 14. Edited by Ine Jacobs: 303–17. Leuven and Walden, MA: Peeters.

Ubric Rabaneda, Purificación. 2004. *La iglesia en la Hispania del siglo V*. Granada: Universidad de Granada.

Wardman, Alan E. 1984. "Usurpers and Internal Conflicts in the Fourth Century AD." *Historia* 33: 220–37.

Ward-Perkins, Bryan. 2005. *The Fall of Rome and the End of Civilization*. Oxford: Oxford University Press.

Wickham, Chris. 2005. *Framing the Early Middle Ages: Europe and the Mediterranean, 400–800*. Oxford: Oxford University Press.

3   A child of two courts

As a child you did crawl among shields, fresh-won spoils of monarchs were your playthings, and you were ever the first to embrace your stern father on his return from rude battles, when, reeking with the blood of northern savages, he came home victorious from his conquest over the tribes of the Danube.

Claudian, *On the Third Consulship of Honorius*, 24–30

The hope of the West

The future western emperor Honorius was born in the imperial palace at Constantinople on September 9, 384. The third child of Theodosius and Aelia Flaccilla, he was named simply Honorius to begin with – the designation Flavius Honorius which is sometimes given came later. Theodosius and Flaccilla called their second son after two paternal family members with the same name – his great-grandfather, of whom little is known, and an uncle who died around 379 (*PLRE* I, 441). Theodosius and his brother Honorius had been close, and the emperor never got over his sibling's death. So much so that he adopted his brother's daughters Serena and Thermantia as his own, though he never actually legalized the adoptions. Claudian tells us that the emperor gave his dead brother's name to his son 'hoping in some way to discover in that son the image of the brother he had loved and lost' (Cl. *c.m.* 30.109–10). Theodosius doted on Honorius and had dynastic ambitions for him, taking the little boy with him on state visits to Rome and the West. Family meant everything to Theodosius, and he was prepared to do anything to protect it. His efforts in establishing a hereditary dynasty were successful and ensured its continuation for the best part of a hundred years.

Theodosius I and Flaccilla's eldest child, Arcadius, was about seven when his brother arrived, and was already his father's co-Augustus in the East. Next after Arcadius came Pulcheria, perhaps five or six when her younger brother was born. It was vital for the imperial line that Theodosius had more male children in the event that anything befell Arcadius. The emperor was therefore relieved with the birth of another son. The imperial couple's happiness did not last, however. When Honorius was about a year old, their daughter

Pulcheria died (*PLRE* I, 755; cf. Graham 2010). Her parents' loss was palpable, and they ensured she received a state funeral, at which Gregory of Nyssa paid tribute to her short life with a sensitive oration (Samellas 2002). It is worth noting that infant and child mortality rates were high throughout antiquity and affected every social class. Roman medical practice was rudimentary. Children, including often their mothers, were especially susceptible to disease and other factors. Infants and children had an estimated 50 percent survival rate, and even then, making it past infancy did not guarantee that a child would last through adolescence since infectious disease was rife in the Roman populace (Pilkington 2013). In such an environment, therefore, Flaccilla and Theodosius were fortunate that two of their three children lived into adulthood – more so because the continuity of the Theodosian line hung in the balance. That said, their daughter's death was traumatic for them, and Pulcheria's loss was deeply mourned by her grieving parents (*De ob. Theod.* 40.2–5).

Growing up in the imperial palace, Honorius and Arcadius led a relatively sheltered existence. Perhaps this was to shield them from contagion, but this was not the only consideration. The seclusion of the imperial brothers was paramount against the risk of assassination. It was not paranoia on Theodosius' part: he had good cause to be vigilant. Honorius was born at a time when the usurper Magnus Maximus controlled much of the Roman West, supposedly acting as a colleague of the legitimate Augustus Valentinian II, whose brother he had earlier murdered. For practical reasons, Theodosius tolerated Maximus for a few years, conscious always of the threat the usurper posed both to himself and to his sons. Politically motivated assassination of a rival's children – regardless of age or sex – had been an élite Roman phenomenon since at least the late Republic. In the imperial period, certain Augusti considered it imperative to terminate an adversary's bloodline, particularly in cases where a male heir had held an imperial rank and had coins minted in their image – sure indicators of being prepared for imperial succession. Élite child assassination removed any possibility of a rival's offspring returning to claim power and seek vengeance at some later date. There were many such instances in the late empire, such as that great exponent of Christianity, Constantine I, who murdered his own eight-year-old nephew Licinius Caesar, whose numismatic propaganda proclaimed *Victoriae Laetae Principium Perpetua* (Joyous victory to the eternal prince) for him. Good for Licinius, not so perhaps for the future prospects of Constantine's three sons-in-waiting, hence Licinius was assassinated.

Theodosius was no different to Constantine in this regard. When he eventually moved against Maximus and defeated him in 388, he made sure to eliminate the usurper's five-year-old son Victor as well. Victor's father had first created him Caesar, and then Augustus. He struck coinage for his son bearing the legends *Bono Reipublicae Nati* (Born for the good of the state) and *Spes Romanorum* (Hope of the Romans) (*RIC* IX 75; 55b; 29b; 36b; 87c). Once Theodosius had done away with Maximus, the child's death was assured. Titles of power such as these were clearly very important for promoting imperial rule – but they could also get you killed.

So routine had such crimes become that most literary sources either glossed over or said nothing at all about Victor's killing (*Cons. Const.* s.a. 388; *Pan. Lat.* 2(12).44–5; Oros. 7.35.10; *Epit. de Caes.* 48.6; Zos. 4.47.1). To his credit, though, Theodosius spared the lives of Maximus' wife and daughters, providing financially for the former and finding a foster home with his own family for the latter (Amb. *Ep.* 40.23). Nevertheless, despite his clemency towards Maximus' female relatives, Theodosius sanctioned Victor's murder in order to safeguard his own sons' future. Honorius learned well from Theodosius' example. When he was emperor, facing far more challengers than his father, he too engaged in similar activity in order to protect the state and his family. Such was the reasoning behind the murder of imperial children, a brutal practice that outlived the fall of the Roman West, and endured through the Byzantine and medieval epochs.

Knowing therefore what others were capable of, Theodosius established security protocols around his children. They were secluded in the palace complex at Constantinople, behind walls and guards, their education and care entrusted to selected tutors and advisors. Their father did not intend to, but he did his sons a disservice by effectively quarantining them within the artificial environs of the palace. As they grew up, all Honorius and Arcadius knew were sycophants, many of whom abused their influence for personal gain. How tired – and fearful – Honorius and Arcadius must have grown of such people. Had he lived longer, Theodosius would likely have overseen a fuller, more robust training to properly prepare Honorius for governance, but the emperor's unforeseen death in 395 left both his sons, particularly Honorius due to his age, woefully unready to deal with the internal struggles that lay ahead of them.

An eastern upbringing

Honorius spent his first years at Constantinople with his mother Flaccilla, brother Arcadius, and other close family members, including his cousin Serena, whom Theodosius had unofficially adopted after her father's death. Serena had recently married Stilicho, an ascendant star in Theodosius' camp and the man who would play an instrumental role later in Honorius' life (O' Flynn 1983, 14–24). The emperor had great faith in Stilicho, and had arranged the marriage. Flaccilla herself led Serena from the palace to the ceremony, though the empress's opinion of the bridegroom is not mentioned by contemporary sources. Stilicho first came to prominence as a military tribune in a Roman embassy to Persia in 383 (Cl. *Stil.* I.51–68). At these negotiations a peace was agreed between the two empires, ending decades of conflict (Gutmann 1991). After his return from the Roman-Persian peace talks, around 384 or 385, Stilicho became *comes sacri stabuli* (count of the sacred imperial stable), with administrative charge of the household cavalry. Serena gave birth to their first child in about 385, a daughter they called Maria. This bound Stilicho by blood to the Theodosian house. Having the emperor's trust ingratiated Stilicho with the imperial family and some of the ruling élite. Stilicho, it should be pointed out, was of Roman and Germanic heritage – his mother a Roman, his Vandal father a cavalry officer in the imperial army – facts which do not seem to have mattered much whilst he was in favor (Eun. *fr.* 60; Oros. 7.38.1). Many years later, when Stilicho fell from Honorius' grace, it was his ethnicity that was used to explain dubious conduct on his part. Certain writers, displaying their own prejudice, portrayed him as a half-barbarian (*semibarbarus*) traitor who cared more about non-Romans than his adoptive countrymen (Jer. *Ep.* 123.17; Rut. Nam. 41–60).

Theodosius was regularly absent from his family, seeing to his official administrative and military obligations, and keeping a watchful eye on the pretender Magnus Maximus in the West. The emperor laid the ground-work for his youngest son to succeed him, however. In 386, Honorius, not yet two, was given the title of Most Noble Child (*nobilissmus puer*) and he also held the consulship for that year. Honorius' mother, so Claudian tells us, wrapped her son in a purple cloak and helped him toddle up to his seat on the curule chair to accept his title (Cl. *IV Hons.* 157–8). It was the first of thirteen consulships Honorius would hold in his lifetime. It might seem impractical that a child so young could have been consul, but in the late empire the consular office was little more than an honorific position, similar in some respects to a modern-day marquis, count, or duke. Besides, children had already been consuls before Honorius. His brother Arcadius was eight when he became consul. The emperor Gratian was consul in 366 aged seven, while his younger brother Valentinian II was five when he held his first consulship in 376 (*CLRE* 14, 23; McEvoy 2013). Both Gratian and Valentinian II had also been *nobilisimi pueri*. Other infant consuls included Varronian, the emperor Jovian's son, appointed as a baby in 364, and quite likely murdered by his father's successor Valentinian I (*PLRE* I, 946). Varronian too was styled *nobilissmus puer* (Philos. *HE.* 8.8; McEvoy 2013, 52–3). Another child consul was the three-year-old Valentinian Galates, son of the ill-fated Valens (*CLRE* 14). The infant Honorius, as consul for the year 386, was clearly being marked for future imperial rule.

A much loved empress

After Honorius' birth, his mother's health drastically declined, yet she continued to visit the poor and the sick across the cities, towns, villages, and districts of the eastern empire. Aelia Flaccilla's selflessness and philanthropy toward the lower socio-economic classes were famous.

> [S]he bestowed every kind of attention on the maimed and the mutilated, declining all aid from her household and her guards, herself visiting the houses where the sufferers lodged, and providing everyone with what he

required. She also went about the guest chambers of the churches and ministered to the wants of the sick, herself handling pots and pans, and tasting broth, now bringing in a dish and breaking bread and offering morsels, and washing out a cup and going through all the other duties which are supposed to be proper to servants and maids.

(Theod. *HE.* 18)

Flaccilla's fragile health worried her aides, who tried to dissuade her from continuing with her humanitarian work. She refused to listen to them, firmly convinced it was her duty to help the poor. She believed that since it was God alone who had given her her rank and status she owed it to God to do what she could for her fellow man (Theod. *HE.* 5.18). Such a stalwart of the Catholic faith was Flaccilla considered to be that a certain church official called Faustinus dedicated no less than seven books against the Arian and Macedonian heresies to her (Gen. 16). She was well regarded in the eastern provinces both for her altruism and for being the wife of the emperor who had rescued the state from further disaster after Hadrianopolis. Flaccilla's religious piety was underscored on a special coin series inscribed with the Chi-Rho symbol. Struck in bronze, silver, and gold, these coins were issued for her by her husband and circulated widely. They carried the slogan *Spes Reipublicae* (Welfare of the State) – propaganda intended to remind the public of her role as the imperial mother, thus the guarantor of stable succession through the provision of heirs (Figure 3.1).

Figure 3.1 Gold solidus of Aelia Flaccilla. Constantinople mint, *c.* 383–7. Obv. Flaccilla draped and diademed, her hair in a *Scheitelzopf* (elaborately plaited style), wearing earrings and necklace. Legend: AEL-FLAC-CILLA-AVG (*Aelia Flaccilla Augusta*). Rev. Victory seated right, inscribing Chi-Rho on shield set on column. Legend: SALVS-REI-PVBLICAE (Welfare of the State)-H (*officina* mark). Exergue: CON (Constantinople)-OB (*Obryzum*/pure gold).

Source: *RIC* IX 72.

Honorific statues of Flaccilla were prominently displayed across the Roman East, from Constantinople to the great regional centers of Aphrodisias – renowned for its thriving sculptural industry – Ephesus, Alexandria, and beyond. Even small statuettes of the empress, belonging to private citizens and with regional variations, appear to have been popular, perhaps copied from public statues or from coins of Flaccilla (Kiilerich 1993, 96–8; Roueché 2002). At Ephesus, an extremely important Christian hub, two large bronze statues of Flaccilla were erected in public spaces. The bronzes themselves are long gone, but the surviving base inscription from one of them indicates the degree of deference expressed by local élites towards their empress.

> To Good Fortune. Aelia Flaccilla, most pious Augusta, the mistress of the inhabited world. The Council and the People of the great (city of) Ephesus (set up her statue), Septimius Maeadius, clarissimus, was pro-consul, and Septimius Maeadius the younger, clarissimus, was legate. With Good Fortune …] being logistes … [
>
> (*IEph* 314)

Death's vacancy

The year 386 proved to be a dark period in the lives of the Theodosian family when Flaccilla died in September. Not long beforehand, probably in late summer, she had travelled to Skotoume in Thrace, northern Greece, seeking respite for her health issues, exacerbated by the recent death of her daughter Pulcheria. Skotoume was noted for its sanative natural springs with cura-tive properties for conditions including biliary tract disease and rheumatism. Indeed, northern Greece's natural springs are still used for similar purposes today. Bishop Gregory of Nyssa did not think much of what Skotoume had to offer, however. In his funeral oration for the empress, he said that it was a desolate place – short on sunlight, shorter still on Christian virtue (Greg. Nyss. *In Flacc.* 480; Holum 1982, 23). Be that as it may, Flaccilla had gone there in an effort to prolong her life, but to no avail, and she died in Skotoume aged about twenty-eight. When her remains arrived back at Constantinople, huge, weeping crowds thronged the capital as her funeral cortege wound its way through rain-soaked streets to the imperial mausoleum where she was interred (Angelova 2015, 213–14).

Honorius was too young to have really remembered his mother, though like his father she was never forgotten. Honorius was reminded of her through her image in statuary, art, and coinage – however unrepresentative that may have been of her actual likeness – and through the preservation of her memory in literature. His mother's charitable works and church patronage, alongside his father's religious policies, set a precedent for their son to aspire to. Flaccilla's absence was partly filled by Honorius' cousin Serena, who effectively became his surrogate mother. Claudian, ever able to make the best of a situation, highlighted Serena's role in rearing the future emperor.

Daughter of my uncle Honorius, from whom I derive my name, chief
glory of the land of swift-flowing Ebro, cousin by birth, by mother's love
a mother, to your care was my infancy entrusted, in your arms I grew to
boyhood; save for my birth you, rather than Flaccilla, are my mother.

(Cl. *Nupt.* 39–43)

Flaccilla's death was a heavy blow to her husband and their children. Though
he would find love and marry again, Flaccilla had been his close confidante
and best friend (Zos. 4.43–4). She had been with him long before his imperial
accession. They were from the same cultural background and region, and
together they had traveled east from Spain. Their early years as parents were
happy. Claudian speaks of Flaccilla and Theodosius affectionately playing
with their children (*IV Cons.* 165–8). In their married life, it was Flaccilla who
often counseled the emperor on religious and other matters, and who had had
to manage his moods during his frequent losses of temper.

Yet other opportunities of improvement lay within the emperor's reach,
for his wife used constantly to put him in mind of the divine laws in which
she had first carefully educated herself. In no way exalted by her imperial
rank she was rather fired by it with greater longing for divine things ... to
her husband, too, she was ever given to say, "Husband, you ought always
to bethink you what you were once and what you have become now; by
keeping this constantly in mind you will never grow ungrateful to your
benefactor, but will guide in accordance with law the empire bestowed
upon you, and thus you will worship Him who gave it." By ever using language of this kind, she with fair and wholesome care, as it were, watered
the seeds of virtue planted in her husband's heart.

(Theod. *HE*. 18)

In the months immediately following her death, Theodosius desperately
needed Flaccilla. In early 387, a public order disturbance broke out in the city
of Antioch, Syria – the so-called 'Riot of the Statues' (Williams and Friell
1994, 44–6; French 1998). The commotion was supposedly over Theodosius'
proposed heavy tax increases aimed at collecting funds for the inevitable war
to come against Maximus in the West. During the ensuing fracas at Antioch,
considerable damage was done to public and private property by a rampaging
mob comprised all of social classes, such was the general resentment at the
emperor's hard fiscal demands. Bronze and marble statues of Theodosius'
father, the emperor himself, Flaccilla, and Arcadius were toppled, dragged
through the streets, and vandalized (*Chrys. Hom de. Stat.*; Lib. *Or.* 19–22;
Soz. *HE*. 7.23). Imperial images – of any format – were highly esteemed
and protected by law. To damage them was a capital offense and liable to
poena capitis. An attack upon imperial images was deemed the same as an
attack upon the imperial person (*CTh.* 9.21.1–10; 9.23.1; 9.38.7–8; 11.21.1;
Sirm. 8.317–93). Theodosius, ever prone to excessive temper, was livid that

his family's images, particularly those of his recently deceased wife, should be desecrated in this way. He ordered the execution of all involved. In time past, Flaccilla might well have been able to deter her husband from such a severe action, but in spring 387 he was intent on retribution. Fate intervened, however. Luckily for the Antiochenes the Christian festival of Lent was upon them. It had become custom in the Christianized empire to grant amnesties to anyone sentenced to death during religious festivals. In a show of clemency, Theodosius reprieved most of the rioters. But his mercy stopped short and the suspected ringleaders were tried for sedition and burned at the stake. Antioch's regional imperial status was revoked, and imperial patronage of its public circus games, theatrical shows, and bath houses ceased (Rebenich 1985, 479). Antioch paid a heavy price for its insubordination against the emperor. John Chrysostom, then a young presbyter in Antioch, blamed the popular revolt on demonic possession (*Hom. de Stat.* 3.17). In reality, the chief suspect was poverty. The Antioch riot shows chronic discontent beneath the veneer of late Roman order, although, as Jon Lendon quips, Theodosius' reaction to the riot at least showed that 'great and distinguished cities were listened to, for better or for worse' (Lendon 1997, 124–5). As cherished as Flaccilla and her family might have appeared through the visual arts, fawning prose, and state media, their people wanted something more than propagandist fare.

In love and in war

In 387, Theodosius married Galla at the imperial residence at Thessalonica, an important city with a large state mint. She was the daughter of Valentinian I and his second wife, Justina. Galla was also stepsister to both the murdered emperor Gratian and Valentinian II, the legitimate western emperor. Based in Italy, Valentinian was under increasing political and military pressure from the usurper Maximus in Gaul, who, despite having an understanding with Theodosius to leave Valentinian be, invaded Italy in summer 387. Valentinian and his family fled for their lives to Thessalonica and appealed to Theodosius for aid. Justina, according to Zosimus, offered her daughter Galla in marriage to Theodosius in exchange for his help against the usurper. Zosimus also alleged that it was Galla's exceptional beauty which inspired Theodosius to marry her after he had fallen head over heels in love with her (Zos. 4.43–4). Romantic love might well have played a part, but Theodosius realized that he needed to end Maximus' usurpation before it gained any further momentum and threatened him and his family. His marriage to Galla lasted almost seven years until her death in 394. Considerably younger than her husband, Galla had three children with him, a girl and two boys – Gratian (388/9– 94), Placidia (392/3–450), and Johannes (394) – of whom only their daughter Placidia survived into adulthood (Rebenich 1985, 385). After Italy, Maximus next invaded Illyricum in early 388, and Theodosius responded by leading an expedition west against the usurper. An experienced military strategist,

Theodosius had no doubt been preparing for such a day, as indicated by the increased taxes raised for the army that led to the Antioch riot in the previous year.

In the end, the campaign against Maximus was short. In August 388, Theodosius routed the usurper's army in a bloody encounter at the River Sava, near the city of Siscia in Pannonia (modern Sisak, Croatia) and, as we have seen, Maximus was executed, as was his infant son Victor shortly afterwards. Their barbarian *magister equitum*, Andragathius, committed suicide about the same time. The usurper's memory was officially condemned (*damnatio memoriae*), a process reserved for state enemies (Hedrick 2000; Varner 2004). Maximus' *damnatio* meant that most of his laws were repealed, and his portraiture, in all its forms, was mutilated and destroyed. He was decapitated, and his head publicly displayed as a sign to his troops that the war was over. His mutilated corpse was left as carrion on the side of a road (*Pan. Lat.* 2 (12).37–45; Zos. 4.46.2–3; Soz. *HE.* 7.14). Maximus' depressing fate was typical fare meted out to defeated usurpers (Lejdegård 2002, 131–7; Omissi 2014). A final thought for Magnus Maximus: considering his refusal to hand Gratian's body over to Theodosius for burial in 383, there was likely a personal vendetta involved in the treatment of Maximus' corpse. It was an extremely sacrilegious act – to both Christians and pagans – to leave a body unburied and without the proper funerary rites. Yet, this was the standard treatment of the bodies of enemies of the state (*hostes publici*). Maximus' shameful end made for effective Theodosian propaganda, as depicted by the Gallo-Roman panegyrist Pacatus Drepanius.

> If anyone at any time dreams of draping his shoulders with royal purple may he encounter the depiction of Maximus being stripped … if anyone contemplates placing a diadem upon his head may he gaze at the head of Maximus plucked from its shoulders, and at his nameless corpse.
>
> (*Pan. Lat.* II.45.1–3)

The Theodosians in Rome

The civil war over, Theodosius based himself in Milan and began a reconciliation process with the civilian and military remnants of Maximus' regime. However, it was one year after Maximus' death before the victorious emperor traveled to Rome and made a ceremonial entrance (*adventus*) into the city on June 13 (Hyd. s.a. 389; MacCormack 1981). Theodosius' *adventus* and triumph was held on the first anniversary of the demise of the usurper, whose embalmed head fixed to a spear was likely a key part of the pomp and ceremony (McCormick 1990, 44–5). Honorius, nearly five years old, accompanied his father, who was eager to show off his heir apparent. Together they stayed in Rome from mid-June to August. Theodosius held a magnificent triumph along with games in the Circus Maximus, gladiatorial displays in the Coliseum, and giving public donatives. One can imagine the impression such a momentous event made on the child as he stood beside his father in a gilded chariot pulled by elephants, a gift from the Persian emperor Sapor III (*Pan. Lat.* 2 (12).22.5). Looking up at the towering figure of the emperor as they moved through Rome's beating heart, surrounded on all sides by cheering crowds and soldiers in brightly polished armor, the little Honorius must have felt like he was the most important person in the world. His father made sure that was how his son was seen.

Where was the rightful western emperor, Valentinian, during all the fun? Surely he was present in Rome along with the Theodosians to share in the glory? Zosimus, writing about a century later, says that Valentinian had returned to Rome with his mother prior to the campaign against Maximus, sometime in early 388 (Zos. 4.45.3). Socrates Scholasticus, a near contemporary source, tells us that Theodosius left Valentinian in Rome before heading east for Constantinople in 391 (*HE*. 18). Our only actual contemporary source for the triumph is Pacatus Drepanius, who excludes mention of Valentinian's presence at the victory celebrations. Pacatus praised only Theodosius and his sons, declaring that 'the Roman Empire shall always belong to you or your descendants' (*Pan. Lat.* 2 (12).45.3). That was Pacatus' job, to laud Theodosius' efforts to rid the West of a usurper, not to remind people of a weak, deposed Valentinian. The court poet Claudian was mindful not to detract from Honorius' first visit to Rome. Claudian reworked the triumph of 389 – sans Valentinian – for his panegyric on Honorius' fourth consulship. Whatever other writers on the event said, who probably used the official line as their reference, we should disregard the panegyrists as memory censors of the first order. It is safe, therefore, to assume that Valentinian II was at Rome in the summer of 389, that he took part in the triumphal ceremonies, but that he was intentionally eclipsed by the real stars of the show – Theodosius and Honorius.

A number of modern scholars, with some reservations, have inferred from two particular primary literary sources that Honorius was raised to the rank of Caesar at Rome in 389 (Cameron 1969, 260–1; Matthews 1975, 227; Dewar 1996, 65–6; Barnes 2010, 320; McEvoy 2013, 137–9). This interpretation stems from a line of Claudian's; 'you [Honorius], then Caesar, did become emperor, and were immediately made equal with your brother' (*IV Hons.* 169–70), and from a similar inference made by the much later Byzantine chronicler Theophanes (AM 5881). It has been shown by Gavin Kelly, through analysis of textual and material evidence, that there is no conclusive proof that Honorius became Caesar in 389 (2016, 336–57). There is, however, a hitherto unexamined piece of legal evidence concerning Honorius' rank before becoming Augustus which I explore later in this chapter.

Victory propaganda commemorating Maximus' defeat flowed from the imperial mints and workshops, disseminating the Theodosian triumph across the empire (Humphries 2015, 160–6; Leppin 2015, 207–11). In conjunction with the festivities, Pacatus composed a paean to Theodosius, reciting it to the Roman élite and the emperor in the late summer of 389 (Kelly 2015, 215–38).

Pacatus – as good a propagandist as Claudian – presented Theodosius' war as the liberation of the West from tyranny, an avenging mission to achieve justice for Gratian's murder. More importantly Honorius received his first proper mention in contemporary literature. He, along with his brother, were described as the 'twin hopes and jewels of the state' (*Pan. Lat.* 2 (12).16.4). Serena, pregnant with Stilicho's second child, was also in Rome for the victory celebrations. Stilicho was probably there too. Serena gave birth to a boy while they were in Rome, perhaps explaining why the visit lasted nearly three months. After Rome, the imperial entourage moved on to Milan. In keeping with family tradition, Stilicho and Serena named their son, also their only male child, Eucherius after his mother's great-uncle, a former imperial treasury administrator (*comes sacrarum largitionum*) in the eastern government (*PLRE* I, 288). By this stage Serena and Stilicho had two children, Maria and now Eucherius. Maria became Honorius' first wife in 398, a union arranged by her parents.

The propaganda of Valentinian II and Theodosius

Theodosius officially reinstalled Valentinian II as the sole western Augustus, extending that partnership to include his two sons as well. Statues and monuments reflecting this sprang up right across the empire, such as this statue base inscription from Pamphylia, Asia Minor:

> To the emperors of all the earth under the sun, triumphant, our lords Valentinian, Theodosius, Arcadius, eternal Augusti, and Flavius Honorius the most noble. Flavius Eutolmius Tatianus, of clarissimus rank, prefect of the sacred praetoria [praetorian prefect], set this up with the traditional rites, under the governor … of clarissimus rank.
>
> (*CIG* 3.4350; *LSA* 267)

Yet, the iconography of Theodosius and Valentinian's coinage suggests that the latter was undermined at every opportunity. It was standard minting protocol to inscribe the unbroken or intact form of an emperor's name on a coin's obverse to indicate junior status, e.g. *Valentinianus*, as opposed to the broken or separated coin legend for senior emperors, e.g. *Theodo-sius*. This might perhaps seem a trivial matter: not so, for it was an indication of rank and power. Valentinian II's numismatic output – with very few exceptions – retained the same unbroken formula. Honorius' coins only use his broken name after he became Augustus in 393 (Figure 3.2). Most of the coinage for his co-reign with Theodosius therefore portrayed Valentinian II as subordinate, despite his having been an Augustus for longer. Furthermore, several coin series promoting imperial victory (*Victoria Augustorum*) and unity showed Theodosius and Valentinian enthroned together on the obverse, with Theodosius the larger of the two figures, ostensibly depicting a father and son scene (*RIC* IX Milan 5; Trier 49c, 90a). Whether or not such stylistic

Figure 3.2 Gold tremissis of Honorius. Constantinople mint, 393. Obv. Honorius pearl-diademed and helmeted, draped and cuirassed. Legend: DN-HONORI-VS-PF-AVG (*Dominus Noster Honorius Pius Felix Augustus*/ Our Lord Honorius, pious and fortunate Augustus). Rev. Victory advancing, holding wreath in her right hand, a *globus cruciger* in her left, a star in right field. Legend: VICTORIA-AVGVSTORVM (Victory of the Augusti). CON (Constantinople)-OB (*Obryzum*/pure gold).
Source: *RIC* X 35.

conventions were the result of direct orders from Theodosius is another matter – the imperial mints had a certain amount of leeway with their coin designs – but the evidence suggests that Theodosius was widely perceived as the real power in the collegiate. Coinage, after all, was an exceptionally effective way to spread imperial propaganda to all parts of the state.

Theodosius probably intended to supplant Valentinian II with his own son, when the right moment came. The eastern emperor's dynastic ambitions are evident well before Valentinian approached him for help against Maximus – from the bestowal of status titles on Honorius in 386, to his public display of his son at Rome, and even Pacatus referred to Honorius as the future ruler of the West (*Pan. Lat.* 2 (12).47.5). Theodosius' strategy was to maintain Valentinian's dependence upon him, effectively infantilizing the young man. In all the time he was Theodosius' co-ruler, Valentinian must have suspected his colleague's motives but he could do nothing about it.

In preparation for Theodosius' visit to Rome, the urban prefect Rufius Albinus erected three conspicuous monuments dedicated to the emperor's family. Albinus wanted to present Rome as pro-Theodosian since some of its leading citizens had been on Maximus' side. Theodosius had a hand in influencing Albinus' program. One of the monuments featured a bronze statue of the emperor's mother Thermantia. It was situated in the forum, directly in front of the senate house, with an inscription that recorded Theodosius' family's service to the empire, and promoted his sons' prestige and legitimacy. The message served to remind all concerned that although Theodosius was ruler in the East, he was a westerner by birth and by heritage. The inclusion of Theodosius the Elder's name and accomplishments was part of a program to rehabilitate his previously tarnished memory.

> To Thermantia, a woman of the holiest and most noble memory, wife of the revered Theodosius the Elder, man of illustrious rank and count leading both branches of the military [infantry and cavalry], mother of our Lord Theodosius, emperor forever, [and] grandmother of our lords Arcadius, the strongest ruler, and Honorius, the most pious youth.
>
> (*CIL* 6.36960)

Arbogastes, Thessalonica, and Ambrose

Before Theodosius returned east in late 391, he appointed Arbogastes as *magister militum* under Valentinian with the instruction to look after the young emperor and manage the western empire's administration and defense on his behalf (*PLRE* I, 95–7). Arbogastes, a Roman officer of Frankish descent and a pagan, had served under Theodosius against Magnus Maximus. He was also the man personally responsible for killing Victor, the usurper's child (Zos. 4.47.1). Theodosius had known Arbogastes for about a decade and he trusted the man. As far as Theodosius was concerned, Valentinian and the West were in safe hands, and therefore he felt ready to leave Italy and set out for Constantinople (Eun. *fr.* 58.1). The journey home took longer than intended. Theodosius' first port of call was Thessalonica, presumably in an effort to make amends for a recent massacre in the city for which he was personally responsible. Part of Theodosius' 382 peace deal with the Visigoths was the installation of Visigothic garrisons in certain eastern cities. At Thessalonica, Visigothic *foederati* had arrested and imprisoned a popular charioteer for alleged immorality. The charioteer's fans demanded his release but this was refused, and riots broke out. In the ensuing violence some Visigoths, along with a few Roman magistrates, were killed. Word of the unrest reached Theodosius in Milan; he took it as a violation of his Visigothic treaty, lost his temper, and ordered the execution of thousands of Thessalonians, just like at Antioch in 387. Unlike Antioch, though, there was an extensive bloodbath at Thessalonica. When Bishop Ambrose heard about the emperor's atrocity he refused Theodosius communion unless he performed public penance. In no uncertain terms, Ambrose told Theodosius that he was 'raging against God and trampling on God's laws.' The upshot was that the emperor submitted to Ambrose's demand and did penance (Theod. *HE.* 5.17; Amb. *Ep.* 51; Soz. *HE.* 7.25). This episode has subsequently been taken as the historic moment that the secular state bowed to the power of the Catholic Church. The standoff between emperor and bishop set a precedent for Theodosius' successors. Henceforth, bishops often became power brokers in imperial politics. When not committing crimes against his own people, Theodosius spent his time in the West prudently building a rapport with senior establishment figures – both pagan and Christian – essential in the aftermath of civil war. Theodosius anticipated the day when Honorius would ascend the western throne and would need the support of western élites. Very soon after his humiliation by Ambrose, Theodosius left the West. He probably couldn't wait to get away from Ambrose.

The return east

In 391, while Theodosius was in Thessalonica, barbarian marauders pillaged northern Greece. Taking a modest force with him, the emperor quickly located and slaughtered the barbarians. It was a messy affair, fought at close quarters, and the emperor himself was almost killed in a skirmish. As soon as the mission was concluded, Theodosius headed home to Constantinople, thoroughly sick of war and killing (Zos. 4.48–50). He arrived there by mid-July (*CTh*. 13.9.4. July 18, 391). Honorius was with him on his return, and it appears he had been with him in the West the entire time since their triumph at Rome in 389 (Soc. *HE*. 5.18). A few months later, on November 10, 391, Theodosius, Arcadius, and Honorius held a triumphal procession through the capital to mark Maximus' defeat. The triumph began just outside the city's boundary, at the Hebdomon, the seventh milestone from the central mile marker (*milion*) in Constantinople. The *milion* was the eastern equivalent of Rome's golden milestone (*milliarium aureum*), from which the distances to all cities of the empire was measured – all roads led to Rome, or in this case Constantinople. The triumphal starting point was significant for other reasons: it was the location of the Iucundianae palace, an imperial summer residence, and it was also the army's main parade grounds, an eastern Campus Martius. The Theodosians entered Constantinople from this spot at the head of massed military formations.

From the Hebdomon, the trio, possibly borne by an elephant-drawn chariot, and the assembled soldiery began their triumphal procession into the city through the *mese* (main street), passing under the newly built Theodosian triumphal arch – later the famous *porta aurea*, or Golden Gate (Bardill 1999, 671–96). From there the procession moved along a *via triumphalis* crowded with jubilant onlookers into the city center, before finally arriving at a ceremonial square in front of the church of Saint Sophia, or Hagia Sophia. Following a formal service at what was then the first incarnation of Hagia Sophia, circus games were held in the Hippodrome (Mango 2000, 173–88). Imperial triumphs were therefore highly formalistic demonstrations of imperial power, and by their very nature were memorable affairs (Wienand 2015, 169–97). Theodosius thus followed a long-established tradition. The triumph that he staged in 391 was particularly lavish, and it surpassed its western counterpart of two years previous. The public display of Theodosian harmony in Constantinople was vital in order to present Arcadius in a central role. He had not been present in Rome where his little brother, not yet a member of the imperial *collegium*, had been virtually treated as such by their father. After all, Arcadius was the heir-designate of the eastern empire, but he was beginning to gain a reputation for having a disagreeable personality.

Theodosian house eternal

For centuries, Roman emperors had celebrated victories over foreign and domestic enemies with triumphs, spectacular entertainments, and building programs (Beard 2007). For example, the Flavian dynasty commemorated their success in the first Jewish-Roman war, 66–73, with an ambitious public works program that included an enormous new amphitheater in Rome, the so-called Coliseum (Bomgardner 2000; Futrell 2000; Gunderson 2003, 637–58). Late Roman emperors continued the tradition. The celebrations at Constantinople in 391 resulted in a monumental building program dedicated to the Theodosian dynasty. An example is the well-known Obelisk of Theodosius, a huge ancient Egyptian pink granite obelisk, over 20 meters high, that was placed in the central wall (*spina*) of the Hippodrome. The obelisk, dating from the second millennium BC, was brought by ship from Alexandria to Athens, and then to Constantinople. There, it was raised atop a new marble base in the circus *spina* in 390 in anticipation of the emperor's return from the West. It still stands in situ today, and although the Hippodrome's physical remains are long gone, the outline of its circuit is traceable around what is now a public square, the Sultanahmet Meydani in old Istanbul. The obelisk's base is decorated in relief sculpture of the so-called Theodosian renaissance style – a fusion of pagan and Christian influences. The reliefs are badly worn but were originally vibrantly painted and had gilded bronze fittings, similar to the Trajan and Marcus Aurelius' victory columns in Rome. Despite its erosion, the Theodosian obelisk's relief figures are discernible. They depict chariot races and spectators, the emperor, the empress, and their sons, flanked by palace guards and the eastern élite. Valentinian II is there too, as is Stilicho. On one side, beneath the figures of Theodosius, Arcadius, and Honorius, foreign emissaries – African, Persian, and German – genuflect in tribute (Kiilerich 1993, 35ff.; Elsner 1998, 75–8). Such scenes were designed to project imperial authority and purpose – what McCormick calls the 'collegiality of victory' (1990, 117). A bilingual inscription in Greek and Latin runs across the obelisk's base, the Latin part of which signifies Theodosius' hereditary aspirations:

DIFFICILIS QVONDAM DOMINIS PARERE SERENIS
IVSSVS ET EXTINCTIS PALMAM PORTARE TYRANNIS
   [Maximus].
OMNIA THEODOSIO CEDVNT SVBOLIQVE PERENNI.
TER DENIS SIC VICTVS EGO DOMITVSQVE DIEBVS.
IUDICE SVB PROCVLO SUPERAS ELATVS AD AVRAS

Once it was difficult to conquer me,
but I was ordered to obey mild masters and to carry the subdued
   tyrants' palm.
Everything cedes to Theodosius and his eternal descendants.
Thus conquered I was tamed in thrice ten days.
When Proculus was judge, I was erected to the skies.

                       (*ILS* 821)

Behind the façade

Certainly, Theodosius enjoyed a rapturous welcome from the city of
Constantinople. His personal life was less joyous. While her husband and
Honorius were away in the west, Galla fell foul of Arcadius, who expelled
her and her infant son Gratian from the palace, perhaps even from the city
itself (*Chron. Marcell.* s.a. 390.2). Why this happened is not at all clear, but
we might speculate a little here. Arcadius' immaturity was an issue; he was
an early adolescent when the fallout occurred. Perhaps he resented Galla for
having replaced his mother, though it might equally have been her own family
background that aroused Arcadius' rancor. Her father, Valentinian I, was
responsible for the execution of Arcadius' grandfather, Theodosius the Elder,
in 375. Religious difference could have been another reason for Arcadius'
enmity. Disputes between Christian factions in Constantinople were interfering with the normal run of business. The Catholic hierarchy wanted the
Arians expelled from the city. There was mounting pressure upon the imperial
government to do something about heretics within the capital. Galla's mother,
Justina, was an Arian Christian, as was Galla, at least before she married
Theodosius. Valentinian I had had a laissez-faire attitude towards certain
religious sects, and he was ardently anti-pagan (Amm. Marc. *Hist.* 30.9.5).
Galla's uncle Valens was the complete opposite, an outright Arian who made
life difficult for Catholic Christians, and of course the man who had lost the
army at Hadrianopolis (Oros. 7.33.1–19). These factors were not likely to
endear Galla to her new stepson. Then again, it might have just as easily have
been Arcadius' unpleasant character which was to blame. One suspects that
figures at court had a hand in the matter, bending Arcadius' ear to suit their
own agendas. True, this can only be conjecture, but it gives us some idea of the
unsettling nature of Theodosius' home life.

   Nor was Theodosius' court life much better. There was in-fighting
between his ministers, much of it provoked by the master of offices (*magister
officiorum*) Rufinus, a man in whom the emperor had placed a great deal of
trust. Rufinus – according to his many detractors – murdered and embezzled
his way through the top tiers of eastern high society (Eunap. *fr.* 57; Oros.
7.37.1; Zos. 4.51–2). So detested was Rufinus by the western imperial court
that Claudian dedicated two full invectives against him (Cl. *In Ruf.* I and II).
In religious matters, Theodosius' fellow countryman, the praetorian prefect
Maternus Cynegius, had been busy exceeding his brief through a systematic

persecution of the non-Orthodox. Cynegius closed down and destroyed many synagogues and temples, and broke up heretical congregations across the eastern empire (*PLRE* I, 235–6; Matthews 1967). Cynegius died in 388 while staying in Berytus (Beirut), the great legal center in the Levant. From there he had drawn up a huge body of repressive legislation against religious dissenters (Honorér 1998, 33–57). Maternus Cynegius' war on religious choice led to a rise in sectarianism in the East, of which the most infamous episode was the destruction of the Alexandrian Serapeum in about 392 (Lavan 2011, xv–xvi). Egypt was plagued with religious violence at this time, much of it carried out by the Taliban of their day, the so-called *parabalani*, a group of militant black-clad monks who Eunapius described as 'filthy ... human in appearance but swine in their way of life' (Eun. *fr.* 56). By 392, however, Theodosius was giving carte blanche to extremists through his implementation of laws that permanently closed pagan temples and associations (*CTh.* 16.10.10. Feb 24, 391; 16.10.11. June 16, 391; 16.10.12. Nov 8, 392).

References

Angelova, Diliana. 2004. "The Ivories of Ariadne and Ideas about Female Imperial Authority in Rome and Early Byzantium." *Gesta* 43.1: 1–15.

Angelova, Diliana. 2015. *Sacred Founders: Women, Men, and Gods in the Discourse of Imperial Founding, Rome through Early Byzantium.* Berkeley, CA: University of California Press.

Arce, Javier. 1997. "*Otium et negotium*: The Great Estates, 4th–7th Centuries." In *The Transformation of the Roman World, AD 400–900.* Edited by Leslie Webster and Michelle Brown: 19–32. London: British Museum Press.

Arce, Javier. 2009. *El ultimo siglo de la España romana, 284–409*, 2nd rev. ed. Madrid: Alianza.

Bardill, Jonathan. 1999. "The Golden Gate in Constantinople: A Triumphal Arch of Theodosius I." *AJA* 103.4: 671–96.

Barnes, Timothy D. 2010. "Maxentius and Diocletian." *CP* 105.3: 318–22.

Beard, Mary. 2007. *The Roman Triumph.* Cambridge, MA: Harvard University Press.

Bomgardner, David L. 2000. *The Story of the Roman Amphitheater.* 1st edition. London and New York: Routledge.

Brilliant, Richard. 1963. *Gesture and Rank in Roman Art: Memoirs of the Connecticut Academy of Arts and Sciences* 14. New Haven, CT: The Academy.

Cameron, Alan. 1969. "Theodosius the Great and the Regency of Stilico." *HSPh* 73: 247–80.

Cameron, Alan. 1988. "Flavius: A Nicety of Protocol." *Latomus* 47: 26–33.

Cameron, Alan. 2011. *The Last Pagans of Rome.* Oxford: Oxford University Press.

Canto, Alicia Maria. 2000. "Las quindecennalia de Teodosio I el Grande (19 de enero del 393 d. C.) en el Gran Clípeo de Madrid." In *El Disco de Teodosio.* Edited by Martín Almagro-Gorbea, José M.ª Álvarez Martínez, José M.ª Blázquez, and Salvador Rovira: 289–300. Madrid: Real Academia de la Historia.

Chavarría, Alexandra, Arce, Javier, and Brogiolo, Gian Pietro (eds). 2006. *Villas tardoantiguas en el Mediterráneo occidental.* Madrid: Consejo Superior de

Investigaciones Científicas, Instituto de Historia, Departamento de Historia Antigua y Arqueología.

Croke, Brian. 2010. "Reinventing Constantinople: Theodosius I's Imprint on the Imperial City." In *From the Tetrarchs to the Theodosians: Later Roman History and Culture, 284–450 CE*. Edited by Scott McGill, Cristiana Sogno, and Edward Watts: 241–64. Yale, CT: Cambridge University Press.

Dewar, Michael. 1996. *Panegyricus de sexto consulatu Honorii Augusti*. Oxford: Oxford University Press.

Elsner, Jas. 1998. *Imperial Rome and Christian Triumph: The Art of the Roman Empire, AD 100–450*. Oxford: Oxford University Press.

French, Dorothea R. 1998. "Rhetoric and the Rebellion of A.D. 387 in Antioch." *Hist.* 47.4: 468–84.

Futrell, Alison. 2000. *Blood in the Arena: The Spectacle of Roman Power*. Austin, TX: University of Texas Press.

Graham, Christopher. 2010. "Pulcher: Oratio consolatoria in Pulcheriam." In *The Brill Dictionary of Gregory of Nyssa*. Edited by Lucas Francisco Mateo Seco and Giulio Maspero: 657. Leiden: Brill.

Gunderson, Erik. 2003. "The Flavian Amphitheatre: All the World as Stage." In *Flavian Rome: Culture, Image, Text*. Edited by A. J. Boyle and W. J. Dominik: 637–58. Leiden: Brill.

Gutmann, Bernhard. 1991. *Studien zur ro"mischen Aussenpolitik in der Spätantike (364–395 n. Chr.)*. Bonn: R. Habelt.

Hedrick, Charles W. 2000. *History and Silence: The Purge and Rehabilitation of Memory in Late Antiquity*. Austin, TX: University of Texas Press.

Holum, Kenneth G. 1982. *Theodosian Empresses: Women and Imperial Dominion in Late Antiquity*. Berkeley, CA: University of California Press.

Honoré, Tony. 1998. *Law in the Crisis of Empire, AD 379–455*. Oxford: Oxford University Press.

Hope, Valerie M., and Marshall, Eireann (eds). 2000. *Death and Disease in the Ancient City*. London and New York: Routledge.

Humphries, Mark. 2015. "Emperors, Usurpers, and the City of Rome: Performing Power from Diocletian to Theodosius." In *Contested Monarchy: Integrating the Roman Empire in the Fourth Century AD*. Oxford Studies in Late Antiquity. Edited by Johannes Wienand: 151–68. Oxford: Oxford University Press.

Keenan, James G. 1973. "The Names Flavius and Aurelius as Status Designations in Later Roman Egypt." *ZPE* 1: 33–63.

Kelly, Christopher. 2015. "Pliny and Pacatus: Past and Present in Imperial Panegyric." In *Contested Monarchy: Integrating the Roman Empire in the Fourth Century AD*. Oxford Studies in Late Antiquity. Edited by Johannes Wienand: 215–38. Oxford: Oxford University Press.

Kelly, Gavin. 2016. "Claudian's Last Panegyric and Imperial Visits to Rome." *CQ* 66.1: 336–57.

Kiilerich, Bente. 1993. *Late Fourth Century Classicism in the Plastic Arts: Studies in the So-Called Theodosian Renaissance*. Odense: Odense University Press.

Kiilerich, Bente. 2000. "Representing an Emperor: Style and Meaning on the Missorium of Theodosius I." In *El Disco de Teodosio*. Edited by Martín Almagro-Gorbea, José M.ª Álvarez Martínez, José M.ª Blázquez, and Salvador Rovira: 273–80. Madrid: Real Academia de la Historia.

Lavan, Luke A. 2011. "The End of the Temples: Towards a New Narrative." In *The Archaeology of Late Antique Paganism*. *LAA* 7. Edited by Luke A. Lavan and Michael Mulryan: xv–xvi. Leiden: Brill.

Lejdegård, Hans. 2002. *Honorius and the City of Rome: Authority and Legitimacy in Late Antiquity*. Uppsala: Uppsala Universitet.

Lendon, Jon E. 1997. *Empire of Honour: The Art of Government in the Roman World*. Oxford: Clarendon Press.

Leppin, Hartmut. 2015. "Coping with the Tyrant's Faction: Civil-War Amnesties and Christian Discourses in the Fourth Century AD." In *Contested Monarchy: Integrating the Roman Empire in the Fourth Century AD*. Oxford Studies in Late Antiquity. Edited by Johannes Wienand: 198–214. Oxford: Oxford University Press.

MacCormack, Sabine G. 1981. *Art and Ceremony in Late Antiquity*. Berkeley and Los Angeles, CA: University of California Press.

Mango, Cyril. 2000. "The Triumphal Way of Constantinople and the Golden Gate." *DOP* 54: 173–88.

Matthews, John F. 1967. "A Pious Supporter of Theodosius I: Maternus Cynegius and His Family." *JThS* 18.2: 438–46.

Matthews, John F. 1975. *Western Aristocracies and Imperial Court, AD 364–425*. Oxford: Clarendon Press.

McCormick, Michael. 1990 (1986). *Eternal Victory: Triumphal Rulership in Late Antiquity, Byzantium and the Early Medieval West*. Cambridge: Cambridge University Press. Reprint.

McEvoy, Meaghan. 2010. "Rome and the Transformation of the Imperial Office in the Late Fourth–Mid-Fifth Centuries AD." *PBSR* 78: 151–92.

McEvoy, Meaghan. 2013. *Child Emperor Rule in the Late Roman West, AD 367–455*. Oxford: Oxford University Press.

O' Flynn, John Michael. 1983. *Generalissimos of the Western Roman Empire*. Alberta: The University of Alberta Press.

Omissi, Adrastos. 2014. "*Caput imperii, caput imperatoris*: The Display and Mutilation of the Bodies of Emperors, in Rome and Beyond, 296–416." In *Landscapes of Power: Selected Papers from the XV Oxford University Byzantine Society International Graduate Conference*. Byzantine and NeoHellenic Studies Series. Edited by Maximilian Lau, Caterina Franchi, and Morgan Di Rodi: 17–30. Bern: Peter Lang.

Pilkington, Nathan. 2013. "Growing Up Roman: Infant Mortality and Reproductive Development." *JIH* 44.1: 1–36.

Rebenich, Stefan. 1985. "Gratian, a Son of Theodosius, and the Birth of Galla Placidia." *Historia: Zeitschrift für Alte Geschichte* 34.3: 372–85.

Roueché, Charlotte. 2002. "The Image of Victory: New Evidence from Ephesus." *TM* 14: 527–46.

Samellas, Antigone. 2002. *Death in the Eastern Mediterranean, 50–600 AD: The Christianization of the East, an Interpretation*. Studien und Texte zu Antike und Christentum 12. Tübingen: Mohr Siebeck.

Scheidel, Walter. 1999. "Emperors, Aristocrats, and the Grim Reaper: Towards a Demographic Profile of the Roman Elite." *CQ* 49.1: 254–81.

Varner, Eric. 2004. *Mutilation and Transformation: Damnatio Memoriae and Roman Imperial Portraiture*. Leiden: Brill.

Wardman, Alan E. 1984. "Usurpers and Internal Conflicts in the Fourth Century AD." *Historia* 33: 220–37.

Ware, Catherine. 2012. *Claudian and the Roman Epic Tradition*. Cambridge: Cambridge University Press.

Wienand, Joachim. 2015. "O Tandem Felix Civili, Roma, Victoria! Civil-War Triumphs from Honorius to Constantine and Back." In *Contested Monarchy: Integrating the Roman Empire in the Fourth Century AD*. Oxford Studies in Late Antiquity. Edited by Johannes Wienand: 169–97. Oxford: Oxford University Press.

Williams, Stephen, and Friell, Gerard. 1994. *Theodosius: The Empire at Bay*. London: Batsford.

4   Young lion of the West

And surely after twenty years it was time to come. I am thinking of a child's
vow sworn in vain, never to leave that valley his fathers called their home
William Butler Yeats, *Under Saturn*, 1919

The education of princes

Leaving civil discord, religious disharmony, and political intrigues aside for
a moment, we should consider what Honorius' schooling was like during his
childhood at Constantinople. The panegyrist Nazarius, reflecting on the education of emperors' sons, contended that 'to perfect their inherent good qualities training is given them ... so that their expectation of becoming equal
to their father is assured; since their nature is like his, but with him as director of their learning their circumstances are more fortunate' (*Pan. Lat.* 4
(10).4.2). Imperial children would have had a number of private tutors (Aus.
20.7). Arcadius and Honorius' tutors included the pagan philosopher, orator,
and senator Themistius, and the deacon Arsenius. The future emperors'
younger sister Placidia received a similar education when she came of age.
That their father placed great emphasis on his sons' education is revealed by
a passage from the Byzantine historian Zonaras. In this excerpt, we catch an
interesting glimpse of the temperament of the young Arcadius, then in his
late teens. Honorius must have been about nine or ten. Theodosius had been
looking for a suitable tutor for Arcadius, and wrote to his western colleague
Gratian, and to Pope Damasus in Rome for recommendations. One of the
tutors Theodosius received from the West was Arsenius, a highly educated
man, skilled in Greek and Latin literature. Arsenius spent over a decade at
Constantinople teaching first Arcadius, and then the two boys together. Their
first cousin Nebridius shared the classroom with them. He was Flaccilla's
nephew, and grew up with Arcadius and Honorius, who were like brothers to
him. Later Nebridius served as an officer in the imperial guard, and was well
regarded by all (Jer. *Ep.* 79.2.1–5).

> Since he [Theodosius] wished them [Arcadius and Honorius] to have a
> share of education both in words and in ethics, he brought from Rome

Arsenius the Great, who was a deacon of the church there, famous both for wisdom and for virtue. To him he delivered his sons, after he had enjoined him to behave toward them not as to sovereigns but as to private individuals and ordinary people, to flog them if he saw them being careless or deviating one bit from propriety, and to deal with them as with his own sons. He deemed Arsenius worthy of great honor and greatly enriched him with wealth. After he had taken charge of the boys, he used to seat them on thrones while he himself stood and filled them with his teaching. Once the sovereign unexpectedly surprised them and, when he saw them sitting and Arsenius standing, became upset, roused the boys from their thrones, seated Arsenius, and ordered him to teach them thus. Thereafter, they used to stand beside their teacher while the teacher was sitting.

(Zon. 8.19)

Zonaras' anecdote is interesting on a number of levels. It proffers a small glimpse into daily life in the imperial schoolroom where we find tired, bored children taking not the slightest bit of notice of their teacher. It gives Theodosius a human quality not usually seen in literary sources. His reaction is atypical of parental embarrassment for their wayward children's apparent disregard for authority figures. Theodosius had caught his children acting in a manner contrary to how he felt they should behave, and chided his sons. This was not how future rulers should behave, he felt. We know nothing of Theodosius' own schooling, but he evidently valued education, especially from ecclesiastics. The respect Theodosius had for clerical instruction is further illustrated by an encounter in the court of Constantinople between Theodosius, Arcadius, and the bishop of Iconium, Amphilochius, in 383. The bishop was at court trying to press the emperor into expelling Arian heretics from the city.

The next time he entered the palace and beheld standing at the emperor's side his son Arcadius, who had lately been appointed emperor, he saluted Theodosius as was his wont, but did no honor to Arcadius. The emperor, thinking that this neglect was due to forgetfulness, commanded Amphilochius to approach and to salute his son. "Sir," said he, "the honor which I have paid you is enough." Theodosius was indignant at the discourtesy, and said, "Dishonor done to my son is a rudeness to myself." Then, and not till then, the very wise Amphilochius disclosed the object of his conduct, and said with a loud voice, "You see, sir, that you do not brook dishonor done your son, and are bitterly angry with those who are rude to him. Believe then that the God of all the world abominates them that blaspheme the Only Begotten Son, and hates them as ungrateful to their Savior and Benefactor." Then the emperor understood the bishop's drift, and admired both what he had done and what he had said. Without further delay he put out an edict forbidding the congregations of heretics.

(Theod. *HE*. 16)

Amphilochius was successful in convincing Theodosius to take action against Arians and other heretics in the capital. Not long after Amphilochius' brush with the emperor and Arcadius, a series of proscriptive laws against heretics in Constantinople came into effect (*CTh*. 16.5.10–13. June 20, 383–Jan 21, 384). Still, working in the service of the imperial family had its downside, as Arcadius and Honorius' tutor Arsenius discovered.

> Well now, once the teacher was laying lashes on Arcadius, who had made an error. Wroth with him as a result, he devised a plot against him, began diligently practicing to kill the man, and was planning the slaughter. When he had learned what was being rehearsed, Arsenius secretly retired from the palace and, after he had retreated to Scetis [modern Wadi El Natrun, Egypt], adopted the solitary life and became like an angel. Although the sovereign Theodosius made a massive search for him, he did not know where on earth he was.
>
> (Zon. 8.19)

The young emperor's malice seems to have been the catalyst for Arsenius' leaving imperial service, but the tutor had already had enough of materialism. Fleeing the oppressive palatial environment, Arsenius found his way to the Egyptian desert, to the monastic community of Scetis. There he would spent most of the rest of his life as an ascetic monk, away from the secular world, and farther away from the vindictive Arcadius (*Apoph. Patr.* 42). Arcadius' spitefulness extended to family members, as we have seen with his stepmother Galla. If Arcadius treated his younger brother poorly, it is not recorded by any source. One wonders what their relationship was really like, especially considering that when Honorius took the throne at Milan in 395, he never saw his brother again. Granted, they kept in contact via letters, and Stilicho, for dubious reasons, obstructed Honorius from going east to see Arcadius. Yet it is odd that, from their joint accession in 395 to Arcadius' death in 408, the two brothers failed to meet just once. Their relationship might not have been as close as official sources claimed.

Treachery in the West

Almost as soon as Theodosius had departed Italy in 391, the *magister militum* Arbogastes detained Valentinian II in Vienne, southeastern Gaul, a fortified city on a junction of the Rhône and Gère rivers. While Valentinian tried in vain to rule, he was powerless to prevent Arbogastes acting as the de facto western emperor. Arbogastes was an arrogant, aggressive individual. He murdered members of Valentinian's administration, some of whom he personally killed in front of the emperor, so he could appoint his own people in their place. In hindsight, Theodosius' choice of men for influential positions was poor. Either he was very unlucky, or he was an extremely bad judge of character. That said, it is worth bearing in mind that Theodosius was first and foremost a soldier, whereas his skills as a politician were not quite so honed. He left much of the administration work to others, a facet of his reign that was passed onto his sons after his death.

At Vienne, Valentinian tried his best to halt Arbogastes' rampage. When the young emperor handed him a letter of dismissal, the *magister* ripped it up and threw it at Valentinian. Arbogastes then drew his sword and threatened Valentinian, shouted obscenities at him, and walked out (Zos. 4.53.1–4). Arbogastes ought to have lost his life there and then, but the emperor had no tangible support to do so. Valentinian had no option but to send for help to Theodosius, as his mother had previously done during Magnus Maximus' usurpation. In the meantime, on May 15, 392, Valentinian was discovered dead in his quarters at Vienne. Accounts vary as to how he died – from stabbing to suicide, none are certain – but the timing is suspect (Soc. *HE.* 5.25; Oros. 7.35.10; Soz. *HE.* 7.22; *Cons. Const.* s.a. 392; Zos. 4.54.4). At any rate, if Arbogastes did murder the young emperor, no one challenged him in the West, and he had total support of the army there. In fact, most late Roman insurrections took place in the West where usurpation was an 'activity promoted by western armies' (Wardman 1984, 234). Arbogastes was popular with the military rank and file, and had a contempt for those born into privilege. His class distaste most surely would have extended to Honorius and Arcadius, and was therefore a threat to Theodosius' bloodline. Whichever way Valentinian died was immaterial, the news of his death absolutely devastated his sister, the empress Galla. She blamed Arbogastes, and maybe her husband, and she demanded that he be avenged (Zos. 4.55.1). Up until then, Theodosius had been reluctant to intervene on Valentinian's behalf, despite the latter's repeated calls for assistance. Theodosius' reticence is probably explained by this fresh crisis coming so soon after the war with Maximus (Zos. 4.53.4). Only just settling back into life at Constantinople, the prospect of another western conflict was too much to contemplate.

Arbogastes' next move was to create his own emperor – Eugenius, a former Latin grammarian and a pagan to boot. On August 22, 392, three months after Valentinian's passing, Eugenius' accession took place at Lugdunum. As John Matthews surmised, Arbogastes chose his own emperor when 'it became clear that he was not going to escape Theodosius' retribution' (1975, 239). Arbogastes knew only too well what the consequences of treason were, as the fate of Magnus Maximus proved. So, for Arbogastes it was all or nothing. On the other hand, his nominee Eugenius was none to happy about being propelled to the purple, but he had little say in the affair. From the outset, Eugenius' self-representation on coinage applied the mottos *Spes Romanorum* (Hope of the Romans) and *Gloria Romanorum* (Glory of the Romans) (*RIC* IX Rome 65b; Trier 104d). Eugenius, ergo Arbogastes, constituted a serious threat to Honorius' future. Eugenius sent messages to Theodosius asking to be recognized as his co-Augustus. The latter delayed his response in order to buy time to prepare for what he knew was coming – war. Egged on Arbogastes, Eugenius proclaimed himself joint consul with

Theodosius for 393. Theodosius ignored this, and chose his own consular partner, the *magister militum* Abundantius, a friend of Stilicho's (*PLRE* I, 4–5). Theodosius' refusal to recognize Eugenius guaranteed that conflict was unavoidable. Faced with Valentinian's questionable demise, a pagan usurper on the western throne, a former comrade who hated anyone born to the purple, along with pressure from his wife Galla, Theodosius had no choice but to prepare for war. In addition, Arbogastes had co-opted many Frankish *foederati* into his army, problematic in light of the growing Visigothic presence in the East. Barbarians were gaining power within the state in a way not previously experienced. Theodosius had recourse to military action against yet another western pretender.

There was however, a well-received addition to the Theodosian household during this turbulent period. In either late 392, or early 393, his daughter Galla was born (Rebenich 1985). Called so after her mother, she was also given the name Placidia. Oost thought that Placidia might have been named after a Spanish relative, since the name was quite common there (1968, 48–9). This may well be true, since it would be in keeping with Theodosian tradition, although one wonders where Arcadius' name originated from. It is equally plausible that Galla and Theodosius might have named their daughter after Saint Placidus, martyred in Sicily during the Diocletianic persecutions. Girls were named after both female and male saints. Furthermore, Placidus' feast day was October 5, which lends some credence to placing Galla Placidia's birth in late 392, in correspondence with her namesake's martyrdom. Of course, this is a matter of opinion, but the choice of the name Placidia itself is significant. It means calm or gentle. As often happens where a birth follows a bereavement in families, Theodosius and Galla likely chose Placidia to bring some comfort into their lives during a time of mourning and uncertainty. The empress had recently lost her brother Valentinian, and her first son Gratian possibly died around the same time as well. There is, however, no mention of when or how Gratian died, other than Ambrose's funeral oration for Theodosius that describes the emperor's pre-deceased daughter and son – Pulcheria and Gratian – as the 'sweetest (*dulcissima*) of children' (*De ob. Theod.* 40.2–5).

The first accession of Honorius

Perhaps it was news of Eugenius' usurpation and his demands for recognition which spurred Theodosius to elevate his eight-year-old son to the rank of Augustus. Early on the morning of January 23, 393, at the Hebdomon, scene of Theodosius' grand entrance to Constantinople in 391, Honorius was proclaimed Augustus. In established custom, the boy was raised high upon a shield in front of the assembled army, to their shouts of acclamation (Cl. *IV Cons.* 174) and their swearing of the military oath of fidelity (*sacramentum*) to Honorius. He was now a member of the imperial *collegium* with his father and brother. According to the late sixth-century Byzantine chronicler Marcellinus Comes, there was solar eclipse at the 'third hour of the day,' a Judaic time calculation based on the twelve-hour day. By this reckoning, the third hour of the day meant three hours after sunrise. A steadfast Catholic Christian, Marcellinus Comes equated the day of Honorius' ceremony with gospel accounts of Jesus' crucifixion (Mark 15.25). The solar eclipse was thus interpreted as a good omen for the Theodosians; an ominous sign for the traitors to the West (*Chron. Marcell.* S.a. 393). Other Christian writers associated Honorius with biblical figures, such as Severus of Antioch's likening of the emperor's piety to that of the great Jewish king David (Sev. Ant. 201.6). Claudian took a different tack. Not for him any biblical exegesis; for the pagan poet it was the gods at play on that auspicious day, and Claudian went on to compare Honorius to the legendary Trojan prince Ascanius (Cl. *IV Cons.* 171–211). In 398, as he recited his panegyric for Honorius' fourth consulship to the court, Claudian recounted what had transpired after the accession, when the family had returned home to the palace. There, away from the public gaze, Theodosius counseled his son with sage advice. At least that is what Claudian told Honorius what had happened. In 398, Honorius was thirteen and could hardly remembered everything his father had said to him when he was eight. Theodosius probably did give his son some advice, but in such detail? And who recorded their private conversation? Claudian? The poet doesn't seem to have met Theodosius until maybe 394 (Christiansen and Christiansen 2009). Claudian was probably given the gist of the conversation, and embellished the rest – still, it is good advice by anyone's standards.

"If you are afraid, have evil desires, are swayed by anger, you will bear the yoke of slavery; within yourself will you be a slave to tyrannical rule. When you can be king over yourself then you shall hold rightful rule over the world ... master your emotions and ponder not what you might do but what you ought to do, and let regard for duty control your mind. Of this too I cannot warn you too often: remember that you live in the sight of the whole world ... above all fail not in loving-kindness; for though we be surpassed in every virtue yet mercy alone makes us equal with the gods. Let your actions be open and give no grounds for suspicion, be loyal to your friends nor lend an ear to rumors. He who attends to such will quake at every idle whisper and know no moment's peace. Neither watch, nor guard, nor yet hedge of spears can secure you safety; only your people's love can do that. Love you cannot extort; it is the gift of mutual faith and honest goodwill ... Not for you let spacious tents overflow with princely delights nor luxury don arms and drag to the standards her unwarlike train. Though the storm winds blow and the rain descends yield not to them and use not cloth of gold to guard you from the sun's fierce rays. Eat such food as you can find. It will be a solace to your soldiers that your toil is as heavy as theirs; be the first to mount the arduous hill and, should necessity demand the felling of a forest, be not ashamed to grasp the axe and hew down the oak. If a stagnant marsh must be crossed let

your horse be the first to test the depth of it. Boldly tread the frozen river;
swim the flood. Mounted yourself, ride amid your squadrons of horse or
again stand foot to foot with the infantry. They will advance the bolder
for your presence, and with you to witness glorious and glad shall be the
fulfilment of their task."

(Cl. *IV Hons*. 259–83, 337–52)

Honorius Augustus before 393?

Going by what literary sources tell us, Honorius became Augustus in January
393. Indeed, his first coinage seems to have been minted to correspond to
his accession. Sozomen and Philostorgius complicate things. Sozomen placed
Honorius' proclamation on January 10, thirteen days earlier than the other evidence indicates. The earlier date might relate to a formality whereby Honorius
was created Caesar before his full accession. However, there are many errors
in Sozomen's writing, and this could be another such case (Soc. *HE*. 6.25; cf.
Kelly 2016, 346, 355). Philostorgius maintained that as soon as Theodosius
learned of Eugenius' usurpation, he appointed Honorius his colleague and
'spent the entire winter [of 392] preparing for war' (Philost. *HE*. 11.2). Yet,
this might be down to Philostorgius' condensing of events to fit his overall
narrative. Whatever we might make of the alternative chronologies on offer
from Sozomen and Philostorgius, at least one thing is certain – from January
23 on, Honorius was an Augustus, nominally at least. Meaghan McEvoy
refers to his early years as Augustus as a type of 'phantom accession,' since
he was obviously too young to wield actual power. Honorius' elevation was a
necessary step towards eventual governance in his own right (McEvoy 2013,
138–9). On the other hand, Honorius' name is on imperial laws both from the
time of his formal accession in January 393 (whichever date in that month we
accept), and, as it turns out, well before then.

There is an anomaly in the timeline for Honorius' progression from
nobilissmus puer to Augustus in 393 – and it is not the question discussed
above about whether or not he became a Caesar at Rome in 389. Rather, it
a legal matter concerning seventeen laws given in the names of Theodosius,
Arcadius, and Honorius Augusti between April (*CTh*. 12.1.124) and December
392 (*Cod. Iust*. 9.9.32). This legislation is clearly prior to Honorius' official
promotion in January 393, and some of it predates Valentinian's death by
at least a month. The content of these laws is not at issue here – they deal
with fairly humdrum matters, along with proscription of pagans added for
good measure. It is the fact that these laws exist in Honorius Augustus' name
nearly eleven months before he was officially proclaimed in Constantinople.
These laws were given at Constantinople – indicating Honorius' presence
in the eastern capital for most of 392 – and all bar one were dispatched to
senior officials in the East. The odd one out was sent to the Italian praetorian
prefect Nicomachius Flavianus in Rome, where Valentinian still nominally
ruled, despite his confinement at Vienne (*CTh*. 10.10.20. April 8, 392). This

particular edict is specifically addressed to Flavianus by the three Theodosian emperors – Theodosius, Arcadius, and Honorius. There is no inclusion of Valentinian, still very much alive at this point. Even more curious is that laws continued to be issued in the names of Valentinian, Theodosius, and Arcadius well into 393, many months after the former's death. This could suggest that news of his death did reach the East until then, but that is not borne out by other evidence; and though the imperial postal service (*cursus publicus*) might have been slow by modern standards, it was not that slow.

What does all of this mean? Are all of our literary sources in error about the date of Honorius' accession? Was Theodosius publicly snubbing Valentinian and promoting his own progeny ahead of legal accession? There are no certain answers, and, for the moment, this is an open question.

Propaganda of the Theodosian triumvirate

The iconography and ideology of the Theodosian Augusti was disseminated using standard imperial propagandist formulae: material propaganda, mass entertainments, civic and ecclesiastical construction projects, and philanthropic programs. Even bronze *exagia* (coin weights) featured the imperial trio in profile (Figure 4.1).

One of Theodosius' great building achievements was his forum at Constantinople, which he inaugurated in 393. Originally Constantine I's forum,

Figure 4.1 Bronze *exagium solidi*/coin weight of Theodosius I with Arcadius and Honorius. Constantinople mint, *c.* 393–5. Obv. Theodosius and his sons facing, diademed and draped. Cross above. Rev. Moneta standing, holding scales and cornucopia. Star in right field. Legend: cross above / EXAC-SOL-SVB-V-INL-IOhANNI-Com-S-L (*Exacium Solidi vir Illustris Iohannes comes sacrarum largitionum*/Solidus weight under the illustrious Johannes, count of the sacred largesse). Exergue: CONS (Constantinople).

Source: Bendall 10.

the so-called Forum of the Bull (*Forum Tauri*), Theodosius revamped the massive space with churches and civic building. A triumphal column, topped by a silver statue of Theodosius, stood in the forum's center. The column was modeled on Trajan's in Rome – perhaps emphasizing the Theodosian familial connection with the great first-century Spanish emperor. There was an imposing marble triumphal arch at one end of the forum, surmounted with greater than life-size bronze statues of Theodosius, Arcadius, and Honorius. Only fragments of the forum remain in what is now Beyazit Square, beside Istanbul University. Similar triumphal monuments went up around the eastern provinces, making it abundantly clear that Theodosius' sons were his heirs apparent.

A bittersweet victory

By spring 394, Theodosius and his *magistri* Stilicho and Timasius were putting the finishing touches to their preparations for the western campaign. They had spent the previous year or so requisitioning supplies, conscripting and training troops, gathering allies from all over the East, and were now ready for the battle ahead (*CTh.* 7.4.18–20. July 29–31, 393; Cl. *III Cons.* 68–72). Just as the military expedition was getting ready for the off in April, the empress Galla, pregnant for the third time, went into labor and died along with her baby, a boy named Johannes (Eunap. *Fr.* 60.1; Rebenich 1985; cf. Oost 1965). Eunapius was of the opinion that Theodosius 'mourned the dead empress for about one day. For the demands of the impending war overshadowed his grief for his wife' (Eunap. *Fr.* 60.2). For the second time in less than a decade, Theodosius had lost a wife, and a child for the third time. Just half of Theodosius' six children lived, a reminder of how precarious pregnancy, childbirth, and infancy was in antiquity. Eunapius was unfair to assign Theodosius just a single solitary day of mourning. The emperor's mourning period for his wife was necessarily brief – probably more than a day. He could not afford to lose the element of surprise over Eugenius and Arbogastes, whose agents inside Theodosius' camp kept them informed of the latter's movements. Theodosius was no doubt upset by the loss of Galla and their baby, but he was keen to get away from the sad mood of the palace – his family's future depended on him having a clear focus.

The last law issued by Theodosius from Constantinople was dated April 29, 394 (*CTh.* 7.1.14). It follows, then, that he left the city soon after this date, taking Honorius with him (Cl. *III Cons.* 111–13; Zos. 58.1). Reaching Thrace, the emperor left his son in camp for his own protection, despite the boy's protestations to join in the battle – a 'young lion' filled with 'martial passion' is how Claudian euphemistically described it (Cl. *III Cons.* 73–87; *IV Cons.* 353–63). As Theodosius left at the head of the column, Honorius watched them disappear into the distance, wondering perhaps if he might see his father alive again.

Theodosius made rapid progress, reaching the Julian Alps, the border of Italy, by late August, where he engaged Eugenius' army along the River Frigidus (the modern Vippaco, or Vipava, river which flows through western Slovenia into northeastern Italy). The battle took place over two days, September 5–6, a few days' shy of Honorius' tenth birthday. The literary accounts of the encounter paint a picture of wanton killing, amid inclement weather conditions – the river practically 'choked with corpses' (Cl. *III Cons.* 88–101; Eunap. *Fr.* 60; Soz. *HE.* 7.24; Soc. Zos. 4.58). Theodosius threw thousands of Visigothic *foederati* into the fray on the first day. His Visigothic allies incurred dreadful casualties, which led them to suspect their expendability in the eyes of the emperor – they were right to think so. The Battle of the Frigidus was a milestone in Roman-Visigothic relations (Heather 1991, 199–200; Ferrill 1997, 71ff.). The future Visigothic leader Alaric fought at the Frigidus and, like many of his compatriots, came to the realization that Romans could not to be trusted. Orosius' claim that although ten thousand Visigoths fell in battle, not much slaughter had occurred, reveals Roman attitudes to the foreigners in their midst (Oros. 7.35.11–22). Apparently barbarian lives just did not count for as much as Romans did. On the second day of clashes, Theodosius caught the enemy off-guard and decimated them (Elton 1996). Eugenius was taken alive and decapitated (*Cons. Ital.* s.a. 394). His severed head was sent around Italy as a warning to anyone contemplating revolt. Arbogastes escaped the battlefield and committed suicide (Cl. *III Cons.* 102–10; Zos. 4.58; Soc. *HE.* 5.25). Because of Eugenius and Arbogastes' religious persuasion, Christian writers claimed the Frigidus battle as a victory over the forces of paganism. Whether it is accurate to see the conflict as religiously motivated is debatable, but that is how ecclesiastic sources presented Theodosius' win (Rapp 1998, 281–3). Interestingly, it has recently been claimed that the Frigidus is where Claudian first came to Theodosius' notice (Christiansen and Christiansen 2009).

The new emperor of the West

In just six years, Theodosius had fought two major wars against fellow Romans, both of whom had been supported by barbarian generals, as was he himself – a sign of what imperial governing was becoming (O' Flynn 1983, 6–13). Now, for the first time in thirty years, the Roman Empire had a single ruler, though this was probably intended to be a temporary measure until Arcadius and Honorius could be properly set up on their respective thrones by their father. In the meantime, Theodosius had much work to do to reconcile with those in the West who had supported the usurpation (Matthews 1975, 247ff.; Salzman 2006). After pardoning Eugenius' surviving soldiers, Theodosius went to the great Christian bastion of Aquileia, in northern Italy, from where he sent for Honorius to join him at Milan as soon as possible (Gentili 1992). Bishop Ambrose visited Theodosius in Aquileia and obtained his pledge of clemency toward élite Christian affiliates of Eugenius – he had been one himself, after all. Ambrose then left for Milan to prepare the city for the coming of the emperor, where he said mass in thanksgiving for Theodosius having saved the state from tyranny (Amb. *Ep.* 61).

From Aquileia, Theodosius traveled to Rome, where he tried unsuccessfully to convince the city's senate to renounce paganism, possibly at the behest of Ambrose. Claudian made his first known appearance as a court panegyrist at this time, reciting a poem in honor of the two consuls for 395, the brothers Anicius Probinus and Anicius Olybrius (Cl. *Prob.* 1–279). The brothers were members of one of Rome's oldest and most distinguished Christian families, the Anicii. Theodosius appointed the two Anicii as joint consuls as both a gesture of goodwill to those who had sided with Eugenius, and as a sign of favor towards Christians over pagans. In Claudian's panegyric for the brother consuls, the goddess Roma was rejoined to Theodosius, signifying reconciliation – inclusive rhetoric was an integral part of Theodosius' peace process, just as much as military and political actions.

In spite of his efforts at reconciliation, Theodosius' attempt to compel the Roman pagan aristocracy into accepting Christianity was ill-advised. It was far too soon after the cessation of hostilities. From Rome he went on to Milan for the upcoming victory celebrations there. Honorius arrived in Milan around late December or early January 395, with his sister Placidia and cousin Serena, and possibly his first cousin Eucherius, in tow. The emperor and his son held a triumphal entry into Milan, on a similar scale to those which they had staged in Rome and Constantinople previously, and on January 17, they attended public circus games (Lejdegård 2002, 46–52; Cameron 1969). Claudian asserts that immediately after the procession, in the privacy of the imperial palace, Theodosius made Stilicho *magister praesentalis*, and ordered him to assume guardianship of his children – perhaps he meant just Honorius and Placida due to their youth – and also full protection of both of his sons (Cl. *III Cons.* 121–41; Soz. *HE.* 7.29; Soc. *HE.* 5.26; Zos. 4.59.4, 5.4) – yet another example of a private conversation which Claudian was privy to at a later date.

Thereafter, so Claudian says, the emperor died and ascended to the heavens with the gods, content in the knowledge that Stilicho had sworn lasting loyalty to his family. Other accounts relay it a little differently: that the emperor had complained of feeling ill during the games and retired to his quarters, where he passed away from dropsy possibly brought on by his exertions on campaign. The modern term for dropsy is edema, typically a swelling of body parts caused by several causes, including injury, which might suggest that Theodosius' sickness was the result of the stresses of war and bereavement. He was approximately fifty years of age.

Best intentions

Theodosius' embalmed body lay in state for forty days at Milan, probably within the Basilica Martyrum (Basilica of the Martyrs, built under Ambrose's direction), otherwise known as the Basilica di Sant'Ambrogio. The emperor's body was then taken in cortège to Constantinople for interment with his deceased family members. On February 25, 395, as the cortège prepared to leave the basilica, Ambrose gave a heartfelt oration for Theodosius, a man whom he had loved as his close friend; a man whose death had 'crushed Ambrose's heart' (*De ob. Theod.* 36). Gathered around the emperor's body were Honorius, Placidia, Serena, and Stilicho, and members of the western and eastern élite, listening intently to the bishop's speech. Honorius helped the bishop at the altar (*De ob. Theod.* 3). Liberally using biblical exegesis, Ambrose extoled the dead ruler's virtues. The bishop appealed to the civilian and military establishment to continue to support Theodosius' sons. Ambrose was aware that Honorius' age might be of concern to some as to whether they could support an orphaned child on the throne, particularly considering the fate of imperial children in the past. There was an urgent need to prevent further challenges to power, and to ensure continuity of Theodosian government – in both western and eastern parts of the empire.

> He has left us his children in whom we should recognize him, and in whom we see and possess him. Let not their age disquiet you. The faith of soldiers is the perfection of the age of an emperor; for age is perfect where strength is perfect. This acts reciprocally, for the faith of an emperor is the strength of his soldiers … let us bestow sedulous and paternal affection on the children of the pious prince. Pay to his sons what you owe to their father; you owe more to him now that he is dead than you owed to him while was living. For if among the children of private citizens, the rights of minors are not violated without grave crime, how much more in the case of the children of an emperor … Who then will doubt that he [Theodosius] will be a powerful protector for his sons in the House of God? By the favor of the Lord, the emperor Arcadius is already a robust youth; Honorius knocks forthwith at the door of manhood, a little older than Josias.
>
> (*De ob. Theod.* 6, 11, 15)

Most importantly for the listening Honorius, the eulogy was intended as a model to guide and inspire the young Augustus. The bishop's advice is reminiscent of the instructive Old Testament maxim to 'train up a child in the way he should go; even when he is old he will not depart from it' (Proverbs 22.6). Ambrose's words had a profound and lasting effect upon the tearful ten-year-old. Honorius was thus shown the path he must follow: that of a pious Christian ruler who places God and the state above sentiment and personal desire.

> He is victorious, who hopes for the grace of God, not he who presumes upon his own strength … Theodosius bore the heavy yoke from youth, since those who killed his father, the conqueror, were plotting against his safety … since he assumed the imperial power in the Roman Empire

when it was overrun by barbarians. He bore the heavy yoke that he might remove tyrants from the Roman Empire … You weep, August Emperor, because you yourself will not accompany the honored remains to Constantinople … But Joseph went into a neighboring province. Here many divergent kingdoms intervene; here seas must be crossed. Even this would not be laborious to you, did not the public interest hold you, which good emperors place before parents and children. Finally, then, your father made you emperor. God has confirmed this, so that you might not do military service for your father alone, but that you might have command over all.

(*De ob. Theod.* 25, 53, 55)

With words such as these, Ambrose sought to comfort a grieving little boy, but for all the kind expressions of praise and advice, the truth was that Honorius was alone, save for his infant sister Placidia, and his ambitious surrogate parents Serena and Stilicho. The young Augustus was in an unfamiliar land which he had only briefly visited before with his father. In January 395, Honorius was alone without his great protector and advisor. The child emperor could not have known then that he was destined never to return to Constantinople, to the place where he had been reared. He was not allowed to accompany his father's body to the eastern capital, possibly because his absence from Italy might inspire another to seize his nascent throne. From spring 395 until the end of his life in 423, Honorius remained in Italy, variously residing in the imperial palaces of Milan, Rome, and Ravenna; in effect a hostage by the fact of his position.

References

Blockley, Roger C. 1998. "The Dynasty of Theodosius." In *CAH* 13: *The Late Empire, AD 337–425*. Edited by Averil Cameron and Peter Garnsey: 111–17. Cambridge: Cambridge University Press.

Cameron, Alan. 1969. "Theodosius the Great and the Regency of Stilico." *HSPh* 73: 247–80.

Christiansen, Peder G., and Christiansen, David. 2009. "Claudian: The Last Great Pagan Poet." *AC* 78: 133–44.

Elton, Hugh. 1996. *Warfare in Roman Europe, AD 350–425*. Oxford Classical Monographs. Oxford: Clarendon Press.

Ferrill, Arther. 1997. *The Fall of the Roman Empire: The Military Explanation*. London: Thames and Hudson.

Gentili, Sara. 1992. "Politics and Christianity in Aquileia in the Fourth Century AD." *AC* 61: 192–208.

Heather, Peter. 1991. *Goths and Romans, 332–489*. Oxford Historical Monographs. Oxford: Clarendon Press.

Kelly, Gavin. 2016. "Claudian's Last Panegyric and Imperial Visits to Rome." *CQ* 66.1: 336–57.

Lejdegård, Hans. 2002. *Honorius and the City of Rome: Authority and Legitimacy in Late Antiquity*. Uppsala: Uppsala Universitet.

Matthews, John F. 1975. *Western Aristocracies and Imperial Court, AD 364–425.* Oxford: Clarendon Press.

McEvoy, Meaghan. 2013. "The Mausoleum of Honorius: Late Roman Imperial Christianity and the City of Rome in the Fifth Century." In *Old Saint Peter's, Rome.* Edited by Rosamond McKitterick, John Osborne, Carol M. Richardson, and Joanna Story: 119–136. Cambridge: Cambridge University Press.

O' Flynn, John Michael. 1983. *Generalissimos of the Western Roman Empire.* Alberta: The University of Alberta Press.

Oost, Stewart Irvin. 1965. "Some Problems in the History of Galla Placidia." *CP* 60.1: 1–10.

Oost, Stewart Irvin. 1968. *Galla Placidia Augusta: A Biographical Essay.* Chicago, IL and London: The University of Chicago Press.

Rapp, Claudia. 1998. "Comparison, Paradigm and the Case of Moses in Panegyric and Hagiography." In *The Propaganda of Power: The Role of Panegyric in Late Antiquity.* Edited by Mary Whitby: 277–98. Leiden: Brill.

Rebenich, Stefan. 1985. "Gratian, a Son of Theodosius, and the Birth of Galla Placidia." *Historia: Zeitschrift für Alte Geschichte* 34.3: 372–85.

Salzman, Michele Renee. 2006. "Symmachus and the 'Barbarian' Generals." *Hist.* 55.3: 352–67.

Wardman, Alan E. 1984. "Usurpers and Internal Conflicts in the Fourth Century AD." *Historia* 33: 220–37.

Yeats, William Butler. (1919) 1989. "Under Saturn." In *The Collected Works of W. B. Yeats*, Volume 1: *The Poems.* Revised second edition. Edited by Richard J. Finneran: 325–6. New York: Macmillan.

5   Crisis in North Africa

> Africa ... a province advantageous to emperors for all occasions ...
>
> Ammianus Marcellinus, *Historia*, 21.7.2

A prelude to war

The year 397 began relatively uneventfully for the western empire. Its frontiers were calm enough and imperial propaganda projected order and security through archetypal slogans on coins such as *Gloria Romanorum* (Glory of the Roman People), *Victoria Augustorum* (Victory of the Emperors), and *Virtus Romanorum* (Virtue of the Roman People). Claudian was busy preparing new works for Honorius' court – dark, violent invectives directed against the Gallo-Roman Rufinus, the former eastern prefect who had been assassinated by soldiers in the presence of Arcadius at Constantinople. Rufinus had accompanied Theodosius to the east in 379, and had served him loyally throughout his reign. Stilicho might have had a hand in Rufinus' killing. A glib comment from Claudian posits the soldier who fatally stabbed Rufinus declaring, 'It is the hand of Stilicho that strikes you' (Cl. *Ruf.* II.402–23).

Honorius' legislation for early 397 was generally humdrum, concerning compulsory public services and ecclesiastical privileges (Honoré 1998, 214). By mid-April 397, however, imperial legislature shifted focus to the North African *annona* – that region's food supply to the West. The annonarian system was notoriously corrupt. Many of Honorius' predecessors had tried to reform the African *annona* to make it more effective and less wasteful. Their efforts were never fully successful and embezzlement was widespread through the entire annonarian infrastructure. Honorius' April laws were about more than simple fraud, however. They suggested western unease about the unfolding political situation in North Africa.

> Emperors Honorius and Arcadius Augustuses to the Senate. You have trustworthy proof, O Conscript Fathers, how much care We devote to your interests and to those of the people, and therefore by this law. We sanction that if any remission of the regular grain or oil tribute for the

City is bestowed by special grant of imperial favor, privileges thus elicited against the public interest shall not be valid. Also no person shall dare to touch any grain set aside for the use of the City, if ever such grain should be forced by fortune or some good reason to remain on the shores of Africa, and no one shall dare to change his direct course and, by the alteration of any orders, to transmit his cargo elsewhere than to the sacred City ... [part missing]

(*CTh*. 14.15.3. April 15, 397)

The Emperors Arcadius and Honorius to the Senate and the People. For the reason that grain destined for the public is said to be sometimes sold on various coasts, the vendors and purchasers of such merchandise are hereby informed that they are liable to capital punishment, and that commercial contracts of this kind made with a view to defrauding the public are prohibited.

(*Cod. Iust*. 4.40.3. April 15, 397)

On April 4, as Honorius and his inner council (*consistorium*) were drafting his *annona* legislation, the formidable Bishop Ambrose died at Milan, a man whom Stilicho both feared and respected in equal measure. Ambrose had once compelled the *magister* to do penance for an offense (Paulin. *Amb.* 34, 45). The bishop's death meant that any constraint he might have held over Stilicho's ambitions was removed. Ambrose had also been a vital influence on Honorius since the death of his father, Theodosius. The bishop's passing left Honorius further isolated at the Milanese court. With Ambrose dead, a trusted source of counsel for the young emperor was gone: Honorius was left alone with Stilicho and his wife Serena.

About the time that Ambrose died, the growing challenge posed by the Visigoths and their leader Alaric to both parts of the empire became critical (Robertson Brown 2011,79–96). The western government received reports that Alaric's forces were marauding through the Peloponnese. The Visigoths had looted the ancient cult centre of Eleusis, and sacked several Greek cities, including Corinth and Sparta. Constantinople seemed indifferent – or impotent – to the crisis, so Honorius, in an effort to assist his brother Arcadius, engaged Stilicho to deal with the barbarians. Stilicho took this as the perfect opportunity to intervene in the East. It gave him a chance to exert his own influence over the eastern Augustus. Stilicho took an army by ship to Greece whereupon he routed the Visigoths (Cl. *IV Cons.* 459–83). Sensing Stilicho's ulterior agenda, the chamberlain Eutropius, Rufinus' replacement, maneuvered the Constantinopolitan senate into declaring his western rival an enemy of the state (*hostis publicus*). Just as it seemed that Stilicho was on the verge of annihilating Alaric, the Greek campaign abruptly ended.

Soon after the Greek debacle – or perhaps simultaneously – the *comes Africae* Gildo is alleged to have attempted to cede the African provinces to Constantinople's jurisdiction. It may have occurred, or perhaps not. Either way the timing of Gildo's action seems suspicious. Perhaps it was a feint by Eutropius to remove Stilicho from Greece and tie him down in North Africa. If so, it worked. By now it appeared that Stilicho had passed up two opportunities to eliminate Alaric, both of which had been in Greece – first in 395 and now in 397. These missed chances have been the subject of intense scholarly debate (Cameron 1970; Matthews 1975; Heather 1991; cf. Burrell 2004). However, from a strategic viewpoint, Gildo's treason was correctly judged by Stilicho and Honorius to be the more dangerous challenge facing them at that time. Losing North Africa – which supplied the West with so much of its food security and tax revenue – would have hampered the effort against the Visigoths and other enemies, thus the western army departed Greece. Yet, despite the apparent necessity of dealing with Gildo first, the Greek campaign had been Stilicho's golden opportunity to resolve the Visigothic question. Had he done so, the western empire's destiny might have been different. As it happened, Stilicho's failure to eliminate Alaric would personally cost the *magister* dearly a decade later, and the empire itself much later. The Visigothic presence on Roman soil was to become one of the biggest sources of instability for both Arcadius and Honorius' reigns – much as it had been for their predecessors, including their father. For Honorius and Arcadius, there was little that they could have done to reverse the Visigothic tide, especially since many Visigoths supplemented the Roman army as *foederati*. There was ongoing internal argument about what course of action to take with the barbarians. The pagan orator Themistius adopted a humanitarian approach, suggesting compassion for the Visigoths instead of the customary Roman policy of subjugation through violence (Them. *Or.* 6.83). A less charitable view, from Synesius, bishop of Cyrene, warned that the state was on course for self-inflicted suicide, and that the 'foreign infection must be purged from the army before it spreads' (Syn. *De Reg.* 24–5). For the time being, though, Honorius' gravest concern in 397 was the looming African crisis. The first proper test of his reign had begun.

Roman Africa

Roman North Africa was an immense territory. It encompassed the Atlas and Rif mountain ranges, and their coastal plain, up to the Atlantic Ocean and the Gulf of Gabés, and from the Mediterranean coast to the edges of the Sahara desert (Cherry 1998). Gildo, as *comes Africae*, was directly responsible to Honorius for administering this vast area on his behalf. It is not possible to overstate what the loss of North Africa to Honorius would have meant for the western empire. To give it a modern geopolitical context, it is akin to the forced closure of the Persian Gulf oil shipping route, a scenario that could be catastrophic to much of the world.

For centuries, Rome exploited the North African agricultural heartland – and also those of Egypt – treating them as its personal granary (Laroui 1977). After destroying Carthaginian power in the Third Punic War (149–146 BC), Rome ruthlessly and systematically utilized North African resources to its own advantage. Carthage became Rome's principal hub for cereal exportation, and about twenty other smaller ports along the coast were used to transport cargo such as oil, timber, animals, and slaves (Raven 1993). Following Octavian's annexation of Egypt in 30 BC, Alexandria served as the main center for cereal exportation to Rome. The acquisition of North Africa and Egypt allowed for a massive expansion in Roman wealth, power, and population (Erdkamp 2005).

The African provinces had higher cereal productivity than other areas of the empire due to intensive polyculture. As with most other late imperial provinces, there was rigidly enforced subservience of the African rustic labor force. It has been suggested that only twice ever in late antiquity did the North African poor experience some relief from Roman servitude. The first was during Gildo's revolt; the second occurring when the Vandals ruled there between 435 and 534 (Laroui 1977; cf. Courtois 1955). This notion that Gildo's revolt supported the servile classes stems from imperial legislation and from ecclesiastical writers such as Augustine (*Contra lit. Pet.* 1.10.11). Gildo was alleged to have had close ties with the Donatist Optatus, the bishop of Thamugadi, a Roman city in what is now Algeria (Frend 1985, 208–10, 225–6; cf. Shaw 2011, 48–50). The Donatist Church, among other things, advocated for the rights of the rural African peasantry. Whatever is the truth about the idea of the Vandals being bringers of rustic freedom, though, caution ought to be applied to any interpretation of Gildo as some sort of people's champion (Cameron 1970, 105–6). Gildo was a member of the landowning class, a group comprised mainly of the western senatorial élite. He and his fellow landowners were the *domini* of huge country estates, the *villae rusticae*. On equal footing with senatorial *domini* – in terms of wealth and status – ethnicity is perhaps the only difference between Gildo and his landowning peers. This distinction probably did not carry much weight while Gildo possessed power and authority in his role as *comes Africae*. After the Gildonic War, however, Roman literary propaganda against Gildo went into overdrive to explain his treason. Such sources stressed Gildo's ethnicity, applying literary tropes that portrayed him as a stereotypical, dissolute barbarian. Racial prejudice, it should be remembered, had been a staple of Classical literature for centuries (Isaac 2004). Therefore, authors like Zosimus described Gildo as a crazed barbarian (Zos. 5.11.3), while Honorius' arch-propagandist Claudian denounced Gildo and his fellow countrymen as rabid rapists.

> When tired of each noblest [Roman] matron Gildo hands her over to the Moors. Married in Carthage city these Sidonian mothers' needs must mate with barbarians …
>
> (Cl. *Gild.* 189–91)

Africa's eternal duty

Both the African and the Egyptian *annonae* were legally defined as an eternal duty (*aeneum frumentum*) to the empire (*CTh.* 14.25.1. Dec 12, 315). Sold at subsidized prices, or distributed gratis to Rome's urban poor, provision of the *annona* was fundamental to public order. Supply shortfalls, whether the result of natural or human activity, could very likely lead to famine and certainly riot. Imperial administrations that were not adequately prepared in the event of a food shortage could face potential civil unrest. Food security was therefore of paramount concern for imperial governments. After Constantine I established Constantinople as the permanent eastern capital in the 330s, he diverted the Egyptian *annona* away from the West in order to serve the new city's needs. The western empire, for the last two centuries of its existence, came to depend solely upon the grain supplies from its African possessions. So when Gildo threatened to place North Africa under eastern authority, the West stared into the abyss. There was intense pressure on Honorius to prevent a food crisis in Rome due to Gildo's interference with the African *annona*. Though demographic estimates for late fourth-century Rome are difficult to properly ascertain, it still had a sizeable population, though nothing like that of the early or high empire (Purcell 1999; cf. Lançon 2000). Honorius and Stilicho therefore had to requisition grain from northern granaries normally reserved for the frontier troops, and from Spain (Claud. *Eutr.* I.402–9; *Stil.* I.306–9; *Stil.* III.91–8). They also had no choice but to send an army to North Africa to deal with the crisis.

On the eve of the Gildonic War, Honorius went to see his troops as they prepared to ship out. Climbing a raised platform in front of them, he delivered an impassioned speech, telling them that the fate of the western empire depended on them. Claudian included a version of the speech in the panegyric *De bello Gildonico* which he presented at court a few months later. Claudian no doubt embellished Honorius' original words, with his signature poetic flair. Yet this was standard fare for ancient military orations – for instance, Appian's reported address of Julius Caesar at the Battle of Pharsalus in central Greece (Appian, *BC.* 2.73–4), or Tacitus' charismatic general Agricola at the Battle of Mons Graupius, northern Scotland (Tac. *Agr.* 33–4). The written versions of these speeches were enhanced, of course, but they surely contained some elements of the real thing. In that case, however much Claudian might have spruced up Honorius' actual pep-talk to the troops, it is entirely feasible that the emperor personally addressed them. Whether or not he was any good at motivational speaking is another story, but a later piece of anecdotal evidence suggests that he had some skill as a communicator. A decade after the Gildonic War, Honorius found himself caught up amid a bloody army mutiny in Ticinum (modern Pavia). Alone in the city's streets, his life in danger, he managed to talk his own frenzied soldiers down from a killing spree (Zos. 5.32.3–7). In this particular instance, there was no Claudian around to extol Honorius' virtues, as he seems to have died by that time. Hence there is no grandiose account of what Honorius was supposed to have said at Ticinum. In the year 398, however, perhaps early April, by which time Gildo may have already been defeated, Claudian eagerly recited *De bello Gildonico* at Milan in front of Honorius and the court. Copies of the work reached Constantinople soon after its performance in Milan. Along with other points made in the panegyric, Honorius' pre-campaign speech conveyed a specific warning to Eutropius and any other schemers at the eastern court. The message was clear – Honorius was a resolute emperor when challenged, and therefore should not be tested again.

> My men, so soon to bring defeat upon Gildo, now is the time to fulfill your promises and make good your threats. If you felt indignation on my behalf, now take up arms and prove it. Wash out the stain of civil war by means of a great and deserved triumph ... obedience and discipline are unknown in their [the enemy's] ranks. Their arms a burden to them, their salvation lies in flight. Though each has many wives, ties of family bind them not, nor have they any love for their children whose very number causes affection to fail. Such are the troops. Their chief [Gildo] will come to battle crowned with roses, drenched with scents, his last feast still undigested; drunken with wine, ruined with age, enervated with disease and venery. Let the war trumpet rouse him from a bed of incest ... Is not death preferable to a life disgraced? If, in addition to the loss of Illyria, Africa is to be surrendered to Moorish kings, what lands still remain to us ... go, win back that southern realm a rebel has torn from me. It depends on your arms whether Rome, the unconquerable mistress of the world, stands or falls ... fight but one battle in defense of Libya. Let empire restored attend on your oars and sails. Give back to Africa the laws of Rome she now disregards. Let history repeat itself, and the sword smite from its trunk the head of this third tyrant and so end at last the series of bloody usurpers.
>
> (Cl. *Gild*. 427–66)

There are echoes of earlier military orations here, but it seems Claudian was inspired by an event from forty years earlier, as related by the soldier historian Ammianus Marcellinus. This was the battle speech of the Caesar Julian to his troops outside Argentoratum (Strasbourg) in 357, as they faced the barbarian Alamanni, against whom the Romans won the day. Claudian, while observing speech-writing convention, was able to frame Honorius within the heroic narrative of a Roman victory still fresh in recent memory.

> Behold, fellow-soldiers, the long-hoped-for day is now here, forcing us all to wash away the old-time stains and restore its due honor to the majesty of Rome. These are the savages whom madness and excessive folly have driven on to the ruin of their fortunes, doomed as they are to be overwhelmed by our might.
>
> (Amm. Marc. *Hist*. 16.12.31)

Gildo, servant to which Rome?

Up until his break with the West, Gildo had held a unique position in Honorius' administration. He was the supreme commander for North Africa (*comes et magister utriusque militiae per Africam*) (*CTh*. 9.7.9. Dec 30, 383). Theodosius I gave him this rank as reward for helping to suppress an insurrection led by Firmus, Gildo's own brother, *c*. 372–5 (Matthews 1989; cf. Oost 1962). During that conflict, another two of Gildo's brothers, Mazuca and Mascezel, and a sister, Cyria, aided Firmus militarily and financially. Gildo had been steadfast in his loyalty to the empire, however, fighting against his rebel siblings (Amm. Marc. *Hist*. 29.5.1–55). Firmus and Mazuca were killed, but Mascezel somehow survived, only to resurface twenty years later as Stilicho's choice of commander for the campaign against Gildo. Nothing is known of Cyria's fate, other than that she was an affluent *domina* of a large, fortified *villa rustica* (Amm. Marc. *Hist*. 29.5.28).

Gildo's family were of the Iubaleni tribe. The family was clearly very wealthy and extremely influential. Indeed, Gildo's personal fortune was so great that Honorius later had to establish a special administrative department (*Comes Gildoniaci patrimonii*) to incorporate his estate's confiscated wealth into the imperial treasury (*Not. dig.* [*occ*]. 12.2). The origins of Gildo's familial power derived from a network of tribal loyalties it maintained in late antique North Africa, and from convivial dealings with Rome. His father, Nubel, was chiefly responsible for consolidating the family's power, having cultivated a mutually beneficial relationship with the emperor Valentinian I in the 360s. In the late empire, élite Romano-African families like Gildo's protected the southern frontier (*fossatum Africae*). Their central role was to preserve internal order and to maintain the annonarian system. In exchange, Rome gave them wealth, titles, and status (Blackhurst 2004, 61ff.).

To guarantee élite Romano-African fidelity, the Roman state applied an extra element – hostage provision. Élite North African children were sent to Rome as a pledge of their parents' obedience to the emperor. This was a well-established policy that extended throughout all Rome's peripheral provinces. For instance, after 376, some of the Visigothic nobility surrendered their children to Rome (Heather 1991, 99). Some hostage children were prepared for future roles within the empire – boys to become civil administrators or military officers, girls to be married into high-status Roman families. Around 392, Theodosius I arranged a marriage between Salvina, Gildo's daughter, and Nebridius, a first cousin and childhood friend of Honorius and Arcadius. This union produced two children, a girl and a boy, but Nebridius died young, leaving her a widow. She later sought solace in religion, becoming part of Bishop John Chrysostom's circle. Though Salvina likely led a privileged lifestyle at Constantinople, this does not mean that her time there was happy. She was far from her family and her homeland. Indeed, Jerome described her as a hostage at the eastern court (Pall. *Dial*. 10; Jer. *Ep*. 79.2; 4.6). It is possible that Eutropius and his cabal used Salvina as leverage to coerce Gildo into switching allegiance from the West.

Preparations for war

Honorius' war plans were underway by early June 397, as indicated by a legal constitution which urgently sought new conscripts. Stilicho, a seasoned military tactician, was likely behind this move. It made sense, at this time at least, for Honorius to concede to Stilicho's experience. As part of the recruitment drive, Honorius made it clear that not even his own estates were immune from contributing to the war effort, thereby setting an example for members of the landowning élite to follow.

> The public welfare recommends that We conscript recruits into the army. For this reason We permit not even Our patrimony [estates] to be exempt from the present payment. Through all the provinces, therefore, through which Our property extends, it is Our will that recruits be furnished from the sacred imperial patrimony with the proper expedition.
>
> (*CTh.* 7.13.12. June 17, 397)

Honorius' personal gesture in this law was intended as a selfless example and to arouse patriotism, but not everyone was enthused. Other imperial decrees put obligations on senators to provide recruits from their own estates. Most senators were landowners, many with large North African investments. Some were reluctant to provide able-bodied men to the military levy from their lands. Those men could be working for them on their properties, rather than for the state, the senators reasoned. Either they did not think that Gildo posed a serious enough threat to necessitate their personal contribution in human collateral, or they saw obstruction of the military levy as a means to damage Stilicho's authority and bond with Honorius. Whatever their motivations, in September 397 Honorius was compelled to offer the senate a choice – give men or money (*CTh.* 7.13.13. Sept 24, 397). Thus, the immensely wealthy senatorial class were allowed to buy their way out of their duty. They did this for 25 gold solidi, plus expenses, in lieu of each recruit they otherwise were supposed to have given. If the landowning class took this as a victory, then it was an extremely short-sighted posture on their part, made at the expense of imperial security. Yet, this was neither the first nor would it be the last time that the rich put their interests above those of the state. Honorius' concession to the élites underscores the limited power of the late imperial office.

As autumn 397 wore on, Gildo's rebellion prevented grain supplies from leaving North Africa, raising the specter of famine in the West – a form of invisible invasion of the city of Rome itself. It is worth noting that the use of famine as a weapon of war was a feature of Roman military policy. It was even advocated by a late fourth-century military manual, *On Military Affairs* (Veg. 3.4–6). Rome was not used to being on the receiving end of starvation warfare. Small wonder, then, for the double standards that feature in the literary sources for the Gildonic War. They present Roman civilization under an existential attack from primitive barbarism, whereas barbaric use of famine was part of the Roman art of warfare.

Honorius and Stilicho countered Gildo's threat of starvation warfare by appropriating alternative food supplies, an initiative welcomed by the Milanese court élite and which gained extra support for the African campaign (Cl. *Stil.* I.306–17). Capitalizing on the good-will resulting from his obtaining of food reserves, Stilicho made one more calculated move, which had more to do with his own self-preservation. He invoked the ancient custom – long unused but still valid – of seeking senatorial consensus for the decision to go to war. Stilicho's stratagem worked, and the senate voted for an 'avenging expedition' against Gildo (Cl. *Stil.* I.325–32). With senatorial support and a proxy commander, it would be difficult for Stilicho's numerous enemies to paint the African campaign as purely his war – in the event things went sour on the ground.

Sailing for Carthage

A successful offensive against Gildo was therefore crucial for Honorius' prestige and to Stilicho's continued survival. The campaign had to be quick and decisive. The last Roman commander to fight a North African insurrection was Honorius' grandfather Theodosius the Elder against Firmus in the early 370s. This hard-fought contest had lasted almost three years, and while Theodosius triumphed, he ended up being executed for alleged treason. With this in mind, Stilicho was wise to send Mascezel as his proxy. Claudian made use of the Theodosian family's previous involvement in North Africa. Apparently, the emperor had had a dream in which his dead grandfather's spirit appeared to him, urging him to lead the war against Gildo and uphold his family's honor. Stilicho did not want the emperor to go with the African expeditionary force, and Honorius remonstrated with him to be allowed to.

> Emulous courage roused the emperor ... he burns to set sail ... to assail with the spear the distant Moors. So he summons his father-in-law [Stilicho] and clasping his hand asks what course of action he advises: Full often, reverend sire, is the future revealed to me in dreams; many a night brings prophecy ... my grandfather eagerly urges me to rival his triumphs with my own. Why, he asked, did I delay and hesitate so long? Already my ships should have been manned and the sea's threatened opposition overcome. I myself am ready to cross in the first vessel. Let every foreign nation that is bound beneath my rule come to our aid ... shall I sit here and submit to such disgrace? Shall I relinquish, now that I am a youth, what I ruled and governed as a boy? Twice my father hurried to the Alps to defend another's realm. Am I to be an easy prey, an object of scorn?
>
> (Cl. *Gild.* 349–78)

Claudian, perhaps trying to preserve Honorius' dignity, asserted that Stilicho convinced the emperor there was no need for him to go; that Honorius' very name would suffice to terrorize Gildo into surrender. Stilicho further advised the emperor not to debase himself, or the imperial office, through engaging in combat with a mere Moor. Let the two savages fight it out was Stilicho's advice, who stressed the importance of permitting Mascezel to exact vengeance on his brother (Cl. *Gild.* 379–414). Send a 'Gildo to fight a Gildo,' is how Shaw puts it (2011, 48). Thus deterred, Honorius reluctantly settled for a speech to the troops. As with the pre-campaign speech, the words which Claudian attributed to Honorius are exaggerated. That said, the teenage emperor probably wanted to be part of what he perceived to be an exciting adventure. Considering his illustrious military family background, Honorius likely wished to prove his valor. Nevertheless, Stilicho could not have allowed Honorius to come to any harm. The boy was too valuable an asset to Stilicho's interests. Furthermore, a good deal of the military and civilian establishment were loyal to the Theodosian house, of which Stilicho was not a blood member. Honorius' self-appointed guardian would not place his young charge in a combat environment. That would have been reckless endangerment, with unpredictable consequences for all involved.

On the other hand, the mid-sixth-century Byzantine writer John the Lydian wrote that Theodosius legally prohibited his sons, and therefore all future emperors, from personally going to war. Apparently only generals should be responsible for commanding armies, and the emperors should stay at home. John suggested that this legal restriction came about as a result of Theodosius' lack of faith in his sons' abilities (Lydus, *De Mag.* 2.11.3–4; 3.41.3). This hardly seems true, even more so when one considers that Honorius was only ten when his father died, Arcadius about seventeen or eighteen. While Theodosius might have had worries about Arcadius' military talents, particularly due to his predilection for petty squabbles, that the emperor could have imagined how Honorius might turn out to be as a man is ridiculous. However, Theodosius really did try to protect them in such a manner: we have seen how he cosseted his boys through a secluded childhood. Did he have a realization that he might have spoiled them? Theodosius himself fought many wars and battles; he knew only too well the strains and dangers of campaigning; he had come close to being killed himself on more than one occasion. Is it possible that he was that over-protective? It does of course happen that former soldiers who have experienced combat never want anything so horrific for their children. Are we then to see some sort of novel reform by Theodosius of imperial rule of which no trace has survived in legal codices, or any other source? John the Lydian's claim is doubtful, but needs some explanation. Perhaps the clue lies in his own time of writing, the 550s, a period when Justinian I's reconquest of the former Roman West had ground to a shuddering halt (Maas 1992). The Byzantine world was racked with bubonic plague, famine, and war. The central Roman military figure of the period was not the emperor, but his top general, Belisarius. John's brief note could well be an attempt to justify his emperor's lack of military leadership at that point. John the Lydian's claim is intriguing, but one which unfortunately cannot be verified. At any rate, there were a myriad of other reasons why, for several hundred years after Theodosius I, so few emperors took the field of battle (Lee 2007, 30ff.).

A short spring war

Mascezel arrived in North Africa with the army in late 397. After leaving Italy, the expedition spent a while on Sicily and Sardinia stocking up on supplies and resting. None of our sources give a precise date for what happened between his landing in Africa and the subsequent pitched battle that occurred between him and his brother. Troop numbers for both sides are likewise uncertain. All we can say for sure is that Gildo's forces heavily outnumbered Mascezel's, and that a battle occurred at some time between January and May 398 in which Mascezel routed Gildo's troops. How this victory was achieved is debateable. Claudian's account, the principal source for the Gildonic War, seethes with customary racist and imperialist bias. The poet says that Gildo's forces were predominantly African tribal warriors whose natural cowardice was no match for Roman discipline (Cl. *Eutr.* II. *Praef.* 69–70; *Stil.* I.354–7). Orosius, true to fashion, brought God into his relaying of the story, giving a sanitized narrative of a bloodless victory, ascribing Mascezel's win to divine intercession from the Christian god (Oros. 7.36.12). Gildo's army was broken and he is supposed to have fled the battlefield in craven terror. Any other source that mentions Gildo's spinelessness simply follows Claudian's lead, nothing more (Oros. 7.36.11; *Chron. Marcell.* s.a. 398). What happened to Gildo after the battle is even less straightforward. Zosimus is alone in saying that Gildo committed suicide immediately after the defeat (Zos. 5.11.4). This cannot be right, since several sources place Gildo's death later than the battle, the most precise date being July 31, 398 (*Cons. Ital.* s.a. 298). While contemporary scholarship differs on the date of Gildo's defeat, hardly any mention the date of his death (Cameron 1970, xv; Barnes 1978; cf. Shaw 2011, 48). A problem exists, therefore, in establishing Gildo's whereabouts between the time of his defeat and death. There is a time lapse of at least two months before his eventual capture and death later in the summer of 397. Why is this important? Because it reveals something about the extent of provincial tribal loyalty to the imperial core. Without friends, Gildo could not have escaped Rome's reach for too long. He still had some influence, but eventually his presence in North Africa would become untenable.

Death in Thabraca

Gildo found sanctuary after his defeat, at least for a time, in all likelihood drawing upon old tribal connections, perhaps in outlying mountainous regions. It would have been difficult to move across such terrain, especially as a fugitive. For anyone who has ever visited this region, even with the aid of modern transportation, the Atlas and Rif mountain ranges are a challenge to traverse. It is an immensely beautiful, remote landscape with narrow corkscrew roads and jagged, snow-capped peaks – perfect for guerrilla war-fare and a very good place to evade detection, for a while at least. Gildo's luck eventually ran out, however. Harboring such a sought-after fugitive as Gildo was dangerous and, with an imperial bounty on his head, Gildo's few remaining friends dwindled. He must have been constantly on the move in order to evade capture, so he chose to leave his homeland where he would inevitably have faced a terrible death.

In late July, a ship carrying the fugitive *comes* ran aground near Thabraca, a small fishing town on the Tunisian coast (Cl. *Eutr*. I.410). No destination for this ship is offered by any primary source. Constantinople was the most likely port of call. It was where his daughter Salvina and his grandchildren were, and if the accusations of collusion with Eutropius were true, he might have hoped for asylum from the imperial chamberlain. Constantinople offered the best odds for survival. It was not to be, and Gildo was destined to die as badly as he feared. Strong winds blew his ship back onto the coast. He was captured, dragged, mocked, and beaten by a mob through the streets of Thabraca. A hastily arraigned court convicted him of treason and he was summarily executed (Cl. *Stil*. I.361–2). A much later account, from the sixth-century Gothic historian Jordanes, says that he strangled himself before the sentence could be carried out (*Rom*. 320). Jordanes was perhaps too kind in his appraisal of the incident.

If, as Claudian alleged, Gildo had really conspired with Eutropius to hand the North African provinces over to Constantinople, the fact is that no eastern assistance materialized in Gildo's hour of need. It has been supposed by Alan Cameron that because Honorius and Stilicho's military reaction was so rapid, Eutropius had no time to help Gildo (1970, 95). A more realistic scenario was that Eutropius always considered Gildo expendable in his power games against Stilicho and the western court. It is particularly frustrating trying to ascertain the truth of the Gildonic crisis, since most of the literary evidence is informed by the western government's mouthpiece, Claudian.

Retribution and propaganda

The victory over Gildo held fantastic propaganda value for Honorius – and likewise for Stilicho. The emperor was presented as the West's savior and as the restorer of the African *annona*. This message was relayed to the Roman public through coinage (Figure 5.1) and inscriptions.

The following text comes from an inscription which once formed part of Honorius' triumphal arch. It was erected in Rome in the early 400s and was one of two of the last triumphal arches of antiquity constructed in the city. The arch has long since disappeared, but Claudian makes brief reference to it (Cl. *VI Cons*. 370–3). Only fragments of the physical structure remain, from which a reconstruction of the original text is possible (Kalas 2015, 90–6). Arcadius' name is included, as it always is on coinage, laws, and other inscriptions of the two brother emperors. As previously mentioned, it was customary to

Figure 5.1 Silver miliarense of Honorius. Constantinople mint, *c.* 398–403.

Obv. Honorius pearl-diademed, draped, and cuirassed. Legend: DN-HONORI-VS-PF-AVG (*Dominus Noster Honorius Pius Felix Augustus*/Our Lord Honorius, pious and fortunate Augustus). Rev. Honorius nimbate, in armor, wearing cloak, standing, gesturing with raised right hand, globe in his left, a star in right field. Legend: GLORIA-ROMANORVM (Glory of the Romans). Exergue: CON (*Constantinopolis*).

Source: *RSC* 19a.

include all concurrent, legitimate emperors on inscriptions, coins, laws, and other official state documents, even if there were divisions behind the scenes. Imperial unity was promoted thus. It is curious that Stilicho's name is not included. Perhaps this would not have been well received by Arcadius and his government.

> To the unconquered and most fortunate emperors, Our Lords, the brothers Arcadius and Honorius, delivering the senate and people of Rome from rebellion and happily reinstating Africa; powerful Honorius defended Libya.
>
> (*CIL* 6.1187)

Honorius held an imperial triumph at Rome in 404 to celebrate, amongst other achievements, Gildo's defeat. Obviously Stilicho was ultimately responsible for much of the logistics and planning for the Gildonic War. He too was afforded accolades via similar propagandist media to that used for the emperor, except state coinage. No coins were ever struck in Stilicho's name or image. Only emperors, their heirs, and certain empresses could be represented on official coinage. Stilicho wisely never attempted such a thing; it was better to rule from behind the throne.

Very soon after Gildo's death, Mascezel died in Italy in murky circumstances. This was rather convenient for Stilicho, who assumed even greater credit for the victory, even though he was not involved in the fighting. Claudian was silent about Mascezel's death. Either he was unaware, or he avoided the subject because it involved his patron Stilicho in a distasteful act. Orosius justified Mascezel's killing on the grounds that Mascezel had committed sacrilege. Zosimus clearly suspected Stilicho of murder, especially since the North African died on his way to Milan to speak with Honorius about a pressing concern (Oros. 7.36.13; Zos. 5.11). If Stilicho was involved in Mascezel's death, then the real reason was likely to have been nuanced.

Punishment and propaganda

From the moment the western imperial army arrived in North Africa Gildo was finished. Beaten on the battlefield, he sought sanctuary, but soon realized that he had little chance of surviving if he stayed in the African provinces. If he had had Donatist support – from Optatus or others – they could not have helped him. Optatus died in prison along with countless others during Honorius' subsequent purges of Gildo's supporters (Aug. *Contra lit. Pet.* 2.92. 209; Shaw 2011, 58ff.). Once Honorius regained control of the African provinces and reincorporated them into the Italian prefecture, he viciously pursued anyone even remotely linked to the former *comes Africae*. A case in point is Marcharidus, one of Gildo's officials, who was subjected to a rigorous legal examination (*quaestio*), an ordeal involving torture. The use of torture was perfectly legal, an aspect of the Roman judicial system that perhaps seems inconceivable to the modern eye. It seems to have been generally accepted, almost stoically so, for, as Jill Harries has observed, 'even that most subtle of thinkers, Augustine of Hippo, was not averse to the infliction of pain, if good could come of it' (1999, 132). Why does that sound familiar? Torture, along with capital punishment, was widely applied for a plethora of misdemeanors such as adultery, homicide, heresy, and pagan worship (MacMullen 1990, 204–17). The unfortunate Marcharidus was tortured in an effort to extract information about hidden wealth, though how successful this line of questioning was in obtaining its aim is unclear.

> [Arcadius and Honorius] to Bathanarius, Count of Africa. When Marcharidus was proscribed, he left much of his property in the possession of different persons, as was revealed by the trial which was held. Therefore, if any person who retains something from said property should return it of his own free will within two months and if he should faithfully deliver at once what he received, he shall know that will obtain pardon. Otherwise, he shall know that his patrimony will be annexed to the fisc and that he will undergo the penalty of deportation.
>
> (*CTh.* 9.42.18. July 13, 401)

No local tribal magnate ever occupied a senior imperial post in North Africa again, as they had done previously. Gildo's downfall and the ensuing violent investigations created a political and administrative vacuum which was filled by men from outside the African provinces – men of proven loyalty or familial connection to Honorius and Stilicho, such as Bathanarius, *comes Africae* after Gildo, who was actually Stilicho's brother-in-law. Honorius' extensive purge of Gildonian elements was a blatant signal that regional insubordination or external meddling in African affairs would not be tolerated. Inevitably, this policy did not succeed; there would be more trouble in North Africa.

Orosius declared that Gildo was a 'licentious heathen' (Oros. 7.36.3). This was a serious allegation. Ever since Theodosius I's oppressive measures against non-adherents to Catholic orthodoxy, it became common literary practice to charge *hostes publici* with the additional charges of heresy or paganism – capital crimes all. Honorius and Arcadius continued their father's religious policies, as did their successors. Orosius' assertion that Gildo was a pagan does not bear fruit. Thirteen years after Gildo's death, at the Council of Carthage in 411, an episcopal delegate's chance remark suggested that Gildo's remains were interred in a Catholic church in the nearby town of Lamzelli (Frend 1985, 225; *Gesta Coll. Carth.* i.206.1343–4). Is it likely that a pagan was buried in a Catholic church? Probably not. Like Claudian, Orosius also had an agenda. By highlighting Gildo's supposed religious differences, Orosius could hold Honorius up as a shining light of Christian piety against the darkness of pagan treason. Gildo's alleged association with heretical Christians gave Honorius further cause to persecute the African Donatist Church. The real winner in this entire affair, however, was the Roman Catholic Church, as another of its rivals was eliminated by the secular authorities.

Our primary sources diverge on practically every part of the Gildonic War. Which ones are accurate? Did Gildo really revolt or was he set up to fall? Did he run from the battlefield – the quintessential cowardly barbarian? Was he executed or did he take his own life? These are questions for which there are no definitive answers. Even in the modern age, with the technological means to view events in real time, there are often multiple versions of a story in circulation. For example, consider the Libyan leader Muhammad al-Gaddafi's final moments in October 2011 – broadcast globally, practically as it occurred. With so many visual sources available, Gaddafi's dreadful fate should be apparent – no questions at all. Yet, the exact details of his death vary significantly, depending on the particular media source. How much more difficult, then, is it to discern the truth of Gildo's fate, some sixteen centuries ago. There were probably a number of reasons why Gildo was toppled – overt and covert. Officially, he was an upstart African, another Hannibal Barca, a *hostis publicus* who threatened the Roman West's food security and way of life. Worse, he was a *tyrannus*, because he had struck at the very center of imperial power, or so Claudian alleged. In the late empire the term *tyrannus* had several interpretations – an individual who had been illegally made an emperor; a once legitimate but now deposed emperor; or, simply, the loser in a civil war. Presenting Gildo as an imperial claimant was far-fetched. He did not appropriate imperial titles, nor did he strike his own coinage, but the idea that he was a *tyrannus* certainly fueled negative public sentiment towards him. Along with the charges of religious dissent and sexual perversion, it is easy to see how the Gildonic War formed the defining narrative for the early part of Honorius' reign.

References

Barnes, Timothy David. 1978. "An Anachronism in Claudian". *Historia* 27: 498–9.

Blackhurst, Andy. 2004. "The House of Nubel: Rebels or Players?" In *Vandals, Romans and Berbers: New Perspectives on Late Antique North Africa*. Edited by Andrey H. Merrills: 59–75. Aldershot: Ashgate.

Blockley, Roger C. 1998. "The Dynasty of Theodosius." *CAH* 13: 111–37. Cambridge: Cambridge University Press.

Burrell, Emma. 2004. "A Re-Examination of Why Stilicho Abandoned His Pursuit of Alaric in 397." *Historia* 53: 251–6.

Cameron, Alan. 1970. *Claudian: Poetry and Propaganda at the Court of Honorius*. Oxford: Clarendon Press.

Cherry, David. 1998. *Frontier and Society in Roman North Africa*. Oxford: Oxford University Press.

Conant, Jonathan. 2012. *Staying Roman: Conquest and Identity in Africa and the Mediterranean, 439–700*. Cambridge Studies in Medieval Life and Thought: Fourth Series 82. Cambridge and New York: Cambridge University Press.

Courtois, Christian. 1955. *Les Vandales et l'Afrique*. Paris: Publications du Gouvernement Général de l'Algérie.

Dewar, Michael. 1994. "Hannibal and Alaric in the Later Poems of Claudian." *Mnemosyne* 47: 349–72.

Di Vita, Antonio. 1999. "Sabratha." In *Libya: The Lost Cities of the Roman Empire*. Edited by Antonio Di Vita, Ginette Divita-Evrard, and Lidiano Bacchielli. Cologne: Konemann.

Erdkamp, Paul. 2005. *The Grain Market in the Roman Empire: A Social, Political, and Economic Study*. Cambridge: Cambridge University Press.

Frend, William H. C. 1985. *The Donatist Church: A Movement of Protest in Roman North Africa*. Oxford: Oxford University Press.

Harries, Jill. 1999. *Law and Empire in Late Antiquity*. Cambridge: Cambridge University Press.

Heather, Peter. 1991. *Goths and Romans, 332–489*. Oxford Historical Monographs. Oxford: Clarendon Press.

Honoré, Tony. 1998. *Law in the Crisis of Empire, AD 379–455*. Oxford: Oxford University Press.

Isaac, Benjamin. 2004. *The Invention of Racism in Classical Antiquity*. Princeton, NJ: Princeton University Press.

Jones, Geraint D. B., and Mattingly, David J. 1980. "Fourth-Century Manning of the *Fossatum Africae*." *Britannia* 11: 323–6.

Kalas, Gregor. 2015. *The Restoration of the Roman Forum in Late Antiquity: Transforming Public Space*. Austin, TX: University of Texas Press.

Kulikowski, Michael. 2004. *Late Roman Spain and its Cities*. Baltimore, MD: Johns Hopkins Press.

Lançon, Bertrand. 2000. *Rome in Late Antiquity: Everyday Life and Urban Change, 312–609*. Edinburgh: Edinburgh University Press.

Laroui, Abdallah. 1977. *The History of the Maghrib: An Interpretative Essay.* Translated by Ralph Manheim. Princeton, NJ: Princeton University Press.

Lee, A. D. 2007. *War in Late Antiquity: A Social History.* Malden, MA: Blackwell.

Maas, Michael. 1992. *John Lydus and the Roman Past. Antiquarianism and Politics in the Age of Justinian.* London and New York: Routledge.

MacMullen, Ramsay. 1980. "Roman Élite Motivation: Three Questions." *Past and Present* 88: 3–16.

MacMullen, Ramsay. 1990. (1986). "Judicial Savagery in the Roman Empire." In *Changes in the Roman Empire: Essays in the Ordinary*: 204–17. Princeton, NJ: Princeton University Press.

Matthews, John F. 1975. *Western Aristocracies and Imperial Court, AD 364–425.* Oxford: Clarendon Press.

Matthews, John F. 1989. *The Roman Empire of Ammianus Marcellinus.* Baltimore, MD: The Johns Hopkins University Press.

Modéran, Yves. 1989. "Gildon, les Maures et l'Afrique." *MEFRA* 101: 821–72.

Oost, Stewart Irvin. 1962. "Count Gildo and Theodosius the Great." *CP* 57: 27–30.

Purcell, Nicholas. 1999. "The Populace of Rome in Late Antiquity: Problems of Classification and Historical Description." In *The Transformation of Vrbs Roma in Late Antiquity*. Edited by W. V. Harris: 135–61. *JRA* Supplement 33. Portsmouth, RI: Journal of Roman Archaeology.

Raven, Susan. 1993. *Rome in Africa.* 3rd edition. London: Routledge.

Robertson Brown, Amelia. 2011. "Banditry or Catastrophe? History, Archaeology, and Barbarian Raids on Roman Greece." In *Romans, Barbarians, and the Transformation of the Roman World: Cultural Interaction and the Creation of Identity in Late Antiquity*. Edited by Ralph Mathisen and Danuta Shanzer: 79–96. Farnham: Ashgate.

Shaw, Brent D. 1986. "Autonomy and Tribute: Mountain and Plain in Mauretania Tingitana." In *Désert et montagne au Maghrib: hommage à Jean Dresch*. Edited by P. R. Baduel: 66–89. *Revue de l'Occident Musulman et de la Méditerranée* 41–2.

Shaw, Brent D. 2011. *Sacred Violence: African Christians and Sectarian Hatred in the Age of Augustine.* Cambridge: Cambridge University Press.

Turcan, Robert. 1961. "Trésors monétaires trouvés à Tipasa: la circulation du bronze en Afrique romaine et vandale aux Vᵉ et VIᵉ siècles ap. J.-C." *Libyca* 51: 201–57.

Ware, Catherine. 2004. "Gildo *tyrannus*: Accusations and Allusion in the Speeches of Roma and Africa." In *Aetas Claudianea*. Edited by Widu-Wolfgang Ehlers, Fritz Felgentreu, and Stephen Wheeler: 96–103. Leipzig: De Gruyter.

Woolf, Greg. 1997. "Beyond Romans and Natives." *World Archaeology* 28: 339–50.

6 Restoration and manipulation

> We have joined Europe again to Africa, and unswerving singleness of purpose unites the brother emperors
>
> Claudian, *Gildonic War*, 4–5

The first marriage of Honorius

At the start of 398, perhaps February, Honorius married Maria, his first cousin once removed, and eldest daughter of Stilicho and Serena. Maria was only twelve or possibly thirteen years of age, Honorius just slightly older. This looks appalling to the modern mind, but it was typical for adolescent girls and boys to marry at this age in antiquity, though the law did at least prohibit marriage under the age of twelve. The prevalence of adolescent marriage in the ancient world was primarily due to low life expectancy, particularly for females, for whom pregnancy and childbirth held a large degree of risk (Bradley 2005; Rawson 2003).

Claudian describes Honorius and Maria's courting and wedding celebration in two elaborate poems: the *Epithalamium*, a tediously long, hexametric poem, and the *Fescennine Verses*, in four short parts (Nathan 2000, 77–83; Wasdin 2014). Traditionally, *epithalamia* and *fescennina* were sung or recited as the marital couple progressed to their bedchamber on their wedding night, and continued outside until completed. The sexual nature of these poems meant that they were not performed during Christian wedding ceremonies, as they would have been considered inappropriate.

> Blessed is she [Maria] who will soon call you husband and unite herself to you with the bonds of first love … Maiden shame now overcomes the anxious bride; her veil now shows traces of innocent tears. Hesitate not to be close in your attacks, young lover, even though she opposes you savagely with cruel finger-nail. None can enjoy the scents of spring nor steal the honey of Hyla from its fastnesses if he fears that thorns may scratch his face. Thorns arm the rose and bees find a defense for their honey. The refusals of coyness do but increase the joy; the desire for that which

flies us is the more inflamed; sweeter is the kiss snatched through tears … Breathe a new loyalty into your breasts and let your sense kindle a flame that shall never be extinguished. May your clasped hands form a bond closer than that between ivy and leafy oak tree or poplar and pliant vine. Be the frequent kisses that you give and receive breathed more softly than those of plaintive doves, and when lips have united soul to soul let sleep still your throbbing breath. Be the purple couch warm with your princely wooing, and a new stain ennoble coverlets ruddy with Tyrian dye. Then leap victorious from the marriage bed, scarred with the night's encounter. All night long let the music of the flute resound and the crowd, set free from law's harsh restraints, with larger license indulge the permitted jest. Soldiers, make merry with your leaders, girls with boys. Be this the cry that re-echoes from pole to pole, among the peoples, over the seas: "Fair Honorius weds with Maria!"

(Cl. *Fesc.* 1.40–1)

As though Honorius needed reminding, Claudian stressed the role of his new wife's parents, Stilicho and Serena, who had, after all, arranged the whole affair. The union of their daughter and Honorius was a calculated maneuver designed to tighten Stilicho's power over the emperor. Intended for Honorius and Maria's ears, then, Claudian's *fescennina* emphasized Stilicho's special relationship to the Theodosian house, and his role as father to Honorius.

Twine with a soft garland, Stilicho, the locks whereon a helmet is wont to shine. Let the trumpets of war cease and the propitious torch of marriage banish savage Mars afar. Let regal blood unite once more with regal blood. Perform a father's office and unite these children with your illustrious hand. You who married an emperor's daughter, now, in turn, your daughter shall marry an emperor. What room is here for the madness of jealousy? What excuse for envy? Stilicho is father both of bride and bridegroom.

(Cl. *Fesc.* 3.1–12)

That Honorius and Maria were cousins does not appear to have been an issue to prevent their marriage. Claudian certainly does not draw attention to the fact. In the pre-Christian Roman world, inter-cousin marriage, though apparently not very common in the main population, did occur among the élites, though it was discouraged (Shaw and Saller 1984, 432–44; Evans Grubbs 2002, 165). With the advent of Christianity, however, marriages between first cousins and other family members became illegal and could incur severe penalties. Theodosius I prohibited marriage between first cousins in about 384, and indeed one of Honorius' earliest laws expressly forbade the practice (Amb. *Ep.* 58; *Epit. de Caes.* 48.10; *CTh.* 3.12.3. Dec 7, 396). How, then, was Honorius and Maria's marriage exempt from the law on close-cousin marriage? Perhaps the fact that they were first cousins once removed? If so, this loophole must have been used again, because after Maria's death, Honorius subsequently married her younger sister Thermantia in 407/8. The law therefore appears to have been biased, at least in favor of the imperial household. Exactly how widely observed imperial laws of this nature were is a matter of debate. Furthermore, it has been suggested that inter-cousin marriage was less of a taboo in the Roman East than it was in the West (Evans Grubbs 2002, 161–6). Seven years after his brother's marriage to Maria, Arcadius partially repealed their father's law against marriage in relation to maternal first cousins (*consobrinos*) (*Cod. Iust.* 5.4.19. June 11, 405).

Even Augustine of Hippo weighed in on the matter of inter-cousin marriage, saying that even pagans frowned upon the practice. The question to consider here, then, is, if Honorius was really the strict and observant Catholic that our ecclesiastic sources say he was, how did marrying his own family members sit with his values? What's more, even Serena seems to have been averse to the idea. Did the benefit of marrying her daughter to Honorius outweigh the morality, not to mention the legality, of the act? This is what Augustine thought about the issue:

> For custom has very great power either to attract or to shock human feeling … the man who neglects and disobeys it is justly branded as abominable … with regard to marriage in the next degree of consanguinity, marriage between cousins, we have observed that in our own time the customary morality has prevented this from being frequent, though the law allows it. It was not prohibited by divine law, nor as yet had human law prohibited it; nevertheless, though legitimate, people shrank from it, because it lay so close to what was illegitimate, and in marrying a cousin seemed almost to marry a sister – for cousins are so closely related that they are called brothers and sisters, and are almost really so … But who doubts that the modern prohibition of the marriage even of cousins is the more seemly regulation – not merely on account of the reason we have been urging, the multiplying of relationships, so that one person might not absorb two, which might be distributed to two persons, and so increase the number of people bound together as a family, but also because there is in human nature I know not what natural and praiseworthy shamefacedness which restrains us from desiring that connection which, though for propagation, is yet lustful and which even conjugal modesty blushes over, with anyone to whom consanguinity bids us render respect?
>
> (Aug. *De civ. Dei.* 15.16)

Naturally, Claudian passes no overt comment on the young couple's blood ties, but he does pass a cryptic comment, 'though no ties of blood united you to the royal house, though you were in no way related thereto [Honorius]' (Cl. *Nupt.* 10.261–2). This line was perhaps inserted to allay any moral concerns that either Maria or Honorius might have had about the fact that they were cousins. Would they really have not known this was the case? And was it an issue in their marriage? Maybe this played a role in their not having children. To give extra legitimacy to the marriage, Claudian claimed that Theodosius I had organized it years beforehand. Ultimately, though, as the poet tells us, it was really Honorius who instigated the whole thing, after he fell madly in love with Maria just from seeing her painted portrait. This can hardly be true. Honorius and Maria already knew each other; they had grown up side by side in the palace at Constantinople. Claudian labors the romance between them a little too much, with the effect that it feels artificial.

> Unfelt before was the fire the emperor Honorius had conceived for his promised bride, and he burned, all unexperienced, with passion's first fever, nor knew whence came the heat, what meant the sighs – a tyro and as yet ignorant of love. Hunting, horses, javelins – for none of these he now cares nor yet to fling the spear; how often a blush, mantling to his cheeks, betrayed his secret; how often, unbidden of himself, his hand would write the loved one's name.
>
> (Cl. *Nupt*. 10.1–10)

Claudian, perhaps unwittingly, suggested that Maria had no idea that she was to be married to her cousin, or anyone else for that matter, until the wedding hour was at hand. How surprised she must have been! The poet tells us that Maria was in the process of being schooled in the Classics by her mother, Serena, when the goddess Venus – no less – arrived at their door to intercede on Honorius' behalf to convince Maria to marry him. And, just as he did for Stilicho, Claudian emphasized Serena's position in Honorius' life.

> Unannounced [Venus] sought the bride's home. But Maria, with no thoughts of wedlock nor knowing that the torches [for the marital procession] were being got ready, was listening with rapt attention to the discourse of her saintly mother [Serena], drinking in that mother's nature and learning to follow the example of old-world chastity; nor does she cease under that mother's guidance to unroll the writers of Rome and Greece, all that old Homer sang, or Thracian Orpheus, or that Sappho set to music with Lesbian quill ... Venus stood and addressed Maria with these gentle words: "All hail! revered daughter of divine Serena, heir of great kings and destined to be the mother of kings. For your sake have I left my home in Paphos' isle and Cyprus; for your sake was I pleased to face so many labors and cross so many seas lest you should continue to live a private life little befitting your true worth, and lest young Honorius should still feed in his heart the flame of unrequited love. Take the rank your birth demands, resume the crown to bequeath it to your children and re-enter the palace from where your mother sprang ... Go, mate with one who is worthy of you and share with him an empire co-extensive with the world ... The whole world alike shall be your dowry."
>
> (Cl. *Nupt*. 10.228–81)

It is only much later that a different picture emerges of Honorius and Maria's marriage. Writing in the late fifth century, Zosimus expressed his distaste by calling it a 'crime against nature' for a girl so young to be forced into wedlock (Zos. 5.28.1–3). This is a stark contrast to Claudian's romanticized vision. Zosimus also related a curious story in which he claimed that Serena was unhappy about her teenage daughter's marriage; so much so that she secretly hired a herbalist to concoct a drug which left Honorius 'neither willing nor able to fulfill his conjugal duty' (Zos. 5.28.2). Since the marriage is usually thought to have lasted nearly a decade until Maria's death in 407 without any children, this would imply that Serena administered drugs to the emperor for years! Another interpretation is that Maria died earlier, in 404/5 (see below). Outlandish as Zosimus' story sounds, neither Maria nor her sister Thermantia's marriages to Honorius produced any children. While it is true that there were – and still are – herbal concoctions that cause erectile dysfunction, the question of whether Serena actually did something to restrain Honorius' sexual impulses – for any amount of time – is pure speculation. Besides, if both of her daughters' marriages to Honorius were politically motivated, in anticipation of heirs that would consolidate both Serena and Stilicho's power and prestige, then making Honorius impotent seems a strange way to achieve that end. The simplest answer is that Honorius might have been sterile. And how Zosimus knew anything at all about this is anyone's guess. He could have taken the herbalist anecdote from any one of the primary sources that he ransacked in order to produce his own work. Or he could have just as easily have made up the story. Zosimus certainly disliked Serena and Stilicho, that much is clear – perhaps therein lies his penchant for gossip.

Arcadius was not present at his brother's wedding, nor was he represented, at least not according to Claudian, our only contemporary source for the event. However, since the wedding occurred while the North African proxy war was playing out between the western and the eastern imperial courts, this might explain Arcadius' absence. Honorius's sister Placidia, aged about five in 398, must surely have been present at her older brother's wedding, but Claudian omits her presence there. In fact, he refers to Placidia only once in his entire body of work. This was a hypothetical scenario where Placidia was a possible bride for Stilicho's son Eucherius, yet even then, Placidia was not named (Cl. *Stil.* II.354–61). As Oost remarked, 'the mission of Claudian was to glorify Stilicho and his family, even when celebrating Honorius; the latter's family is irrelevant when it does not serve this purpose' (1968, 72). The omission of Placidia from the court propaganda of Honorius' early reign could be due to her age, and consequently her perceived insignificance on the political stage. On the other hand, it infers a less than cordial relationship with her surrogate parents Serena and Stilicho. As the next chapter shows, Placidia was alleged to have been directly involved in Serena's execution in 408. If that is true, that one act might well have been the culmination of years of resentment that Placidia had harbored towards Serena.

The restoration of harmony

The aftermath of the Gildonic War was a drawn-out business that proved exceptionally beneficial to both Honorius and Stilicho – financially and politically. In 399, the eunuch Eutropius, Arcadius' former chamberlain, now consul for that year, fell from power through an eastern intrigue. Eutropius was already deeply unpopular at the eastern court, and Stilicho seems to have played a clandestine role in the eunuch's overthrow. Eutropius' meddling with the North African annonarian system had threatened the West's stability, and so Honorius determined to exact vengeance. Eutropius' many enemies rounded on him, and thus he fell from Arcadius' favor. Realizing the game was up, Eutropius sought refuge in the church of Saint Sophia at Constantinople but he was forcibly removed and exiled to Cyprus. Soon afterwards, he was brought back to Constantinople, where he was beheaded in a suburban district (Soz. *HE*. 8.7.2.3). Contemporaries had no sympathy for Eutropius. He had been greatly feared, and his greed and arrogance were notorious. Eunapius said that Eutropius was a 'true serpent … coiling through the halls of the palace … seizing everything and dragging it off to his lair' (Eunap. *fr.* 65.2). Claudian took a great deal of pleasure from Eutropius' ruination. A month after Eutropius' execution in August 399, Claudian performed two powerful invectives against him at the Milanese court, just as he had done for Eutropius' predecessor, Rufinus, in 395 (Cl. *Eutr.* I, II). Eutropius was not only demonized in the West. While awaiting transportation to Cyprus, he was savagely denounced by the Constantinopolitan senate, and his memory was condemned (*damnatio memoriae*) through a jointly issued law of Arcadius and Honorius. This proclamation marked an important step in the official re-establishment of harmony between the brother emperors.

> [Emperors Arcadius and Honorius] to Aurelianus, Praetorian Prefect.
>
> All the property of Eutropius, who was once grand chamberlain, We have annexed to the account of Our treasury; he shall be stripped of his splendor, and his consulship shall be vindicated from the foul stain and from the memory of his name and from his low meanness. All his acts shall be annulled, that all ages may be mute about him, that a blot may not appear on Our age through the recital of his deeds, and that neither those men who by their courage and their wounds extend the Roman boundaries nor those who guard these territories by preserving the equity of the law may lament the fact that this vile monster defiled the divine gift of the consulship by his contagion. He shall know that he has been despoiled also of the dignity of the patriciate and of all the lesser dignities which he has polluted by the perversity of his morals. All his statues, all his images, in bronze as well as in marble, in pigments, or in whatever material is suitable for portraiture, We order to be destroyed in all cities

and towns, both in private and public places, in order that the stigma of our age, so to speak, may not pollute the sight of those who look at such images ...

(*CTh.* 9.40.17. Aug 17, 399)

The elimination of Eutropius allowed for rapprochement between the eastern and western courts. Coins, such as the *Concordia Augustorum* type (Figure 6.1), were another medium used by both imperial governments to project a renewed age of reconciliation. And yet, despite the bitter political climate which existed between Theodosius' death in 395 to Eutropius' downfall in 399, both Roman governments maintained communication with each other, through embassies and other means (Cl. *Stil.* III.81–3). The propaganda campaign, in the wake of Gildo's defeat and Eutropius' *damnatio*, was therefore to reassure the entire Roman world that all was well between West and East once more. It was important to convey an impression of domestic imperial cohesion so as to deter the possibility of internal challenges arising to either Honorius or Arcadius' positions.

The Gildonic War really was a bonanza for Honorius – a gift that kept on giving. After Gildo's death, he was officially condemned as a *hostis publicus*

Figure 6.1 Gold solidus of Honorius. Constantinople mint, 1st officina, *c.* 395–402. Obv. Honorius cuirassed, wearing diademed helmet, facing, holding a spear in his right hand, a shield with horseman motif in his left. Legend: DN-HONORI-VS-PF-AVG (*Dominus Noster Honorius Pius Felix Augustus*/ Our Lord Honorius, pious and fortunate Augustus). Rev. Constantinopolis seated, holding scepter in her right hand, Victoriola in her left, her right foot on ship's prow. Legend: CONCORDI-A-AVGGG (Concord of the Augusti)-A (officina). Exergue: CON (Constantinople)-OB (*Obryzum*/ pure gold).

Source: RIC X 24.

(*CIL* 9.4051), and for well over a decade afterwards a range of legal sanctions were enacted against his satellites and property across North Africa. Honorius made it abundantly clear that disloyalty and eastern interference in that region would not be tolerated again. Honorius hoped that the example set by Gildo's punishment would prevent a repeat of the same thing. The earliest Honorian law, in this respect, had the sole purpose of administering Gildo's immense estates in North Africa. As we have seen, because of their size, Honorius had to create an entirely new department for the purpose of incorporating Gildo's wealth into the imperial treasury (*Not. dig.* [*occ*]. 12.2). It seems that this was a complex task, for Honorius continued to enact legislation concerning Gildo's wealth well into the early fifth century.

> [Arcadius and Honorius] to Peregrinus, Count and Procurator of the Imperial Household. We order that the regular tax of all accounts due from the landholding of Gildo which have devolved upon Our treasury shall (now) be paid in full, with receipts for payment taken into account in the usual manner.
>
> (*CTh*. 9.42.16. Dec 1, 399)

> Emperors Honorius and Theodosius II Augustuses to Sapidianus (Vicar of Africa). Whereas We recently ordered, by establishing a fine of five pounds of gold, that the landed estates brought to Our treasury from the property of Gildo should be exempt from compulsory quartering, We now further command that all houses which come from the same right of confiscation, in whatsoever municipalities they are located, shall be exempted from compulsory quartering, so that lessees (tenants) may be found more easily. If any person, therefore, should violate Our order, he shall be punished by the fine previously imposed.
>
> (*CTh*. 7.8.9. Aug 6, 409)

Wedded bliss?

A year or so into their marriage, and with no children in sight, Maria and Honorius must have been under incredible pressure to produce an heir for the western throne, and this likely went on for the nearly ten years they were together – all the more so in view of Arcadius and his wife Aelia Eudoxia's growing, healthy family at Constantinople. The eastern emperor had married Eudoxia in April 395, very soon after Theodosius I's death (*PLRE* II, 410). They would have five children in the course of their marriage: Flaccilla (397–c.408), Pulcheria (399–453), Arcadia (April 3, 400–44), Theodosius II (April 10, 401–50), and Marina (Feb 10, 403–49). Contrary to his parents' tragic experiences, all bar one of Arcadius' children lived to adulthood. Flaccilla was born just a few months before her uncle's wedding, and Pulcheria was brought into the world less than a year after Honorius and Maria's marriage.

The fairly quick succession of babies born to the eastern imperial couple must have a been a source of embarrassment to Honorius, and likely did not help his relationship with his father-in-law. After the first few years without grand-children, Stilicho and Serena perhaps began to consider other possibilities to bring new blood for the imperial line. Their son, Eucherius, Honorius' cousin and now brother-in-law, was not far off adolescence, when he could marry. By 398, Eucherius held the minor rank of *tribunus et notarius* (imperial notary/ clerk). He does not seem to have held any other titles later on, which would have been a sign of his preparation for some important role in Honorius' civilian or military administration (Barnwell 1993, 26–8). Later historians were sure that Stilicho wanted Eucherius to replace Honorius as emperor, which, considering Honorius' lack of heir, might have seemed logical to the *magister*, at least from the perspective of preserving political stability (Zos. 5.31.1; Soz. *HE*. 9.4.1; Oros. 7.38.6). The famous ivory diptych (Figure 6.2) preserved at Monza Cathedral, northern Italy, alternately titled *The Diptych of the Young Office Holder* or *The Stilicho Diptych*, is identified by some as Eucherius and his parents, but this is a view contested by others. Alice T. Christ neatly synthesizes the debate surrounding this artwork (2015, 173–88; cf. Kampen 2009, 123–38). It would indeed be helpful to conclusively identify the figures in this diptych as Stilicho, Serena, and Eucherius, but unfortunately this has not been the case thus far.

As the wives of an emperor, Maria and Thermantia both held a pos-ition comparable to Eudoxia. The three women also had a similar ethnic background: Eudoxia's father was Frankish, her mother Roman, as were Maria and Thermantia's grandparents. This is where the comparison ends. Eudoxia attained Augustal status, whereas Maria and Thermantia did not. This was not a question of ethnicity, since the three women had barbarian blood. Rather, it was due to Maria and Thermantia's childless marriages to Honorius, as opposed to Eudoxia's five offspring with Arcadius. This fits with a pattern in the late empire whereby certain imperial women who had borne children achieved the rank of Augusta, for example, Constantine I's mother, Helena, and second wife, Fausta, or Theodosius I's first wife, Aelia Flaccilla. It appears that childless imperial wives were not entitled to such honors. An Augusta was represented and venerated through sculpture and coinage, as evidenced by the representation of Flaccilla and Eudoxia through this media (Figure 6.3). However, while it is certain that Honorius' wives were not portrayed on coinage, they may well have been depicted in other media. Some possibilities include a late Roman cameo in the Rothschild Paris Collection, which may or may not portray Maria and Honorius; a miniature on the so-called *Stilicho Diptych* (Figure 6.2); and a gold repoussé medallion from Rome depicting a wedding couple that could be Honorius and either one of his wives. All things considered, there are, unfortunately, no verifiable images of Maria or Thermantia (Kiilerich 1993, 93–4; *DOCat* 2, 2–4).

A further ingredient that worked in favor of an imperial woman being elevated to the position of an Augusta was if they patronized the Church,

Figure 6.2 Diptych of the Young Office Holder/Stilicho Diptych. Late antique ivory
diptych depicting a high-status family: a middle-aged bearded military
officer, a younger woman, and a young boy. The standing trio are facing,
their eyes looking left. The man's right hand holds a spear, his left hand
rests on a shield depicting two miniature figures (Honorius and Maria?).
A *parazonium* (ceremonial sword) on his left side, his long cloak (*chlamys*)
fastened at the right shoulder by a crossbow shaped brooch (*fibula*). The
chlamys is intricately decorated with human figures, as is his tunic, which
has a swastika frieze hemline. A circular pattern on his left shin, either
a fabric pattern, or a tattoo, perhaps a military mark (*stigma*). The boy
holds a closed diptych in his left hand; his right hand, with two fingers
raised, is held to his chest in an oratorical gesture. His cloak is also fastened
with a crossbow *fibula*. The woman's long-sleeved tunic (*tunica manicata*) is
held up by her left hand which also holds a table napkin (*mappula*), a late
antique aristocratic symbol. Her right hand holds a stylized rose between
her forefinger and thumb. This floral motif is part of the iconography of
Venus and Spes (Hope). It is not uncommon to find pagan imagery like this
in late Roman art of the Christian era (Kiilerich 1993, 137–41).

Source: © Museo e Tesoro del Duomo di Monza, Italy.

Figure 6.3 Gold solidus of Aelia Eudoxia. Constantinople mint, *c.* 400–1. Obv. Eudoxia rosette-diademed and draped, crowned by the *manus Dei* from above. Legend: AEL-EVDO-XIA-AVG (*Aelia Eudoxia Augusta*). Rev. Victory seated on cuirass, shield behind, inscribing Chi-Rho on a shield set on column. Legend: SALVS-REI-PVBLICAE (Health of the State)-Є (officina mark). Exergue: CON (Constantinople)-OB (*Obryzum*/pure gold).

Source: *RIC* X 14.

or performed charitable works. We have already seen this in regard to Honorius' mother, Aelia Flaccilla. As his sister-in-law, Eudoxia was a passionate Catholic, who organized nocturnal protests against Arian heretics in Constantinople, and this helped secure her rank as the eastern Augusta (Soc. *HE*. 6.8). There are no accounts about her western counterparts, Maria and Thermantia, doing anything remotely like this. If we discount Claudian's idealized, insipid portrait of Maria, there is no historical evidence for what Maria, and later Thermantia, actually did, other than marry an emperor. No acts of charity, no piety, no endowment of the Church – nothing! This is a pity, as it clouds our knowledge of what their lives were like as members of Honorius' household.

In praise of Stilicho

Stilicho was the western consul designate for the year 400, the highest honor he ever received from the Roman state. Since 398, he was already Count and Master of Both Branches of the Military Service (*comes et magistro utriusque militiae*), but the consulship was the greatest political office Stilicho achieved (*CTh*. 7.22.12. Sept 26, 398). It is unclear why, but he refused to recognize his eastern consular colleague Aurelian. He had similarly refused to acknowledge Eutropius' consulship in 399, but that is understandable given that individual's behavior (*CLRE* 16, 78). In Aurelian's appointment as co-consul, Stilicho may have held off recognizing him until a serious crisis at Constantinople had been resolved. Some Visigothic commanders were attempting to force Arcadius to submit to their will, which ultimately did not end well for them. The eastern situation aside, Stilicho's solitary consulship was celebrated by Claudian with no less than three lavish panegyrics. The poet performed the first two at Milan; the third he gave at Rome. From these poems, it is clear that Stilicho was the more feted figure in Honorius' administration, far above the emperor himself. The short excerpts below demonstrate the general tenor of Claudian's three works. The panegyrist laid special emphasis on Stilicho's all-encompassing role as Honorius' guardian, mentor, father figure, and all-round Roman hero.

> Defended by this shield (Stilicho), Honorius did not mourn his noble father, he dictates laws to conquered races and sees his triumphs increase with his years. Him, you (Stilicho) do seek to shape as with kindly so with severe mind; neither to laziness do you deliver him by a ready yielding to all his wishes, nor by opposing do you crush his eager spirit: as a youth you teach him in secret a king's lesson – his duty to his people; as a reverend senior you (Honorius) pay him honor, and govern the empire at a father's bidding … so it was that he (Honorius) knew not passion before matrimony and preferred to vindicate his manhood not in a youth of debauchery, but in the chaste bonds of legal wedlock. Blessed art you in having an emperor for a son-in-law; more blessed he with you for father … by means of fair Maria he endows Rome with a dynasty? That he is looked to as the ancestor of kings?
>
> (Cl. *Stil.* II.64–78, 239–40)

> O blessed mortal, whom the Rome you have saved calls her father … thanks to your victories, Stilicho, salvation has dawned on all beyond their hopes … Stilicho gives scope for the virtues of a bygone age and rouses a people, forgetful of their former glory … thanks to him dishonor is banished, and our age blossoms with Rome's ancient virtues … consul, all but peer of the gods, protector of a city greater than any upon earth …
>
> (Cl. *Stil.* III.51–108)

What did Honorius think of such presumptiveness, in particular Claudian's quip urging the emperor to provide an heir to the throne? Now in his sixteenth year, the emperor had still not been able to emerge from behind Stilicho's shadow. It would not be surprising if resentment festered in the emperor's mind at this man's usurpation of his own father's place, never mind the fact that Stilicho was behaving as de facto ruler. If the young emperor did have his doubts about Stilicho, however, he kept them to himself for the moment, for who could he trust in his own palace? His wife Maria? She was hardly an impartial confidante.

Claudian's adulation of Stilicho must have made at least some of the western hierarchy uncomfortable. Elevating Stilicho to the status of Rome's savior, instead of the emperor, was a step too far, even if it was the truth. By doing so, Claudian confirmed any suspicions that members of the senatorial aristocracy must have had about Stilicho's allegiance to Honorius. This begs the question, did Stilicho not inspect the panegyrics before their recital? Even if he missed vetting the first two, given at Milan, he would have heard them and have had the good sense to read the third one before its performance at Rome. Either he was satisfied with the content of Claudian's verse, or Stilicho just did not appreciate the power of poetry.

Goths on the western stage

As the implications of Claudian's words sank in among western élite circles, Italy, for the first time in many years, was invaded by a hostile force. In late 401, Alaric crossed the Italian border from the Balkans with his army. Eutropius had already conferred Alaric with a Roman military command, *magister militum per Illyricum*, and the Visigoth had used that position to his advantage in order to move unobstructed throughout the Balkans (Heather 1991, 204–8). Alaric perhaps viewed the West as a softer target than the eastern provinces, and so turned his attentions towards Italy, bent on extorting wealth and land from Honorius. Alaric had some justification to expect recompense. Ever since the Visigoths had crossed the Danube in 376, eastern emperors had promised them land to settle on in exchange for their military service as *foederati*. As we have seen, all of these repeated promises came to nothing, and the Visigoths were treated as an expendable imperial asset. It is understandable, therefore, that Alaric probably felt that Rome owed him and his people a debt. How to claim that debt was the question.

So, in about November 401, Alaric marched on Milan and besieged it. His intelligence revealed Stilicho's absence from Honorius' court – the *magister* was engaged against the Franks along the northern border of Raetia (eastern Switzerland and northern Italy) – and therefore Alaric chose that moment to attack Honorius in Milan. Some historians think that Alaric's 401 invasion was the catalyst for Honorius strengthening Rome's defenses, the Aurelian Wall, but restorative work was already in progress when Alaric arrived in the north (Matthews 1975, 273; Ferrill 1997, 95; Lejdegård 2002, 76–7; cf. Dey 2011, 33–48). Honorius had appointed Macrobius Longinianus as Rome's city prefect (*praefectus urbi*) in late 400, and tasked him with overhauling the city's defensive system. The work which Longinianus undertook at Honorius' behest is supported by commemorative inscriptions from three of Rome's city gates (*portae*) – the Tiburtina/San Lorenzo, Praenestina, and Portuensis. As ever, Stilicho's name was included on these dedications.

The Senate and the People of Rome, under the supervision of his Excellency Flavius Macrobius Longinianus, City Prefect, in devotion to their authority and majesty, set up effigies to the Emperors Caesars our Lords the two invincible princes Arcadius and Honorius, victors and conquerors, forever Augusti, for restoring the walls, gates, and towers of the Eternal City, with the removal of a vast amount of rubble, in accordance with the prompting of his Excellency Flavius Stilicho, distinguished Count and master of both services, to the everlasting memory of their name.

(*CIL* 6.1189)

The Aurelian circuit is an enormous structure that stretches around the ancient capital for 19 kilometers. The Honorian building project was expensive, labor-intensive, and time-consuming. Honorius doubled the wall's height to 16 meters, extended the existing defensive towers, and constructed new ones (Dey 2011, 33–48). Anyone who has ever had the pleasure of visiting modern Rome, and has passed beneath any of the old city gates, or walked the Aurelian circuit, has seen how imposing the walls are. It is the Honorian building phase that makes this great Roman landmark what it is. Claudian mentions Honorius' renovations in a panegyric written for the emperor's sixth consulship in 404. Here, the poet assigns Rome's renewal to Honorius, and puts him on a par with the first emperor, Augustus, whose building program transformed the city landscape. Claudian's reference to the Visigoths' approach suggests that the western government had prior knowledge of Alaric's intentions before he set foot on the soil of Italy. The following excerpt is part of a larger description of Honorius' triumphal procession through Rome in 404.

Rome … more glorious since now her hills rise higher, and greater than the City that we knew, reveal herself to your (Honorius) vision. The new walls but recently completed at the rumor of the Goths' approach increased the beauty of her face, and fear was a craftsman working to her enhancement, and, by a strange reversal, the creeping age that peace had brought upon her was scattered by war, now girt by one unbroken wall, to grow young again.

(Cl. *VI Cons.* 529–36)

If Honorius knew there was a good chance Alaric would soon invade Italy, why then did Stilicho choose that time to leave for the northern frontier? The Gallo-Roman aristocrat Rutilius Namatianus was convinced that Stilicho betrayed Honorius to Alaric – and to other barbarians as well. Writing about six years after Alaric's sack of Rome in 410, Rutilius accused Stilicho of having brought this calamity on the Roman state. Indeed, after Alaric's initial and subsequent forays into Italy, many among Honorius' civilian and military establishment began to suspect Stilicho of collusion with the Visigoths and others. The truth, however, is not clear cut and it is impossible to either prove or disprove the charge of Stilicho's collusion with any barbarians. In all likelihood, Stilicho thought he could manage the Visigoths, as both he and Theodosius had done for years, but, ultimately, it did not matter what the real story was. Stilicho was blamed for the West's barbarian crisis, as we will see in the next chapter.

Furthermore, Rutilius was a pagan who says that Stilicho burned the ancient Sibylline Books, a prophetic collection traditionally consulted in time of peril to the state. Thus, in Rutilius' opinion, Stilicho's sacrilege caused the old gods to abandon Rome to its fate. Like so much else from this period, religious affiliations seriously affect the judgment of our primary sources.

> [B]itter is the crime of cursed Stilicho in that he was betrayer of the empire's secret (the Alpine passes into Italy from the east) ... cruel frenzy turned the world upside down ... he let loose the arms of the barbarians to the death of Latium: he plunged an armed foe in the naked vitals of the land, his craft being freer from risk than that of openly inflicted disaster. Even Rome lay exposed to his skin-clad menials ... nor was it only through Gothic arms that the traitor made his attack: before this he burned the fateful books which brought the Sibyl's aid.
>
> (Rut. Nam. 41–52)

Leaving aside the notion of Stilicho as a barbarian fifth columnist for a moment, we see instead a pragmatist who, faced with simultaneous threats, used subterfuge against his main adversary, Alaric. In the late summer of 401, Frankish war bands were pillaging Raetia, all along the Danubian *limes*. Stilicho headed to the northern frontier to repel the invaders, thinking perhaps he had time enough to deal with the Franks, but misjudging the timing of Alaric's arrival. It is also conceivable that Stilicho's strategy was to draw Alaric into pitched battle on the open Italian plain, where he could eliminate the Visigoth once and for all. Whatever his intentions were, Stilicho's failure to check Alaric at the Italian border added fuel to the fire of suspicion among his peers that he had concerted with Rome's eternal enemies.

Honorius among the wolves

As the Visigoths neared Milan, Honorius, for the first time, had a real chance to show that he would do whatever it took to defend his people, and take the field against the enemy. Claudian tells us that Honorius personally trained with his men for the coming Visigothic invasion, yet his verse is deeply frustrating in its vagueness. Did the emperor just parade his troops, or did he have a bigger contribution in the war effort against Alaric?

> Before the emperor's face, as he practiced his cavalry upon the plain, two wolves savagely attacked his escort. Slain by darts, they disclosed a horrid portent, and a wondrous sign of what was to be. In each animal, on its being cut open, was found a human hand, in the stomach of one a left hand, in that of the other a right was discovered; both still twitching, the fingers stretched out and bathed with living blood. Would that you search out the truth, the beast, as messenger of Mars, foretold that the enemy would fall before the emperor's eyes. As the hands were found to be living when the

stomachs were cut open, so, when the Alps had been broken through, the might of Rome was to be discovered unimpaired. But fear, ever a poor interpreter, read disaster in the portent; severed hands, it was said, and nursing wolf, threatened destruction on Rome and her empire ... It was Stilicho alone who by his courage assured despairing Rome the promise of a better fate; at this crisis he showed himself by his courage at once general and seer.

(Cl. *Get.* 249–269)

The episode of the wolves is clearly a metaphor for the danger facing Honorius and the West, but it is curious nonetheless. The wolf, or more precisely the she-wolf, was a very common motif in Roman mythology and iconography. According to legend, the she-wolf rescued and nursed the mythological twins Romulus and Remus, and thus the animal was revered in religion and culture. It is therefore exceptionally rare to find negative Roman artistic or literary references to wolves, never mind cases that involved wolves devouring human flesh. For instance, a bronze coin of Philip II (244–9) depicts a wolf with a human hand in its mouth, the meaning of which is unclear (*MFA* 69.1093). Ammianus' narrative on the Battle of Hadrianopolis has a similar ring to Claudian's wolven tale. Just prior to the battle, omens of howling wolves appear to the emperor Valens, and it is apparent that nothing good will come of such signs (Amm. Marc. *Hist.* 31.1.1–2). It is tempting to make a biblical allusion to Honorius as the good shepherd protecting his flock from the wolves, but it is hard to think of Claudian as an exegete (John 10.1–14). Rather, Claudian's wolves are aberrant, and used to to convey an impression of the Visigoths as rabid beasts. An interesting connection between Claudian's anecdote and a modern American urban legend calls such animals 'ambiguous guardians,' whose role is defense against intruders – in our case the Visigoths. Adrienne Mayor's article also suggests that these animals can be seen as 'mistrusted protectors,' the idea being that Rome's ancient totem animal itself was such a creature (Mayor 1992).

Even though Claudian praises Honorius for swapping the comforts of the palace for the martial field in order to muster his troops, the poet follows this by accrediting Stilicho the real honor for defending Italy from Alaric. In one stroke, Claudian stripped Honorius' dignity from him. Was this intentional or misjudged? It was true that Stilicho's military skills (*ars militaris*) helped counter the barbarian menace. His martial talent was the reason why he had earned Theodosius' trust, and it was why he was successful in most of the campaigns that he waged in Honorius' name. Be that as it may, Honorius was head of state, not Stilicho. After years of writing material favorable to Stilicho, Claudian ought to have realized that perhaps he was pressing his luck by diminishing Honorius' image. In one particularly long passage of the *Gothic War*, the poet went too far. Claudian declared that the emperor was overjoyed that Stilicho had saved him, and that Stilicho was akin to Rome's ancient heroes. Stilicho, according to Claudian, was 'Mars in human form' (Cl. *Get.* 404–68). Perhaps the court poet had no choice but to continue paying lip service to Stilicho's authority, just as the emperor had had to do. Catherine

Ware has discussed how Claudian constructed the image of Stilicho as an epic hero, and how the panegyrist impressed upon his audience that it was Stilicho alone who was capable of defending the Roman West (Ware 2012, 44–8, 86–8). In effect, though, Claudian's praise for Stilicho, especially in relation to Alaric's invasion, made a coward of Honorius. It should come as no surprise, therefore, that the poet disappears entirely without trace sometime around 404. Perhaps, as eventually happened with Stilicho in 408, Claudian crossed a line with Honorius, but, as our opening chapter speculates, how exactly that happened is unknown.

Honorius brave, Stilicho braver

The wolf omens were proven right when Alaric invaded Italy in November 401. His first port of call was Milan, where Honorius was at that moment (Barnes 1976; Dewar 1996, xxix–xliv; cf. Heather 1991, 208; Lejdegård 2002, 73–9). The now seventeen-year-old emperor, so Claudian says, was not at all frightened by the Visigothic assailants on his city and, in an address to the goddess Roma, Honorius exhibited defiance.

> He (Alaric) threatened to block me in, cherishing the hope that perhaps, in vain terror, with the garrisons all gone and with fear pressing hard upon me, I might make terms with him on any conditions that he liked; but no fear shook my constancy, since I was both confident that my general was on his way and mindful, Roma, of your generals, who never, even though death awaited them, bartered the loss of their good name for base love of life.
>
> (Cl. *VI Cons.* 446–52)

After describing Honorius' bravado, Claudian then had Honorius make an overture to Stilicho. Even if we allow for a certain amount of poetic license, it is improbable that Honorius said this. Like so much of Claudian's hyperbole, this acknowledgement of Stilicho's military skill on the emperor's part negates Honorius' own fortitude in the face of barbarian aggression. How much longer could Claudian expect to continue undermining Honorius? As long as Stilicho called the shots, it seems. It is interesting how Claudian manages to elevate a subordinate's status over the emperor. His work is a departure from earlier panegyrists, notably those of the fourth century, who do not ever give pride of place to someone lower in rank than the emperor. Then again, none of those emperors were children when they assumed the supreme office.

> It was night, and far and wide I saw the barbarian campfires burning like the stars … when from the snow-chilled north the glorious Stilicho arrives … the dangers that I faced permitted no delay … he struck out to hammer those who threatened me, and inflamed by a loving valor, forgetful of his own safety, he drove through the midst of the enemy.
>
> (Cl. *VI Cons.* 453–67)

Stilicho returned from Raetia in the nick of time and defeated the Visigoths in two pitched battles in northern Italy. The first was at Pollentia (modern Pollenzo) on April 6, 402; the second occurred at Verona later that summer, or, as some historians argue, in the following year, 403 (Barnes 1976; cf. Cameron 1970; McCormick 1990, 51). What is agreed, however, is that on both occasions Alaric evaded capture. In the first instance, after Pollentia, it seems that Stilicho brokered some sort of deal with Alaric that allowed him to leave Italy (Cameron 1970, 185–7). This looks like misjudgment on Stilicho's part, which in hindsight it was, but he may not have had another option. In both engagements with Alaric, Stilicho used many barbarian *foederati*, but these proved ill-disciplined and prone to looting, and thus he was prevented from conclusively destroying Alaric (O' Flynn 1983, 37–41).

After a hard contest fought under a scorching hot sun at Verona, Alaric's forces were badly mauled by Stilicho, but he managed to escape from Italy into Illyricum to lick his wounds.

An interesting line from Claudian claims that the rest of the northern *barbaricum* watched with keen interest to see how Alaric's invasion would fare (Cl. *Get.* 567–70). Claudian therefore made monumental importance of Pollentia and Verona – they were the West's existential fight for survival. If other barbarian peoples or disenchanted Roman military units thought that Alaric could extort what he wanted from Honorius, they might become emboldened. Ironically, this is actually what transpired just a few years later, notwithstanding Alaric's defeats, because, although he was down, Alaric was far from a spent force. In essence, the Roman victory of 402/3 was pyrrhic, for it opened the path for challenges to Honorius' government.

Despite its title, Claudian's *Gothic War* actually gives us very little information about the battles themselves (Cl. *Get.* 580–97). Orosius is pleased enough to tell us that he has much nothing to say about Pollentia except that atrocities were committed by a pagan barbarian, Honorius' general Saul, an Alan who had fought under Theodosius at the Frigidus in 394 (*PLRE* I, 809; *PLRE* II, 981). The Christian poet Prudentius, visiting Honorius' court in Milan after Pollentia, provides a flavor of how the battle went. Prudentius was far more complimentary and sincere towards Honorius than his pagan counterpart Claudian was. Like other ecclesiastical authors of the age, Prudentius emphasized Honorius' religious piety as the prime reason for his military successes. Yet, Prudentius had sense enough to see who it was that was pulling the strings at the emperor's court at that time.

> The leader of our army and empire was a young man strong in Christ and his companion and father, Stilicho, and the one God to both was Christ … the spear which carries higher the standard of Christ, goes before the military banners … the (Visigoths) were at last destroyed and paid the penalty … the widely scattered unburied corpses which covered with their bones the fields of Pollentia … On the other hand, our Stilicho fought hand-to-hand and forced the armored enemy to flee

from the battle. In this case, Christ our God was close to us as was real strength … Living glory is your due O prince; gain a living reward for courage, immortal glory. As ruler of the world, you will be joined to Christ for ever …

(*Contra Symm.* II.709ff.)

Over a century after these events, Jordanes, a Byzantine historian of Gothic history, expressed a very different opinion about Alaric's reasons for entering Italy. Jordanes claimed that the Visigoths came to Italy in good faith after receiving a surety from Honorius of land on which to settle, but were attacked without provocation by Stilicho en route to their promised land. What is more, Alaric caused no damage while in Italy (Jord. *Get.* 30.152–5). Jordanes' view is reminiscent of Orosius, Hydatius, and others' softly-softly approach to Alaric's sack of Rome in 410.

One place where Honorius' authority could not be diminished by Stilicho, Claudian, or anyone else was the medium of coinage. During and after Alaric's siege of Milan, Honorius commissioned a series of gold and silver coins – all of which were minted at Milan – to be struck in order to commemorate the victories over Alaric, and to pay his troops with. One of these coin types was a *Victoria Augustorum* gold tremissis, intended by Honorius to assure the public of his commitment to protecting the state (Figure 6.4).

Figure 6.4 Gold tremissis of Honorius. Milan mint, 402. Obv. Honorius pearl-diademed, draped, and cuirassed. Legend: DN-HONORI-VS-PF-AVG (*Dominus Noster Honorius Pius Felix Augustus*/Our Lord Honorius, pious and fortunate Augustus). Rev. Victory advancing, holding globe in her left hand, a wreath in her right. Legend: VICTORIA-AVGVSTORVM/Victory of the Augusti). Field: M/D (Mediolanum), cross above. Exergue: COM (*Comitatensian* mint).

Source: *RIC* IX 37c; *RIC* X 1215.

Other coin types that Honorius issued carried the legends *Virtus Exercitum* (Valor of the Army), commemorating the Roman military's achievements; *Virtus Romanorum* (Valor of the Romans), emphasizing the Roman people's endurance against adversity; and *Triumfator Gentium Barbarum* (Victor over Barbarian Peoples). Both the legend and the emperor's iconography on the latter, silver, coin – Honorius proudly holding a military standard, towering above a bound captive – were directly copied from a unique coin of his father's. This was the coin that celebrated Theodosius' victory after Hadrianopolis (Figure 2.1). Through his coinage, at least, Honorius could demonstrate to his subjects that he still held control and authority.

The move to Ravenna

A subject that has been often debated is Honorius' transfer of his court to Ravenna. Consensus holds that this occurred in 402 as a result of Alaric's siege of Milan, although no Honorian-era written primary source attests to this as the year or the reason (Matthews 1975; Ferrill 1997; Honoré 1998; cf. Gillett 2001; Deliyannis 2010). The first law that Honorius issued from Ravenna was not until the end of the year he is supposed to have made the move (*CTh.* 7.13.15. Dec 6, 402). The last law issued from Milan was in September 401, but this does not necessarily mean that Honorius did not personally move to his new capital before his entire administration had (*CTh.* 1.15.16. Sept 10, 401). It is strange, though, that there are no western legal pronouncements for over a year. Even more problematic is determining when Honorius struck his first coinage at Ravenna, a must for an official imperial capital. All that can be safely said is that Honorius' first coins, bearing the Ravenna mintmark, were made at some some point between mid-402 and early 403. Gillett, however, makes a good argument for Honorius' waiting until early 408 to make Ravenna his imperial residence, and only then for strategic reasons (2001, 140–1).

It makes sense that, after Milan's siege, Honorius would have considered Ravenna a much safer location, surrounded as it was by marshes on one side and the Adriatic Sea on the other. Ravenna had a reputation for being a secure haven in times of crisis (Lejdegård 2002, 77–9). Whatever the date was when Honorius actually moved to Ravenna, the city became a main – though not the only – imperial residence of western emperors for most of the fifth century (Gillett 2001). Ravenna became so associated with imperial governance that after the western empire's final disintegration in the 480s, the city continued to operate as an administrative center for Italy under the Ostrogothic monarchy.

The year 402 was notable for another important occasion, this time at Constantinople. Arcadius and Eudoxia raised their eight-month-old son, Theodosius, to the rank of co-Augustus in January of that year. Arcadius issued coinage proclaiming his son as his heir, colleague, and the New Hope of the State (Figure 6.5). Honorius and Maria had still not had such good fortune, and the young Theodosius' elevation surely preyed on the western

Figure 6.5 Gold solidus of Arcadius. Constantinople mint, *c.* 402–3. Obv. Arcadius pearl-diademed and helmeted, cuirassed, facing, spear in his right hand, shield with horseman motif in his left. Legend: DN-ARCADI-VS-PF-AVG (*Dominus Noster Arcadius Pius Felix Augustus*/Our Lord Arcadius, pious and fortunate emperor). Rev. Victory seated on cuirass, inscribing XX/XXX (*Votis Vicennalibus, Multis Tricennalibus*/Prayers for the twentieth anniversary of reign, more offered for the approaching thirtieth anniversary) on shield, star in field. Legend: NOVA-SPES-REIPVBLICAE (New Hope of the State). Exergue: CON (Constantinople)-OB (*Obryzum*/pure gold).

Source: *RIC* X 29.

imperial couple's minds. Zosimus, ever the gossip merchant, alleged that Theodosius was not really Arcadius' son, but was born from an alleged affair that the empress Eudoxia had had (Zos. 5.18.8). Eudoxia had many enemies at the eastern court due to her refusal to bow to Bishop John Chrysostom's authority. Eudoxia was a far stronger character than either Maria or Thermantia, and she was often out in public without her court-bound husband, something that Chrysostom considered immoral. The rumors of impropriety therefore probably stemmed from such misogynistic attitudes. In fact, it is a recurring feature for antique male writers, particularly churchmen, to make serious allegations against strongminded Byzantine empresses who seemed to exert influence over their husbands, an infamous example being Procopius' vile *Anecdota* written against Theodora (527–48).

Honorius formally recognized his nephew as his colleague through legislation; the first laws to include Theodosius II's name, along with his father and uncle, date from early 403, considerably later than the infant's accession (*CTh.* 7.13.21. Jan 30, 403; 12.6.29. Feb 20, 403). We do not know whether Honorius planned to go to Constantinople for his nephew's accession, but if he did, Stilicho would probably have convinced him not to leave the West at such a critical time. In fact, Stilicho did just this in 408 when, after Arcadius' untimely death, Honorius wanted to travel east to protect his nephew. Stilicho persuaded Honorius otherwise, on the grounds of state security. Zosimus suspected that Stilicho's motives were more to do with his fear that Honorius might succumb to eastern intrigue against himself than a genuine concern for the emperor's safety (Zos. 5.31.1–6). It seems that Honorius thought so too, for very shortly afterwards he had Stilicho executed. Yet, even though Honorius could not attend his nephew's accession, he very likely wrote to Arcadius congratulating him. For while the two brothers never again saw one another after their father's death, they kept in touch by letter about matters of state and religion (Pall. *Dial.* 3).

Triumph and tragedy

At the very end of December 403, Honorius entered Rome in a ceremonial *adventus*. On January 1, he inaugurated his sixth consulship with a military triumph to commemorate the Visigothic victory, and also Gildo's defeat, some six years after the fact (Cl. *VI Cons.* 372–83). It was an impressive affair that moved slowly through thronged streets to the city center. Honorius' triumph also gave the population a rare opportunity to see their sovereign in the flesh, something they had not done since he accompanied his father as a child on their triumphal visit in 389. As he rode through the ancient capital, surrounded on all sides by cheering crowds, Honorius must have thought about being with his father in the summer of 389. Then a small boy, he had looked up at Theodosius with admiration and love. Now, in 403, with Stilicho standing right next to him, what must Honorius have felt about this surrogate parent, Stilicho – this man who would not relax his control over the young emperor?

As discussed in Chapter 5, Honorius' recently built triumphal arch in the forum was a focal point of the procession when it reached the heart of the city. Not only was this the last triumphal arch erected in Rome, it was also the penultimate imperial triumph ever held in the eternal city, the last being held in 416 (MacCormack 1972; Lejdegård 2002, 122; Kalas 2015, 90–6). Arriving at the forum, Honorius addressed the Roman senate inside the Curia, and then it was off to the Circus Maximus for a full itinerary of games. Traditionally, Roman victory celebrations culminated with the giving of free public spectacles in the amphitheater and the circus, an ancient Republican gesture designed to curry favor with the masses – a form of 'political theater' (Hopkins 1983). By the early fifth century, circus races were still a popular form of entertainment, gladiatorial combats far less so: Christianity had seen to that (Curran 2000, 230ff.). In the late empire, it was a new consul's responsibility to provide public games, something which incurred enormous expense (*CLRE* 18ff.). As western consul designate for 404, therefore, Honorius was duty-bound to put on a public show. As emperor, he was expected to stage a lavish spectacle, which, it appears, he did at Rome. This, as much as the *adventus*, triumph, and senate speech, was a necessary element in establishing a good rapport with the old capital (Lejdegård 2002, 82–3).

Figure 6.6 Gold semissis of Honorius. Rome mint, *c*. 404. Obv. Honorius pearl-diademed, draped, and cuirassed. Legend: DN-HONORI-VS-PF-AVG (*Dominus Noster Honorius Pius Felix Augustus*/Our Lord Honorius, pious and fortunate Augustus). Rev. Victory seated on cuirass, holding an inscribed shield (VOT-X-MVLT-XX) supported by small Genius. Legend: VICTORIA-AVGVSTORVM/Victory of the Augusti). Field: R/M (Roma). Exergue: COMOB (*Comitatus obryziacum*/pure gold mark).
Source: *RIC* X 1257.

Rome's mint struck coinage for Honorius to coincide with his consulship and triumph (Figure 6.6). Some of these coins commemorated Honorius' rule from 393, when he was co-Augustus with his father. The coins, the Victoria Augustorum type, were inscribed with VOT-X-MVLT-XX (*Votis Decennalibus*/prayers for ten years of rule–*Multis Vicennalibus*/hopes for more years to come). Through such buoyant slogans, a new, happy future for both emperor and state was projected.

Claudian's contribution to the triumphal festivities was the recital of a grandiose panegyric in the presence of the senatorial assembly, as well as the emperor, Stilicho, and their entourage. Inside Rome's ancient Curia where, Claudian declared, the goddess Victory herself was present, Honorius' sixth consular appointment was praised with great panache. As far as we know, this was the poet's last work; and although it ostensibly honored the emperor, inevitably Stilicho had a pivotal part. This panegyric is intensely optimistic and overly stylized.

All the space that extends from the Palatine Hill as far as the Milvian Bridge, and from the ground up as far as the roofs could soar, was filled by a crowd that wore a single face; you could see the ground flooded with waves of men and the high buildings ablaze with matrons. Young men rejoice in an emperor as young as themselves; old men dismiss the past in scorn and congratulate themselves on a prosperous destiny that has lasted till this very day, and praise the moderation of the times, because, as mild to approach as he is mild of heart, he would not permit Rome's conscript fathers (the senate) to march before his chariot, when even Eucherius, whose blood on either side is royal and whose sister is the empress, did a common soldier's service for his triumphant brother-in-law … this man (Honorius) has come as fellow-citizen, but those before had come as the masters of slaves …

(Cl. *VI Cons.* 543–59)

If Stilicho or Claudian thought that Honorius' triumph at Rome was a successful public relations stunt, they were mistaken. It was customary for a Roman triumph to parade high-value prisoners in front of the populace, but there were none on this occasion. No matter how sumptuous the carefully orchestrated event was, the fact remained that Alaric had evaded being captured or killed. He was still at large, a foreboding shadow lurking somewhere to the not so distant east of Italy. Where once upon a time, a slave would have stood at the rear of a triumphal chariot whispering to the victor to remember his own mortality, now Stilicho stood (Beard 2007, 81–2), not behind but beside the triumphal honorand. Who was the slave and who was the victor, in this instance, is a matter of opinion, but there was unease among western élites that perhaps Stilicho was no longer fit to defend the state. As for Honorius, after Verona he may well have sensed an opportunity to rid himself of his domineering father-in-law. Time would tell.

Exit Claudian

After 404, we hear no more of Claudian, who disappears completely from the historical record. What a relief, one might say! However, for all Claudian's poetic ostentation, most primary written sources on the rest of Honorius' reign are either unimaginative or incredibly fragmented. Whatever else one may think about Stilicho's favorite spin-merchant, Claudian was nothing if not entertaining. While not the most historically dependable source, his output for the early Honorian period is fairly chronologically consistent, and unashamedly pagan as well (Cl. *Carm. Min.* 50). From 404 on, practically everything that Honorius says or does, outside the legislative record, is predominantly narrated by ecclesiastical authors, whose descriptions of the emperor are in tandem with his Christian virtues, love of God, and patronage of the Church.

The passing of empresses

404 may have begun on a high note for Honorius, but it drew to a sad conclusion, both for his brother and himself. Arcadius' wife Eudoxia, expecting their sixth child, miscarried and died in October. She was interred in her favorite

ecclesiastical building in Constantinople, the Church of the Holy Apostles, built in the 330s by Constantine I (*Chron. Pasch.* s.a. 404).

Eudoxia's death is recorded by multiple sources and thus we are able to date this precisely to October 6, 404. Arcadius, never one for the limelight, retreated into near total seclusion for the remaining few years of his life. Whatever unkind things were said about his mental faculties or physical appearance, Arcadius obviously loved Eudoxia, and he took her death very badly.

It is widely held that the empress Maria died in 408, aged approximately twenty-two. This belief originates from just one line in Zosimus' *New History*, which says that she died a short time before the twin consulate of Anicius Auchenius Bassus and P. Flavius Philippus, whose terms officially commenced on January 1, 408 (Zos. 5.28.1). This could mean that Maria died at any time between 400 and late 407. It is odd that Maria's death is not recorded by any contemporary source. Even her sister's death was recorded later in 415, but by now we have seen how unreliable, or confused, Zosimus can be as a historian. Why then should Maria's death be accepted as 407 instead of earlier, based solely on one careless writer's testimony? If Maria died sometime in 404 or 405, she would have been aged about eighteen or nineteen, Honorius about twenty. Oost, following the calculations of the great twentieth-century French historian Émilienne Demougeot, posited 404 as the year in which Maria died (Demougeot 1951, 373; Oost 1968, 74–5; cf. Mackie 2003, 58–9). I am inclined to take their side on this issue.

If it is indeed the case that Maria was deceased by 405 at the latest, then this goes some way to explain a particular point of interest. This is the depiction of Honorius with a short, straggly beard and moustache on an ivory consular diptych of Anicius Probus from 406 (Figure 8.1). In the Graeco-Roman tradition, this style of beard was a mark of funeral mourning, while longer beards were typically associated with philosophers (Hamelink 2015). Honorius also appears with a beard on coins as well (Figure 7.7). Honorius' beard in imperial art has usually been taken as a sign of mourning for his brother Arcadius, who died in April 408 (*RIC* 10, 132). Going by the earlier date from the consular diptych, of 406, Honorius' short beard could equally be construed as his expression of grief for Maria. However, having a beard did not just signify sorrow or philosophy, it also conveyed maturity, and since Honorius was about twenty-two when he first appears with facial hair in imperial art, his image began to reflect his advancing age. There are precedents from earlier Roman history, for example, Severus Alexander (222–35), just thirteen when he ascended the throne. By his nineteenth year, Alexander's coinage began depicting him with a short beard, a political statement designed to project his maturity (Cohen 4.331; *RIC* 4 (2).71). Imperial Roman art was carefully conceived to construct a specific public image. If Maria had died earlier than Zosimus claims, Honorius would have been expected to demonstrate genuine mourning. Coinage and art ensured this.

Maria's remains were interred in an Egyptian porphyry sarcophagus, in a crypt beneath Old Saint Peter's Basilica in Rome. In January 1544, her tomb was discovered by workmen who were leveling the decrepit old Constantinian church in order to make way for the present edifice on Vatican Hill (Mackie 2003, 58–60; Johnson 2009; Lapatin 2015, 257). According to notes made around the time of the discovery, the empress's sarcophagus was filled with luxury grave deposits, most of which have long since disappeared (Marliano 1548, 5.20; Frey 1913, 84).

> In this month of January, 1544, in the shrine of [our] lord Peter, to the left of the main altar, the tomb of Maria, wife of the emperor Honorius, and daughter of Stilicho, has been uncovered.
> (*Archivio di S. Pietro*, 1544, 26.1; in Frey 1913, 84)

She herself was wrapped in a gown and burial shroud made from woven gold, and it seems that another female was interred alongside her, perhaps her mother, Serena, or her sister Thermantia. Most likely the gold thread from her vestments was melted down, as was a very large quantity of gold and silver jewelry – earrings, amulets, rings, hair clips, headbands – and other artifacts. There was also a huge amount of precious gemstones – sapphires, emeralds, and rubies – and agate and crystal vessels (Johnson 1991; Paolucci 2008; McEvoy 2013, 121). Marliano states that there were inscribed items among the grave goods; an *Agnus Dei* (Lamb of God) shaped item with the inscription MARIA NOSTRA FLORENTISSIMA (Maria, our shining flower); a gold plate inscribed in Greek, with the names of four archangels – Michael, Gabriel, Raphael, and Uriel; and a gold band inscribed with DOMINO NOSTRA MARIA – DOMINO NOSTRO HONORIO (Our Lady Maria – Our Lord Honorius).

From the brief sixteenth-century inventories, the contents of Maria's sarcophagus were truly a dazzling sight, a treasure trove in every sense of the word. A great deal of thought and care had gone into the young empress's burial. Notwithstanding the perils of attempting to decipher emotion from inanimate objects, as the opening quote of this book suggests, we can, however, surmise several things from Maria's tomb. Probably everyone in the imperial household contributed something of sentimental and high status value to accompany Maria in death. The items likely included her personal possessions, Theodosian family heirlooms, and also wedding gifts from her marriage to Honorius; perhaps those mentioned in Claudian's *Epithalamium* (Lanciani 1892, 204–5). If, as other sixteenth-century reports claim, there was a second body in the tomb with Maria, then some of the grave goods may be from this unknown person's interment. Honorius must have had a hand in deciding what went into his wife's casket, as would have her parents, Serena and Stilicho.

Apart from two items, everything else from Maria's tomb has vanished. The two surviving pieces are a crystal agate *simpulum* (ladle), held by the Museo degli Argenti in Florence, and an intricately decorated pendant made from agate, gold, emeralds, and rubies, now in the Louvre (Figure 6.7). This hollow

Figure 6.7 Maria *enkolpion/bulla.*
Source: © Louvre Museum, Paris. Photograph by Frederique Kartouby.

pendant – also the frontispiece of this book – is long been considered to be a *bulla* (seal), but more recently has been described as a religious *enkolpion*, a reliquary worn on the breast (Evans and Wixom 1997, 560; Hendrix 2016). When it was first found, Maria's *enkolpion* contained musk-fragranced earth, perhaps a relic from pilgrimage to the Holy Land. One side of the *bulla/enkolpion* is inscribed HONORI, MARIA, STELICHO, SERENA, and cut across with the word VIVATIS (Live!). The other side has STELICHO, SERENA, ECHERI (Eucherius), THERMANTIA, and also VIVATIS. The names on both sides combine to form the Chi-Rho symbol. For a woman about whom we know so little, we may infer from her grave goods that Maria was held in high esteem as a pious Christian.

Maria's remains were found in Honorius' mausoleum. This was either a new structure or an existing one that he reused for his family vault. Whichever was the case, Maria's death was the most likely reason that Honorius commissioned a personal sepulcher, but Saint Peter's resting place held significant meaning for the emperor. At some point during his 404 triumph in

Rome, Honorius visited the apostle's tomb, laid down his diadem, and struck himself on the breast, a curious gesture within a military triumphal context, since in Christian symbolism, to beat one's chest mean either sorrow or repentance. Perhaps Honorius sought forgiveness for the sin of pride, i.e. his ostentatious triumph. At any rate, Claudian does not mention it. The incident is instead referred to in a number of Augustine's sermons (McEvoy 2013, 172–4; Wienand 2015, 169–97).

When Honorius died in 423, he was interred in his mausoleum alongside his two wives, though his remains have yet to be found. Unless his tomb was looted during one of the several sacks that Rome endured through the Middle Ages, Honorius' mortal remains may still lie awaiting discovery, beneath the tread of the millions of pilgrims and tourists who visit Saint Peter's annually. Then again, the Church itself might simply have disposed of the emperor's remains, for Honorius' mausoleum was rededicated in 757 to an early Christian martyr, Saint Petronilla. Before this, however, the papacy was already using Saint Peter's crypts for their mausolea. McKitterick (2013) suggests that that late Roman popes did this in order to preserve that sacred space closest to the apostle's tomb for themselves. Thus, the papacy protected its role as Christ's representative on earth against any imperial claim. As for Maria and her unknown female companion, it is unclear as to what happened to their remains post-discovery.

References

Barnes, Timothy D. 1976. "The Historical Setting of Prudentius' *Contra Symmachorum.*" *AJP* 97: 373–86.

Barnwell, Paul S. 1993. *Emperor, Prefects and Kings: The Roman West, 395–565.* Chapel Hill, NC: University of North Carolina Press.

Bayless, William N. 1976. "The Visigothic Invasion of Italy in 401." *CJ* 71.1: 65–7.

Beard, Mary. 2007. *The Roman Triumph.* Cambridge, MA: Harvard University Press.

Bradley, Keith. 2005. "The Roman Child in Sickness and Health." In *The Roman Family in the Empire: Rome, Italy, and Beyond.* Edited by Michele George: 67–92. Oxford: Oxford University Press.

Cameron, Alan. 1970. *Poetry and Propaganda at the Court of Honorius.* Oxford: Oxford University Press.

Christ, Alice T. 2015. "The Importance of Being Stilicho: Diptychs as a Genre." In *Shifting Genres in Late Antiquity.* Edited by Geoffrey Greatrex and Hugh Elton with the assistance of Lucas McMahon: 173–88. Farnham: Ashgate.

Curran, John. 2000. *Pagan City and Christian Capital.* Oxford: Clarendon Press.

Deliyannis, Deborah M. 2010. *Ravenna in Late Antiquity.* Cambridge: Cambridge University Press.

Demougeot, Émilienne. 1951. *De l'unité à la division de l'Empire romain, 395–410: essai sur le gouvernement impérial.* Paris: Adrien-Maisonneuve.

Dey, Hendrik W. 2011. *The Aurelian Wall and the Refashioning of Imperial Rome, AD 271–855.* Cambridge and New York: Cambridge University Press.

Evans, Helen C., and Wixom, William D. 1997. *The Glory of Byzantium: Art and Culture of the Middle Byzantine Era, AD 843–1261.* New York: Metropolitan Museum of Art.

Evans Grubbs, Judith. 2002. *Women and the Law in the Roman Empire: A Sourcebook on Marriage, Divorce and Widowhood*. London and New York: Routledge.

Ferrill, Arther. 1997 (1986). *The Fall of the Roman Empire: The Military Explanation*. London: Thames and Hudson.

Frey, Karl. 1913. "Zur Baugeschichte des St. Peter: Mitteilungen aus der Reverendissima Fabbrica di S. Pietro." *JbPrKs* 33. Beiheft 84. 411: 1–153.

Gillett, Andrew. 2001. "Rome, Ravenna and the Last Western Emperors." *PBSR* 69: 131–67.

Hamelink, Anique M. 2015. *By My Beard! The Symbolic Value and Meaning of the Beard in Antiquity*. Case Studies in Roman Coinage: 1–18. Unpublished research paper. Leiden. Leiden University.

Heather, Peter. 1991. *Goths and Romans, 332–489*. Oxford Historical Monographs. Oxford: Clarendon Press.

Hendrix, David. 2016. *The Byzantine Legacy*. Online resource. https://thebyzantinelegacy.com.

Hersch, Karen K. 2010. *The Roman Wedding: Ritual and Meaning in Antiquity*. Cambridge and New York: Cambridge University Press.

Honoré, Tony. 1998. *Law in the Crisis of Empire, AD 379–455*. Oxford: Oxford University Press.

Hope, Valerie, and Marshall, Eireann (eds). 2000. *Death and Disease in the Ancient City*. London and New York: Routledge.

Hopkins, Keith. 1983. *Death and Renewal*, Volume 2. Sociological Studies in Roman History. Cambridge: Cambridge University Press.

Johnson, Mark J. 1991. "On the Burial Places of the Theodosian Dynasty." *Byzantion* 61: 330–9.

Johnson, Mark J. 2009. *The Roman Imperial Mausoleum in Late Antiquity*. Cambridge: Cambridge University Press.

Kalas, Gregor. 2015. *The Restoration of the Roman Forum in Late Antiquity: Transforming Public Space*. Austin, TX: The University of Texas Press.

Kampen, Natalie Boymel. 2009. *Family Fictions in Roman Art: Essays on the Representation of Powerful People*. Cambridge: Cambridge University Press.

Kiilerich, Bente. 1993. *Late Fourth Century Classicism in the Plastic Arts: Studies in the So-Called Theodosian Renaissance*. Odense: Odense University Press.

Kiilerich, Bente, and Torp, Hjalmar.1989. "Hic Est: Hic Stilicho: The Date and Interpretation of a Notable Diptych." *JDAI* 104: 319–71.

Lanciani, Rodolfo. 1892. *Pagan and Christian Rome*. Boston, MA and New York: Houghton, Mifflin and Co.

Lapatin, Kenneth. 2015. *Luxus: The Sumptuous Arts of Greece and Rome*. Los Angeles, CA: Getty Publications.

Lejdegård, Hans. 2002. *Honorius and the City of Rome: Authority and Legitimacy in Late Antiquity*. Uppsala: Uppsala Universitet.

MacCormack, Sabine. 1972. "Change and Continuity in Late Antiquity: The Ceremony of Adventus." *Hist.* 21.4: 721–52.

MacCormack, Sabine G. 1981. *Art and Ceremony in Late Antiquity*. Berkeley and Los Angeles, CA: University of California Press.

Mackie, Gillian. 2003. *Early Christian Chapels in the West: Decoration, Function, and Patronage*. Toronto: University of Toronto Press.

Marliano, Bartolemeo. 1548. *Le antichità di Roma*. Rome.

Matthews, John F. 1975. *Western Aristocracies and Imperial Court, AD 364–425*. Oxford: Clarendon Press.

Mayor, Adrienne. 1992. "Ambiguous Guardians: The 'Omen of the Wolves' (A.D. 402) and the 'Choking Doberman' (1980s)." *Journal of Folklore Research* 29.3: 253–68.

McCormick, Michael. 1990. *Eternal Victory: Triumphal Rulership in Late Antiquity, Byzantium and the Early Medieval West*. Cambridge: Cambridge University Press.

McEvoy, Meaghan. 2013. "The Mausoleum of Honorius: Late Roman Imperial Christianity and the City of Rome in the Fifth Century." In *Old Saint Peter's, Rome*. Edited by Rosamond McKitterick, John Osborne, Carol M. Richardson, and Joanna Story: 119–136. Cambridge: Cambridge University Press.

McKitterick, Rosamond. 2013. "The Representation of Old Saint Peter's Basilica in the Liber Pontificalis." In *Old Saint Peter's, Rome*. Edited by Rosamond McKitterick, John Osborne, Carol M. Richardson, and Joanna Story: 95–118. Cambridge: Cambridge University Press.

Nathan, Geoffrey S. 2000. *The Family in Late Antiquity: The Rise of Christianity and the Endurance of Tradition*. London and New York: Routledge.

Oost, Stewart Irvin. 1968. *Galla Placidia Augusta: A Biographical Essay*. Chicago, IL and London: The University of Chicago Press.

O' Flynn, John Michael. 1983. *Generalissimos of the Western Roman Empire*. Alberta: University of Alberta Press.

Paolucci, Fabrizio. 2008. "La tomba dell'imperatrice Maria e altre sepolture di rango di età tardoantica a San Pietro." *Temporis signa: archeologia della tarda antichità e del medioevo* 3: 225–52.

Parkes, Ruth. 2005. "Model Youths? Achilles and Parthenopaeus in Claudian's Panegyrics on the Third and Fourth Consulships of Honorius." *ICS* 30: 67–82.

Rawson, Beryl. 2003. *Children and Childhood in Roman Italy*. Oxford: Oxford University Press.

Scheidel, Walter. 1999. "Emperors, Aristocrats, and the Grim Reaper: Towards a Demographic Profile of the Roman Elite." *CQ* 49.1: 254–81.

Shaw, Brent D., and Saller, Richard P. 1984. "Close-Kin Marriage in Roman Society?" *MAN* 19.3: 432–44.

Shelton, Kathleen J. 1982. "The Diptych of the Young Office Holder." *JbAC* 25: 132–71.

Ware, Catherine. 2012. *Claudian and the Roman Epic Tradition*. Cambridge: Cambridge University Press.

Wasdin, Katherine. 2014. "Honorius Triumphant: Poetry and Politics in Claudian's Wedding Poems." *CP* 109.1: 48–65.

Wienand, Joachim. 2015. "O Tandem Felix Civili, Roma, Victoria! Civil-War Triumphs from Honorius to Constantine and Back." In *Contested Monarchy: Integrating the Roman Empire in the Fourth Century AD*. Oxford Studies in Late Antiquity. Edited by Johannes Wienand: 169–97. Oxford: Oxford University Press.

7 Pro patria

> The emperor Honorius, seeing that with so many usurpers opposing him he was unable to do anything against the barbarians, ordered that these usurpers be suppressed first.
>
> Orosius, *Historia adversum paganos*, 7.42.1

Into the abyss

Stilicho was western consul in 405, his second such appointment. He continued to press Arcadius to help him against the Visigoths, by now firmly entrenched in the Balkans, but had no success. A poisonous atmosphere existed at the eastern court, caused by greedy court eunuchs and their agents (Zos. 5.24). After the death of his wife, Eudoxia, Arcadius closed himself off even further from the outside world. Consequently, his palace bureaucracy gained more and more power in his court. Like Rufinus and Eutropius before them, these officials opposed Stilicho's attempts at improving relations between the brother emperors.

With Alaric at bay, and no indication of assistance from Constantinople, Stilicho thought to pacify the Gothic leader with a military command. Thus, Alaric became a Roman *magister militum*. He was no fool though. Alaric had first-hand experience of the true meaning of gifts and alliances with those Rome called barbarian. Time and again, Alaric had seen just how disposable foreign peoples like his own were to Roman interests. Nevertheless, Alaric accepted his commission, and retired to his stronghold at Epirus on the north-eastern Greek coast to bide his time and see what might present itself.

Alaric was not the only barbarian seeking fortune in the West. At the close of 405, a large barbarian force descended upon Italy under their leader Radagaisus, a Goth and a 'worshipper of demons' according to Augustine (*De civ. Dei*. 5.23). Primary written sources differ over the size of Radagaisus' force – anywhere between two to four hundred thousand warriors. Such figures are clearly exaggerated, but still, the numbers must have been significant to inspire such fear (Zos. 25.6.3; Oros. 7.37.4.13; Chron. Marcell. s.a. 406). Our sources also diverge on the length of time it took to bring Radagaisus to heel. It seems that nearly a year passed before Stilicho managed to deal with Radagaisus (Kulikowski 2007, 171). If so, the western Roman army must have been overstretched or undermanned. Consequently, Stilicho had to use Visigothic and Hunnic mercenaries against Radagaisus. These groups operated under their own commanders – the Visigoths under Sarus, the Huns under Uldin. In August 406, near Faesulae (modern Fiesole), Stilicho's mixed army routed Radagaisus' forces, slaughtering thousands of his men, and selling many thousands more into slavery. Stilicho also recruited a huge amount of surrendered Visigoths into the Roman army (Olymp. *fr.* 9). Radagaisus, meanwhile, was captured and beheaded. Stilicho had won a great victory for Honorius and the realm. Zosimus tells us that Stilicho was widely praised, but others like Augustine and Orosius, the latter ever hateful of the *magister*, censured Stilicho's role in Radagaisus' defeat (Zos. 5.26.1–5; cf. Aug. *De civ. Dei.* 5.23; Oros. 7.37.12–17).

In times like these

In the eye of the barbarian storm, Honorius called on the civilian populace of Gaul and northern Italy to enlist in the army in the defense of their home-land (*pro patria*). The emperor issued his call to arms from Ravenna through two edicts (*CTh.* 7.13.16. Feb 15, 406; 7.13.17. Feb 15, 406). Even slaves were included, despite there being strict laws against this. Furthermore, it was a capital offense for slaves to join the army without express approval (*CTh.* 7.13.8. Jan 29, 380; 7.13.11. May 15, 382; *Dig.* 49.16.8). But, in early 406, slaves were being urged to enlist, in exchange for their freedom. In the past, this had only happened in a national crisis, such as during Marcus Aurelius' German wars along the Rhine (SHA *Mar. Ant.* 21.6–7; 23.5). On occasions when slaves did enlist in the army, they were generally separate from regular units, poorly trained and equipped, and placed on the frontline (Le Bohec 1994, 72, 87). We do not know how many, or indeed if any, slaves heeded Honorius' call, but if they did, they were likely not well treated.

> Emperors Arcadius, Honorius and Theodosius Augustuses to the Provincials: In the matter of defense against hostile attacks, We order that consideration be given not only to the legal status of soldiers, but also to their physical strength. Although We believe that freeborn persons are aroused by love of country, We exhort slaves also, by the authority of this edict, that as soon as possible they shall offer themselves for the labors of war, and if they receive their arms as men fit for military ser-vice, they shall obtain the reward of freedom, and they shall also receive two solidi each for travel money (*viaticum*). Especially, of course, do We urge this service upon the slaves of those persons who are retained in the armed imperial service, and likewise upon the slaves of federated allies and of conquered peoples, since it is evident that they are making war also along with their masters.
>
> (*CTh.* 7.13.16. Feb 15, 406)

[Arcadius, Honorius, and Theodosius II] to the Provincials: On account of Our imminent necessities (*inminentibus necessitatibus*) by this edict We summon to military service all men who are aroused by the innate spirit of freedom. Freeborn persons, therefore, who take arms under the auspices of military service for love of peace and of country, shall know that they will receive ten solidi each from Our imperial treasure when affairs have been adjusted; however, We order that three of the aforesaid sum be paid each man now. For We believe that the best soldiers will be those whose courage and concern for the public welfare have brought them forward for the present needs.

(*CTh*. 7.13.17. Feb 15, 406)

CTh. 7.13.16 offered a *viaticum* (travel expense) of 3 gold solidi to any 'freeborn' – remember what this term meant in the late empire – citizens if they joined the army. It has been argued that Honorius' financial subvention meant his treasury was in the red by early 406 (Ward-Perkins 2005, 42–3). However, the *viaticum* was a standard military recruitment practice for centuries. Domitian, for instance, had paid his soldiers a *viaticum* of 3 gold aurei (Suet. *Dom*. 7.3; Alston 1994). Honorius' small down payment was sensible, therefore. It was designed to stop potential recruits reneging on their commitment. As the barbarian crisis deepened, not only did money matter for military payment, but for propaganda as well. Honorius' coinage of this period emphasized the virtues of fortitude and courage (Figure 7.1). Through

Figure 7.1 Silver siliqua of Honorius. Rome mint, 407. Obv. Honorius pearl-diademed, draped, and cuirassed. Legend: DN-HONORI-VS-PF-AVG (*Dominus Noster Honorius Pius Felix Augustus*/Our Lord Honorius, pious and fortunate Augustus). Rev. Roma seated on cuirass, Victoriola in her right hand, an inverted spear in her left. Legend: VIRTVS-RO-MANORVM (Strength of the Romans). Exergue: RM (Roma)-PS (*Pusulatum*/pure silver).
Source: *RIC* X 1267; *RSC* V 59.

coinage, Honorius could at least reassure and inform his subjects that the state still functioned under his authority.

The barbarian Rubicon

After Radagaisus' defeat in August 406, more barbarians transgressed the northern frontier. Our fragmented sources are confusing, but, at some point in late 406, a tribal confederation that included Vandals, Alans, and Sueves breached the Rhine *limes* and crossed into Gaul. In terms of its size and impact, the barbarian crossing of the River Rhine has caused endless controversy among historians (Clinton 1850, 134; Stevens, 1957, 317ff.; Kulikowski 2000, 325–425; Liebeschuetz 2003, 63–5; Birley 2005, 457–9; Ward-Perkins 2005, 39–40; Heather 2005, 376ff.). Contemporary observers certainly did not dispute the effects of the Rhine incursion upon western provinces. Regions were devastated, and lawlessness reigned throughout Gaul, northern Italy, and eventually in Spain (Kulikowski 2004, 151ff.). The dam had well and truly given way. Orientius of Auch declared that 'throughout every neighbourhood, villa, crossroad and rural district … there was death, grief, destruction, slaughter, fire, and mourning' (*Comm.* II.181–4). A good many other primary sources provide similar narratives of barbarian atrocities. Such accounts are far too numerous for them all to be exaggerated or fictitious, as some historians have claimed. Jerome's comment – 'we dread the barbarians more than shipwreck' – written near Bethlehem in 399, was given new definition by the events of the early 400s (*Ep.* 77.8). Whichever way modern historians prefer to see them, the barbarian incursions were not peaceful, and they terrified the Roman world. So much so, that just a few years later, an anonymous Christian poet looked in vain to God for answers.

> When the image of our smoking fatherland has passed before our mind, and universal destruction stands before our eyes, we are broken and the tears water our cheeks without restraint … why have so many cities perished … why have so many peoples deserved such evil … For ten years we have been cut down by the slaughtering swords of the Vandals and of the Visigoths. No forts set on rocks, no towns on lofty mountains, or cities protected by mighty rivers, not all together have been able to overcome the wiles of the barbarians and their raging weapons – we have suffered the ultimate calamity. The same tempest destroyed both the good and the wicked … there was no order in such a compounding of evils.
>
> (*De prov. Dei.* 15–63)

Britain, the far removed island

By 407, Honorius was confronted with a multitude of challenges. The Rhine frontier had collapsed, and barbarians ran wild through Gaul. In response to the unfolding disasters on the mainland, the Roman army in Britain

Figure 7.2 Gold solidus of Constantine III. Lyon mint, *c.* 407–8. Obv. Constantine rosette-diademed, draped, and cuirassed. Legend: DN-CONSTAN-TINVS-PF-AVG (*Dominus Noster Constantinus Pius Felix Augustus/* Our Lord Constantine, pious and fortunate emperor). Rev. Constantine in armor and cloak, standing, *labarum* in his right hand, Victoriola in his left, his left foot trampling a bearded captive. Legend: VICTORIA-AAAVGGGG (Victoria Augustorum/Victory of the Augusti). Field: L/D (Lugdunum). Exergue: COMOB (*Comitatus obryziacum/*pure gold mark).

Source: *RIC* X 1506.

revolted and raised three emperors in a row. The first two had very short tenures, but the third, known to us as Constantine III (407–11), had more luck. Zosimus states that the British revolts were the direct consequence of the Rhine crossing (Zos. 6.3.1–3). Yet, the catalyst for the Romano-British mutiny could well have been Honorius' policy of civilian and slave enlistment – a difficult pill to swallow for professional soldiers, all the more so for those in Britain whose salaries had been sporadic for several years (Frere 1991, 363–4). In Spring 407, Constantine crossed to Gaul and captured Lyon, and by 408, had established his court at Arles, from where he minted coins (Figure 7.2) proclaiming himself as a imperial colleague with Honorius, Arcadius, and possibly Theodosius II (Lafaurie 1953; Stevens 1957; Bastien 1987; Drinkwater 1998; Kulikowski 2000; Doyle 2014). Until his defeat and execution in 411, Constantine III continued to be a problem for Honorius, who even recognized the usurper for a short period, just as Theodosius I had had to do with Magnus Maximus.

On the subject of the end of Roman Britain, much has been made of a line from Zosimus, perhaps in about 410, that claims 'Honorius sent letters to the cities in Britain, urging them to fend for themselves' (6.8.10). The reference to Britain is an error of mistranslation. David Woods has convincingly put to rest any debate about Honorius' role in abandoning Britain. Honorius did urge the administration of certain cities to look to their own defenses, just not

Romano-British ones. The emperor's advice seems to have been for the cities of Raetia, on the northern Danubian frontier (Woods 2012, 818–26).

Honorius in Rome

In 407, Honorius was consul for the seventh time, an event he celebrated in Rome. Though not well documented, Honorius' visit to Rome in early 407 is nonetheless attested by three laws he issued from there between February and March (*CTh*. 16.5.40; 7.13.18; 7.20.13; Gillett 2001; Lejdegård 2002, 88–90). The interesting point here is that two of these laws were addressed directly to Stilicho, who seems to have been in Ravenna at this point. Does this mean that relations were less than cordial between the two men? Stilicho had been present at Honorius' side for every major ceremony thus far in the emperor's reign. It has been suggested that the reason why Stilicho was in Ravenna was that he was fortifying Ravenna's defenses (Gillett 2001, 140). This may be so, but it is also possible that Honorius was in Rome acting on his own behalf, seeking out potential allies to help him free himself of Stilicho.

The second marriage of Honorius

Serena was also in Rome in early 407, just as Honorius seemed to be taking matters into his own hands. She attempted to rein him in by arranging his marriage to her other daughter, Aemilia Materna Thermantia. Zosimus says that Honorius was enthusiastic about the prospect, but that Stilicho was not so keen. Be that as it may, we are given no convincing explanation for Stilicho's reluctance, or, for that matter, Honorius' eagerness (Zos. 5.28.1). Indeed, we know nothing of the wedding itself other than that it happened (Olymp. *fr*. 3; Zos. 5.28.1–3; Chron. Marcell. s.a. 408). Honorius' marriage to Thermantia is so noticeably unremarkable for several reasons. Firstly, it was a rushed effort designed to retain Serena and Stilicho's waning control of the emperor, now nearly twenty-three years of age. Stilicho's reticence was therefore out of concern that his political enemies would think him desperate, and thus vulnerable. Secondly, there was a question of morality. As well as being related by blood, Thermantia was the emperor's sister-in-law. Although Honorius' first marriage seems to have been generally accepted, would a second such union be well received, by the Church or the public?

The price of friendship

By 408, with the threat from Constantine III growing and no sign of relief from Constantinople, Stilicho persuaded Alaric to move into Gaul in order to suppress the usurper. However, Alaric claimed that first he needed to be paid for prior services to the empire. It was extortion, of course, but Stilicho needed the Visigoths, and so he went to Rome to request funds from the senate to pay the barbarians. There was outcry on the senate floor when Stilicho delivered

Alaric's bill of 5,000 pounds of gold, 30,000 pounds of silver, and an enormous quantity of spices and silks. One incensed senator, Lampadius, declared 'this is not peace but a pact of slavery,' but instantly regretted his candor, and sought sanctuary in a church, fearful of what Stilicho might do (Zos. 5.29.9). Despite senatorial resentment, Alaric was paid, but many among the western élite saw this as appeasement. The complaint about the amount which Alaric demanded is odd. As we have already seen, the average annual income from a rich Roman senator's estates was well over 5,000 pounds of gold. Even moderately wealthy Roman élites had yearly incomes of about 1,500 pounds of gold (Olymp. *fr*. 41.2). What was the problem, then, with the amount that Stilicho needed to pay Alaric? The senatorial class could surely afford to pay this between them. But, as Lampadius had pointed out, if Rome conceded to the barbarian this time, more ultimatums would inevitably follow, and nobody knew where it all might end.

Elements in the Roman military and civilian hierarchy saw Stilicho's policy towards Alaric as defeatist. Yet, as difficult as this strategy was to accept, the situation facing the West in 408 was dire. Honorius was surrounded by hostile forces – Alaric, Constantine, and the various other barbarian groups. Hence, as this chapter's opening quote from Orosius states, Honorius chose to deal with his domestic enemies first. Then, fate intervened through an unexpected event in May 408 which irrevocably changed everything for Honorius and Stilicho. Aged just thirty-one, Arcadius died unexpectedly at Constantinople. His seven-year-old son Theodosius II was now the sole eastern emperor. Honorius wanted to travel to Constantinople to secure his nephew's succession, but was persuaded by Stilicho to remain in the west to deal with Constantine's revolt (Zos. 31.1–6). Instead, Stilicho reasoned with the emperor that he should go east to fulfill a promise he had made to Theodosius – to protect the imperial dynasty. Unfortunately for Stilicho, as he readied to leave, plans were already in motion to remove him from power.

Coup d'état, August 408

Stilicho's downfall has been told and retold many times. In the modern era, i.e. from Gibbon to the present, Stilicho's rise and spectacular disgrace has served as a warning about the folly of overreaching for ultimate power. The following section therefore details the central events of how Stilicho met his end and shows how, when that end came, at the direction of Honorius, it was swift, thorough, and merciless.

By the summer of 408, a court official named Olympius, the master of the imperial secretarial bureau (*magister scriniorum*), had gained the emperor's confidence. Stilicho had helped Olympius attain his high office, but now in mid-408, he turned against his patron, and plotted against him (Olymp. *fr*. 2). It has been questioned whether or not Honorius was directly involved in overthrowing Stilicho, but he must have been, since he saw the entire operation through with determined resolve. On August 13, 408, Honorius convened his military high command at Ticinum (modern Pavia). Most of this group were Stilicho's favorites. The emperor, Olympius, and the high command were in Ticinum to oversee the army's deployment to Gaul for the coming campaign against Constantine. The plan was that Honorius' troops would rendezvous with Alaric's *foederati* en route to the western front. All of this was Stilicho's arrangement. Sozomen takes up the narrative.

> After the death of Arcadius, Honorius projected a journey to Constantinople, on behalf of his nephew, to appoint officers faithful to his security and empire; for he held his nephew in the place of his son, and he was fearful lest the boy might suffer on account of his youth, since he would be exposed to plots; but when Honorius was on the very point of setting out on this journey, Stilicho dissuaded him from his design, by proving to him that his presence was requisite in Italy, to repress the schemes of Constantine, who sought to possess himself of the sovereign power at Arles. Stilicho then took (an imperial scepter) ... obtained some letters from the emperor, with which he set out, at the head of four legions, to carry on war in the east; but a report having been spread that he had conspired against the emperor, and had formed a scheme, in conjunction with those in power, to raise his son (Eucherius) to the throne, the troops rose up in sedition, and slew the Praetorian Prefect of Italy and of Gaul, the military commanders, and the chief officers of the court.
>
> (Soz. 9.4.4–8)

Sozomen did not exaggerate. With one decisive blow, practically all of Stilicho's senior allies in government and the military were wiped out. Under the searing August sun, the soldiers embarked on a frenzied killing spree through the streets of Ticinum. Zosimus informs us that the soldiers lost all control, indiscriminately butchering many innocents in the process (5.32.1–7). In fact, Honorius himself intervened to try to stop the bloodshed, at great risk to his person. The emperor showed real courage and complete disregard for his own life. Eventually, Honorius realized that he had no choice but to get off the streets, yet his actions in the face of danger ought to be commended.

> When the evil had advanced beyond cure, the emperor donned a short tunic, without cloak or diadem, and came out into the middle of the city. With very great difficulty, he managed to check the soldiers' rage ... even clasping the emperor's feet did not suffice to save (them) from death. The mutiny continued until late afternoon and the emperor withdrew for fear of being harmed himself ... magistrates fell victims to the soldiers' insanity, but there also perished a host of ordinary people not easy to calculate.
>
> (Zos. 5.32.5–7)

Stilicho was still in the old Etruscan town of Bononia (Bologna), preparing to travel east, when he first heard of the massacre. Unsure whether Honorius was living or dead, Stilicho was deliberating on what to do next to restore order, when he received news that the emperor was alive and well, but had issued an arrest warrant for Stilicho himself, charging the *magister* with plotting to place his son Eucherius upon the western throne. Stilicho promptly left Bononia for Ravenna, hoping perhaps to work things out with the emperor (Zos. 5.33–4). It proved impossible to get anywhere near Honorius, however, and Stilicho had to take refuge inside a church in Ravenna, accompanied by a few bodyguards. On August 22, nine days after the Ticinum bloodbath, Honorius' agents tracked Stilicho down and delivered a letter of clemency from the emperor to him. In front of the bishop of the church, Stilicho was assured safe passage to Honorius' court if he surrendered quietly. Stilicho accepted, walked out into the sunlight, whereupon he was handed a second imperial letter ordering his summary execution. His bodyguard went to protect him, but he refused their aid and, after thirteen years at the helm of Honorius' government, Stilicho was put to death at Honorius' command (Olymp. *fr.* 5; Zos. 5.34.4–5). Orosius later remarked that 'thus provoked, the army rightly cut Stilicho down,' though the ecclesiastical historian's glibness had more to do with a dislike of the man's ethnicity and undue influence over Honorius than anything else (7.38.5).

The order of death

When Stilicho was killed, Eucherius fled to Rome to join his mother, Serena, but never reached her and, like his father, was forced to take sanctuary in a church. Meanwhile, a wave of anti-foreign hysteria swept across Italy, stoked by wild rumors of Stilicho's treason and double-dealings with Alaric. In the ensuing turmoil, Roman troops massacred the families of Stilicho's barbarian *foederati*, probably those captured after Faesulae who had joined the imperial army (Heather 1991, 213–14). These men subsequently deserted to Alaric's cause en masse. Who, if anyone, ordered the civilians' massacre is unknown. Events were rapidly spiraling out of control. Furthermore, now that Stilicho was gone, Alaric's direct means of extorting money from the empire vanished. Thus, the Visigoths marched on Rome, intent upon further financial gain (Zos. 5.37.4).

Honorius' next move was to locate and eliminate Eucherius, who, as our main sources allege, was part of his father's plot against the emperor (Zos. 5.32.1; Oros. 7.38.1–6; Soz. 9.4.1; Jord. *Rom.* 322). How did Honorius feel about ordering Eucherius' execution? The two young men had known each other all their lives. Did the emperor struggle to suppress his personal feelings for the sake of the state's security, or had he long harbored resentment for his young kinsman? It is hard to discern, but perhaps it was the latter sentiment. Honorius seems to have repudiated his wife, Thermantia, immediately after Stilicho's execution, which suggests the emperor's desire for total total separation from Stilicho's family. Alternatively, Honorius did not want to face his wife after killing her father, which he was about to do to her brother.

The emperor Honorius then ordered that his wife, Thermantia, be dismissed from the imperial throne and restored to her mother, although she was not under any resulting suspicion. He also ordered Stilicho's son, Eucherius, to be tracked down and killed, but when he was found in some church at Rome where he had taken refuge, out of respect for the place they let him be.

(Zos. 5.35.3–4)

Honorius' agents returned to Eucherius' church refuge and demanded that its bishop hand him over to the emperor's authority. The bishop refused – he had probably heard how church asylum had fared for Eucherius' father. Undeterred, the assassins gave the bishop a letter from Honorius which apparently superseded the fugitive's claim to church protection (Olymp. *fr.* 7). The bishop acquiesced to Honorius' order, and Eucherius was taken beyond the church precincts and put to death. The execution was carried out quickly since Alaric was close to Rome, for, as Zosimus charged, if the Goth had reached Eucherius before Honorius' men, he would have elevated the young man to the western throne.

Next, it was the turn of Serena, the woman who, according to Claudian, was more dear to Honorius than his own mother, Flaccilla (Cl. *Nupt.* 38ff.). All that affection, if indeed it had ever existed, disappeared. Serena became caught up in the savage proscriptions of her husband and his affiliates, though this seems to have been more by chance than by design. What happened was that when Alaric reached Rome in late September, and tried to reach an agreement with Honorius for land and pay, the emperor refused. Olympius and others were virulently anti-barbarian, and persuaded Honorius to follow the same line. Aggrieved at this response, Alaric put the city under siege. Mass terror convulsed the city, and consequently anti-barbarian feeling erupted within its walls. Serena was an easy target for the mob. Hoping to quell the public anger, the Roman senate accused her of collusion with Alaric and sentenced her to death (Zos. 5.38; Olymp. *fr.* 7). Placidia's presence in Rome somehow lent legitimacy to the senate's judgment, and Theodosius' favorite niece was garroted for the crime of high treason.

Actually, the condemnation and death of Serena is where we encounter our first proper mention of Placidia in the historical record. It is, however, vague as to why Placidia's mere presence gave the senate carte blanche to execute Serena. Honorius' sister had not played any role in his administration thus far. If Placidia had played a more central part in Serena's death than indicated, we are not told what that was (Oost 1968, 81–6). The fact that the senate went through with Serena's execution, apparently with no fear of backlash from the court, tells us that they were aware of the emperor's true feelings towards Serena. It may well be that Placidia's role in all of this was to reassure them that her brother would not seek retribution if they removed their troublesome foster mother.

No tangible evidence was uncovered by Honorius' administration that could prove Stilicho's guilt. In other words, there was no 'smoking gun.' Nonetheless, Stilicho was condemned via *damnatio memoriae*, which involved legal censure, property confiscation, and the erasure of his name from most public inscriptions (*CIL* 6.41381; 6.1731). In the months following Stilicho's death, Honorius' new *consistorium*, headed by Olympius, who helped the emperor select this group, went to great effort to find proof of Stilicho's treason. A significant number of Stilicho's former associates were subjected to trial by torture – a legal requisite in late antiquity – but nothing these victims had to say incriminated the deceased *magister* (Olymp. *fr.* 2; Oros. 7.38.6; Soz. 9.4). The executioners of both Stilicho and Eucherius were promoted. For example, Heraclianus, Stilicho's killer, became the new *comes Africae*. Heraclianus replaced Bathanarius, Stilicho's brother-in-law, who was himself executed as part of the crackdown. A series of imperial constitutions were enacted against Stilicho, Eucherius, and their circle. One law in particular dealt with the executed men's alleged crime of aiding and abetting barbarians against the state.

> [Emperors Honorius and Theodosius II] to Theodorus, Praetorian Prefect. We order that every avenue for the recovery of property shall be closed to those persons who have given their resources, either incorporeal or corporeal, to the public brigand (Stilicho) or to his son (Eucherius) or other satellites, which resources that brigand used to enrich and to incite all the barbarians.
>
> (*CTh.* 9.42.22. Nov 22, 408)

Retribution

After the coup of 408, Honorius' problems rapidly mounted. Alaric, though he had lifted his siege of Rome for a ransom, was still threatening Italy and continuing to press Honorius for somewhere to settle his people permanently. Constantine III ruled most of Gaul and Spain, and made his eldest son Constans his colleague. However, Constantine had his own dilemma. His *magister* Gerontius rebelled against him, murdered Constans, and installed his own puppet, Maximus, at Barcino (Barcelona) in Spain (Figure 7.3). Two of Honorius' Spanish cousins, Didymus and Verenianus, had resisted Constantine's takeover of the Iberian peninsula, but failed and were executed, an act which sealed Constantine's fate later (Zos. 5.43.2).

By April 409, Honorius was frustrated by Olympius' arrogance. Since helping to depose Stilicho, Olympius had become *magister officiorum* at Ravenna, and abused his position by interfering with peace talks with Alaric. In addition, Olympius failed to organize an effective resistance against Constantine III. The western branch of the Theodosian house was in serious danger, and Olympius was a liability to its existence. Honorius therefore

Figure 7.3 Silver siliqua of Maximus of Spain. Barcelona mint, *c.* 410–11. Obv. Maximus pearl-diademed, draped, and cuirassed. Legend: DN-MAXIM[V]S-PF-A[VG] (*Dominus Noster Maximus Pius Felix Augustus*/Our Lord Maximus, pious and fortunate emperor). Rev. Roma seated upon cuirass, Victoriola in her right hand, inverted spear in her left. Legend: VICTOR[I]A-AVGGG (*Victoria Augustorum*/Victory of the Augusti). Exergue: [SMBA] (*Sacra Moneta Barcino*).

Source: *RIC* X 1601; *RSC* 1b.

handed Olympius over to his new *magister militum* Constantius to deal with. Constantius, a tough, no-nonsense soldier, had the man mutilated, then beaten to death (Olymp. *fr.* 8.2; Zos. 5.47.2–3).

Constantius then got down to the business of suppressing the western rebellion. In autumn 411, Constantius defeated Constantine III at Arles and compelled him to capitulate. The usurper renounced his imperial claim, took ecclesiastical vows, and cried mercy. The ploy did not save him from Honorius' anger. Constantine's murder of the emperor's Spanish cousins was not forgotten, and the usurper was put to death along with his youngest son (Olymp. *fr.* 16–17; Soz. 9.15.1). Their severed heads were displayed in several major western cities, before finally adorning the walls of Ravenna – a grim reminder of the consequences of treason (Olymp. *fr.* 20). The warning went unheeded, for the removal of Stilicho had opened the floodgates of rebellion against Honorius. Those who took up arms against their emperor believed that, without his old protector, Honorius would quickly fall.

Alaric, Attalus, and the assaults on Rome

As Constantine III gathered his strength in Gaul, another pretender emerged, Priscus Attalus, a Roman senator. Attalus was no military opportunist. His elevation was entirely Alaric's creation, just like Arbogastes' promotion of

Eugenius in 392. How did it happen that, yet again, the West found itself in a similar position in 409?

After learning of Stilicho's execution, Alaric tried to negotiate with Honorius for a land settlement in the northern province of Noricum (roughly modern Austria and Slovenia), along the Danube. Alaric got nowhere with the emperor, despite the best efforts of several high-ranking Romans. So, Alaric blockaded Rome hoping to force Honorius to the table, as we have seen. During this siege, in which Serena lost her life, the city starved to the point that they 'were in danger of turning to cannibalism, after trying every abomination known to man' (Zos. 5.40.1). Rome made its own arrangements and paid the Visigoths to withdraw. Honorius agreed to make an alliance with Alaric, who marched towards Ravenna to meet the emperor and conclude this deal. En route, Honorius' forces attacked the Visigoths, but were defeated. Betrayed by the emperor, Alaric withdrew to deliberate on his next move.

In late 409, Alaric returned to Rome. He tried and failed to come to terms with Honorius, and so he again besieged the city. The Goth had asked not only for gold and provisions, but also for a military position in which he could serve the emperor. Honorius granted the money and food supplies, but not the commission. Sozomen tells us that even the pope of Rome, Bishop Innocent I (402–17), was involved in these talks, as was the pretorian prefect for Illyricum, Jovius, who knew Alaric from their previous dealings through Stilicho (*PLRE* II, 623–4). Yet, try as they might to convince Honorius to accept the Visigoth's proposal, the emperor stuck to his position, and refused Alaric a military command (Soz. *HE*. 9.7).

The historians Zosimus and Procopius criticized Honorius as a weak, indecisive dilettante because, in their view, he ought to have accommodated Alaric, and thereby prevented the subsequent sack of Rome (Zos. 5.36.1–3; Proc. *BV*. 3.2.25–6). This advice comes from historians who regale us with tales of a drugged, impotent Honorius feeding pet chickens as Rome burned! Honorius did exactly what he should have done: nothing. Faced with so much uncertainty – a divided military, reliant on dubious barbarian allies, having just purged his government of suspected traitors, and surrounded by sycophants – Honorius could not give in to the barbarian's extortion. If he did, there was no way of knowing how much more Alaric would demand. If Alaric was seen to get what he wanted simply through intimidating Honorius, it would give others a green light to do the same. No, the emperor had to stand firm, no matter the cost, or the West really was lost.

As Alaric prosecuted his second siege of Rome, unable to assault its walls, so well restored as they had been by Honorius, the food situation in the city grew so bad that some people apparently turned to cannibalism for sustenance (Jer. *Ep*. 127.12; Aug. *De civ. Dei*. 22.12; Soz. 9.8; Olymp. *fr*. 10.2; Zos. 6.11.1–2). In effect, Rome became a giant prison camp. Its people were unable to get out, the enemy outside unable to get in. It is a point of note that this is the first recorded instance of siege cannibalism in a Roman city. Cannibalism was long considered to be a preserve of barbarians. Even more interesting is that starvation was a common Roman military tactic used to subjugate others. It seems that Rome's centuries-old foreign policies had finally come home to roost. Alaric's assault upon the ancient heart of the empire was, to apply a modern term, blowback.

Honorius the delayer

Concerned that he would not have anyone left alive in Rome to take hostage, Alaric raised the siege, and installed the senator Priscus Attalus as western Augustus (Figure 7.4). If Honorius would not come round, Alaric might fare better with an alternative sovereign. To some degree he did, for Attalus made Alaric his *magister militum*. The new *magister* advised Attalus to quickly seize North Africa with Visigothic troops, held for Honorius by the *comes* Heraclianus, thereby securing Africa for the usurper, and denying Ravenna its vital grain supply. However, Attalus did not heed Alaric's advice, perhaps suspicious of sending barbarians to take control of the West's most vital resource, and sent an inadequately sized force to Africa which Heraclianus promptly destroyed as soon as it arrived. Honorius then ordered Heraclianus to withhold grain shipments from Carthage to Rome, thus further pressurizing Attalus' illegal regime.

While these events were taking place, Attalus sent Alaric to attack Honorius in Ravenna. Zosimus alleges that Honorius prepared to flee the capital by

Figure 7.4 Silver siliqua of Priscus Attalus. Rome mint, *c.* 409–10. Obv. Attalus pearl-diademed, draped, and cuirassed. Legend: PRISCVS-ATTA[L]VS-PF-AVG (*Priscus Attalus Pius Felix Augustus*/Priscus Attalus, pious and fortunate emperor). Rev. Roma seated on cuirass, Victoriola in her right hand, inverted spear in her left. Legend: INVICTA-RO-MA-AETERNA (Invincible Eternal Rome). [P]S (*Pusulatum*/pure silver)-T (*officina* mark?).
Source: *RIC* X 1411; *RSC* 7a.

ship until, at the last minute, he was reprieved by the arrival of four thousand troops sent by Theodosius II from Constantinople. Zosimus claimed that these reinforcements had been arranged earlier by Stilicho, but only now arrived, well over a year later (Zos. 6.8.1–3). Olympiodorus, an actual contemporary of this event, says that the eastern detachments were unexpected (Olymp. *fr.* 10). It could well be that both historians are wrong, and that Honorius himself had requested aid from his nephew's government. This is my conjecture, of course, but it would explain Honorius' intransigence in the face of Alaric and Attalus.

Honorius followed his father's technique for how to deal with usurpers when under constraints. He endeavored to buy himself time by offering to share power with Attalus, who took this as a symptom of weakness, and dismissed it out of hand. A more severe response was urged by Jovius, Attalus' new pretorian prefect for Italy. Jovius had been initially sent by Honorius to parley with Alaric, but had betrayed the emperor and joined with the usurper. Jovius advised his new master that the only way to resolve the crisis was the capture, mutilation, and deposition of Honorius. That way at least, Attalus could avoid committing regicide. Attalus was sickened by this suggestion and refused to countenance such an inglorious deed. More than likely, Attalus did not trust Jovius, who had so eagerly betrayed his former emperor (Olymp. *fr.* 14).

Meanwhile, a large Alan, Suevic, and Vandal war band, flushed from their looting of Gaul, overran Spain, taking advantage of Constantine III's internal problems there with Gerontius and his puppet emperor Maximus. Spain fell into absolute chaos, as Hydatius relates.

> Thus, with the four plagues of sword, famine, pestilence, and wild beasts raging everywhere throughout the world, the annunciations foretold by the Lord through his prophets came to fulfillment.
>
> (Hyd. s.a. 410)

Apocalypse in Rome

By the summer of 410, Alaric realized that his tactics were not working. Attalus' elevation had been a mistake, and Honorius had proved more resilient than expected. In a last attempt to get what he ultimately wanted – land and Roman military command – Alaric deposed and exiled Attalus, apparently in an agreement reached with Honorius. Honorius then pardoned the members of Attalus' administration (Soz. 9.8). However, Alaric was thwarted in his attempts to reach terms with Honorius. While traveling north to Ravenna, Alaric was attacked by Sarus, a fellow Visigoth and Honorian loyalist, who had a blood feud with him (Olymp. *fr.* 11; Soz. 9.9.2–5). Angered by what he perceived as the emperor's duplicity, Alaric returned south to Rome, where he besieged the city for the third and final time. The Visigoth knew exactly what the city of Rome meant to Honorius, and what it represented to the empire as a whole. It turned out to be the shortest of Alaric's three sieges.

On August 24, it is alleged that somebody opened the city's Salarian Gate and let the Visigoths in (Proc. *BV*. 3.2.25–9). We can hardly condemn whoever may have done this, since the city's inhabitants had already endured so much deprivation. Whatever else about the physical effects of Rome's sack – and we should be in no doubt that considerable violence was involved – the psychological impact was immense (Oost 1968, 96–8; Lipps et al. 2013). Rome's defenses had been breached by a foreign foe, something which had not happened since the Celts raided the city in about 390 BC.

Between August 24 and 27, the Visigoths spent three days loading up their wagons with as much treasure as they could carry, including many Roman prisoners, rich and poor (Curran 2000, 304ff.). The most famous of all Alaric's captives was Placidia, the emperor's sister. Marcellinus Comes claimed she was abducted (s.a. 410). Actually, it seems that Placidia was already in Visigothic hands prior to the city's sack (Zos. 6.12.3). Thermantia, Honorius's forgotten wife, must have been in the city, but she seems to have escaped detection, perhaps taking refuge in a church, for we are told by multiple sources – Christian and otherwise – that Alaric forbade his men from entering ecclesiastical property (Olymp. *fr*. 11; Soz. *HE*. 9.9; Soc. *HE*.7.10; Hyd. *Chron*. s.a. 410). Zosimus unfortunately cannot help us here, as his history is incomplete, breaking off just a month before Alaric ransacked Rome. It would have been interesting to know his thoughts on barbarian behavior during the city's pillage. Orosius denies any barbarian crimes were committed against Christians, though this is at odds with certain other accounts (7.39.1–18). For Orosius, the Visigoths were the very model of piety, even if they were heretical Arians. Orosius claimed that those who took refuge inside church property were left in peace. Church attendance in Rome must therefore have been at a record high in late August 410.

> Alaric came, besieged, threw into panic, and burst into Rome as she trembled, but he first gave the order that whoever had fled to the holy places, above all to the basilicas of the Holy Apostles Peter and Paul, were to be left safe and unharmed. He also told his men that, as far as possible, they must refrain from shedding blood in their hunger for booty.
>
> (Oros. 7.39.1)

Alaric after Rome

Placidia was taken prisoner, along with many thousands of her fellow Romans, a high-value prize for Alaric whom he meant to use against her brother as a bargaining tool. However, as noted above, Placidia seems already to have been Alaric's hostage. In that case, she may have been used as a bargaining chip against Honorius before the Visigothic leader took the city in frustration at the emperor's obstinacy. Yet, Alaric did not live to see any of his goals through. Having exhausted the city and environs of Rome, Alaric's long troupe of captives, spoils, and soldiers plundered their way south through Campania, and embarked via ship for Sicily (Olymp. *fr.* 11.2; 16). A sudden storm wrecked the Visigothic flotilla, forcing them back to Italy. Alaric became sick and died at Consentia (Cosenza, Calabria). He was buried in a secret tomb, and succeeded as leader of the Visigoths by his brother-in-law Ataulf, who had been with him in Italy since 408 (Olymp. *fr.* 11.4; Zos. 5.37.1). Ataulf stayed in Italy until the following year, and in 412, he crossed into Gaul, taking Placidia as well as the deposed Attalus along with him. In Gaul, Ataulf would marry Placidia in 414.

The age of disobedience

By the beginning of 412, three new usurpers opposed Honorius, two in Gaul, the other in North Africa. As Hydatius put it, 'the brothers Jovinus and Sebastianus within Gaul, and in Africa Heraclianus, were filled with the same mad desire to seize the throne (s.a. 412). Jovinus was elevated at Mainz in late 411, with Alan and Burgundian support, and in 412 he appointed his brother Sebastianus as his co-Augustus (Figures 7.5 and 7.6). Their joint usurpation was really nothing more than a puppet regime for the leaders of their barbarian forces. Their illegal rule lasted until the summer of 413, when they were destroyed by a Visigothic army under Ataulf, acting in Honorius' name.

Figure 7.5 Gold solidus of Jovinus. Arles mint, *c.* 411–13. Obv. Jovinus pearl-diademed, draped, and cuirassed. Legend: DN-IOVIN-VS-PF-AVG (*Dominus Noster Iovinus Pius Felix Augustus*/Our Lord Jovinus, pious and fortunate emperor). Rev. Jovinus, in armor and cloak, standing, *labarum* in his right hand, Victoriola in his left, his left foot trampling a prostrate captive. Legend: RESTITV-TOR-REIP (*Restitutor Reipublicae*/Restorer of the State). Field: A/R (Arelate). Exergue: COMOB (*Comitatus obryziacum*/pure gold mark).

Source: *RIC* X 1708.

Figure 7.6 Silver siliqua of Sebastianus. Arles mint, *c.* 412–13. Arelate (Arles) mint.
Obv. Sebastianus pearl-diademed, draped, and cuirassed. Legend: [DN-SE]
BASTIA-NVS-PF-AVG (*Dominus Noster Sebastianus Pius Felix Augustus*/
Our Lord Sebastianus, pious and fortunate emperor). Rev. Roma seated,
Victoriola in her right hand, inverted spear in her left. Legend: RES[TITV]-
TOR-REIP (*Restitutor Reipublicae*/Restorer of the State). Exergue: KON
(Arelate)-T (*officina* mark).
Source: Unpublished.

The brothers were killed, and their decapitated heads followed the same route
as that of Constantine III (Drinkwater 1998; 2007, 324ff.).

While Jovinus and Sebastianus established their court in Gaul, the *comes
Africae* Heraclianus seized his opportunity and declared war on Honorius.
This is the same Heraclianus who had received his African posting from
Honorius as a reward for executing Stilicho, and who had supported Honorius
against Alaric and Attalus. Like Gildo so many years before, Heraclianus
applied economic pressure on the western government by preventing the
export of North African grain to Italy. Honorius was outraged by this
treachery, and he swore harsh justice.

> [Emperors Honorius and Theodosius II] to the Dignitaries and Provincials
> of Africa. We adjudge that Heraclianus is a public enemy, and with due
> authorization We decree that his accursed head shall be cut off. We pursue
> his satellites also with criminal prosecution …
>
> (*CTh.* 9.40.21. July 5, 412)

In contrast to Gildo, Heraclianus preferred not to wait around for Honorius'
armed response to arrive on his doorstep. The *comes* sailed to Italy with a
substantial military force, intent on defeating and deposing the emperor, but
the Italian campaign was a complete disaster. Heraclianus was met with heavy

opposition. He lost most of his troops in the melee and fled back to North Africa, hotly pursued by Honorius' men. Reaching Carthage, Heraclianus sought sanctuary in the city's Temple of Memory, only to be assassinated beneath its colonnade (Olymp. *fr.* 23; Chron. Marcell. s.a. 413). Honorius had made good on his promise. Now, the emperor could at last go about dealing with the intruders in his empire, beginning with the Visigoths.

Honorius' Christian victory

Honorius struck a gold coin series at Ravenna, at some point between 406 and 412, which marks a distinct change in his triumphal self-representation (Figure 7.7). Entirely Christian in style, this coin omits the goddess Victoria. She is replaced by the *manus Dei* reaching down from heaven to crown Honorius with a laurel victory wreath (Bellinger and Berlincourt 1962; Doyle 2015, 157–71). This coin type's religious iconography emphasizes Honorius' strength as being derived solely from Christ. Although Victoria does not yet disappear from coinage or other forms of imperial art until much later, the appearance of this purely Christian coin is all the more intriguing given the period in which it was minted – time when still practicing pagans blamed

Figure 7.7 Gold solidus of Honorius. Ravenna mint, uncertain date after 406. Obv. Honorius bearded, draped, and cuirassed, wearing diademed helmet with star ornamentation. Legend: DN-HONORI-VS-PF-AVG (*Dominus Noster Honorius Pius Felix Augustus*/Our Lord Honorius, pious and fortunate Augustus). Rev. Honorius standing, in short tunic and cloak, facing, crowned by *manus Dei*, his left hand on his sword hilt, a *labarum* in his right, the scepter transfixed in a prostrate hybrid creature under his feet. Legend: VICTORI-A-AVGGG (*Victoria Augustorum*/Victory of the Augusti). Field: R-V (Ravenna). Exergue: COB (*Comitatus Obryziacum*/Comitatensian mint, or *Comes Obryzi*/count of the treasury).
Source: *RIC* X 1310.

the Christianization of the Roman Empire for the instability plaguing the land, particularly after Rome's desecration.

The coin's reverse depicts a bearded Honorius wearing a short cloak, like that which he is described as wearing during the Ticinum massacre. His triumphal right hand holds a *labarum*, while his left hand rests upon his sword hilt, ready to draw his blade to defend the state. Honorius stands over a hybrid animal, a lion with a serpent's tail, trampling it beneath his right foot, and piercing it with his standard. The image of the *labarum* piercing a serpent had already appeared on the coinage of Constantine I (RIC *VII* 19). The hybrid creature, a type of chimaera, has sometimes been taken to symbolize Honorius' suppression of western usurpers (*RIC* X, 131–2; McEvoy 2013, 206). The idea is that the lion indicates their ferocity, and their betrayal is depicted by the tail of the snake. It is unlikely that the animal indicates barbarians, as they are generally portrayed as human, naked or semi-clothed, with unkempt hair and beards. Another meaning for Honorius' novel numismatic expression is that it is a biblical reference from the Book of Psalms. As a good Catholic Christian emperor, Honorius was obliged to protect his people from the enemies of God. In the troubled days of the early 400s, God's enemies could mean pagan or heretical Romans or barbarians, or even Jewish communities (Demougeot 1986, 94–118). Either way, propaganda like this was specifically created in order to demonstrate and celebrate Honorius' determination to defend the West against its enemies – foreign or domestic, Christian or otherwise.

> He that dwells in the secret place of the most High shall abide under the shadow of the Almighty. I will say of the Lord, He is my refuge and my fortress: my God; in him will I trust. Surely he shall deliver you from the snare of the fowler, and from the deadly pestilence. He shall cover you with his feathers, and under his wings shall you trust: his truth shall be your shield and buckler. You shall not be afraid for the terror by night; nor for the arrow that flies by day; nor for the pestilence that walks in darkness; nor for the destruction that wastes at noonday. A thousand shall fall at your side, and ten thousand at your right hand; but it shall not come near you. Only with your eyes shall you behold and see the reward of the wicked. Because you have made the Lord, who is my refuge, even the most High, your habitation; there shall no evil befall you, neither shall any plague come near your dwelling. For he shall give his angels charge over you, to keep you in all your ways. They shall bear you up in their hands, lest you dash your foot against a stone. You shall tread upon the lion and adder: the young lion and the serpent shall you trample under feet.
>
> (Psalms 91.1–13)

References

Alston, Richard. 1994. "Roman Military Pay from Caesar to Diocletian." *JRS* 84: 113–23.

Bastien, Pierre. 1987. *Le Monnayage de l'atelier de Lyon: du règne de Jovien à la mort de Jovin, 363–413*. Editions Numismatique Romaine 14. Wetteren.

Bellinger, A. R. and Berlincourt, M. A. 1962. "Victory as a Coin Type." *ANS* 149: 1–68.

Birley, Anthony R. 2005. *The Roman Government of Britain*. Oxford: Oxford University Press.

Bury, John Bagnall. 1958 (1889–1923). *History of the Later Roman Empire from the Death of Theodosius I to the Death of Justinian*. 2 volumes. New York: Dover Publications Inc.

Clinton, Henry F. 1850. *Fasti Romani: The Civil and Literary Chronology of Rome and Constantinople from the Death of Augustus to the Death of Justin II*. 2 volumes. Oxford: Oxford University Press.

Curran, John. 2000. *Pagan City and Christian Capital*. Oxford: Clarendon Press.

Demougeot, Émilienne. 1986. "La symbolique du lion et du serpent sur les solidi des empereurs d'occident de la première moitié du Ve s." *RN* 6.28: 94–118.

Demougeot, Émilienne. 1988. *L'Empire romain et les barbares d'Occident, IVe–VIIe siècle*. Paris: Publications de la Sorbonne.

Doyle, Christopher. 2014. *The Endgame of Treason: Rebellion and Usurpation in the Late Roman Empire, AD 395–411*. Unpublished thesis. Galway: National University of Ireland Galway. https://aran.library.nuigalway.ie/handle/10379/4631.

Doyle, Christopher. 2015. "Declaring Victory, Concealing Defeat? Continuity and Change in Imperial Coinage of the Roman West, c.383–408." In *Shifting Genres in Late Antiquity*. Edited by Geoffrey Greatrex and Hugh Elton with the assistance of Lucas McMahon: 157–71. Farnham: Ashgate.

Drinkwater, John F. 1998. "The Usurpers Constantine III (407–411) and Jovinus (411–413)." *Britannia* 29: 269–98.

Drinkwater, John F. 2007. *The Alamanni and Rome, 213–496: Caracalla to Clovis*. Oxford: Oxford University Press.

Esmonde-Cleary, A. Simon. 2000. *The Ending of Roman Britain*. 2nd edition. London: Batsford.

Frere, Sheppard. 1991. *Britannia: A History of Roman Britain*. London: Pimlico.

Gillett, Andrew. 2001. "Rome, Ravenna and the Last Western Emperors." *PBSR* 69: 131–67.

Heather, Peter. 1991. *Goths and Romans, 332–489*. Oxford: Clarendon Press.

Heather, Peter. 2005. *The Fall of the Roman Empire: A New History of Rome and the Barbarians*. Oxford: Oxford University Press.

Icks, Martijn. 2014. "The Inadequate Heirs of Theodosius: Ancestry, Merit and Divine Blessing in the Representation of Arcadius and Honorius." *Millennium* 11.1: 69–100.

Kulikowski, Michael. 2000. "Barbarians in Gaul, Usurpers in Britain." *Britannia* 3: 325–45.

Kulikowski, Michael. 2004. *Late Roman Spain and its Cities*. Baltimore, MD: The Johns Hopkins Press.

Kulikowski, Michael. 2007. *Rome's Gothic Wars*. Cambridge: Cambridge University Press.

Lafaurie, Jean. 1953. "La chronologie des monnaies de Constantin III et de Constant II." *RN* 6: 37–65.

Le Bohec, Yann. 1994. *The Imperial Roman Army*. Translated by Raphael Bate. London: Batsford.

Lejdegård, Hans. 2002. *Honorius and the City of Rome: Authority and Legitimacy in Late Antiquity*. Uppsala: Uppsala Universitet.

Liebeschuetz, 2003. "*Gens* into *regnum*: The Vandals." In *Regna and Gentes: The Relationship between Late Antique and Early Medieval Peoples and Kingdoms in the Transformation of the Roman World*. Edited by Hans Werner Goetz, Jorg Jarnut, and Walter Pohl, with the collaboration of Sören Kaschke: 55–83. Leiden: Brill.

Lipps, Johannes, Machado, Carlos, and von Rummel, Philip (eds). 2013. *The Sack of Rome in 410 AD: The Event, its Context and its Impact*. Proceedings of the Conference held at the German Archaeological Institute at Rome, 04–06 November 2010. Deutsches Archäologisches Institut Rom: Palilia 28.

Mathisen, Ralph. 2013. "Roma a Gothis Alarico duce capta est: Ancient Accounts of the Sack of Rome in 410 CE." In *The Sack of Rome in 410 AD*. Edited by Lipps et al.: 87–102.

McEvoy, Meaghan. 2013. "The Mausoleum of Honorius: Late Roman Imperial Christianity and the City of Rome in the Fifth Century." In *Old Saint Peter's, Rome*. Edited by Rosamond McKitterick, John Osborne, Carol M. Richardson, and Joanna Story: 119–136. Cambridge: Cambridge University Press.

Oost, Stewart Irvin. 1966. "The Revolt of Heraclian." *CP* 61.4: 236–42.

Oost, Stewart Irvin. 1968. *Galla Placidia Augusta: A Biographical Essay*. Chicago, IL and London: The University of Chicago Press.

Stevens, Courtenay E. 1957. "Marcus, Gratian, Constantine." *Athenaeum* 35: 316–47.

Ward-Perkins, Bryan. 2005. *The Fall of Rome and the End of Civilization*. Oxford: Oxford University Press.

Woods, David. 2012. "On the Alleged Letters of Honorius to the Cities of Britain in 410." *Latomus* 71: 818–26.

8   The emperor and his church

Whatever statutes were enacted by Our Fathers at different times with respect
to the sacrosanct churches shall remain inviolate and unimpaired ... We desire
that reverence shall be increased in Our time ...

Codex Theodosianus 16.2.29. March 23, 395

The president and the monk

On the morning of February 2, 1984, the American president Ronald Reagan
addressed the annual national prayer breakfast meeting at the Washington
Hilton Hotel. Reagan's speech was written by Peter Robinson, who had a
keen interest in the works of Augustine of Hippo (*APP* 1984). First, the president spoke about how much daily prayer meant to him personally. To highlight his principles, Reagan related a story which, as it happened, concerned
Honorius' triumphal visit to Rome in 404.

> This power of prayer can be illustrated by a story that goes back to the
> fourth century. [This] Asian monk ... I hesitate to say the name because
> I'm not sure I know the pronunciation, but let me take a chance. It was
> Telemachus ... one day, he thought he heard the voice of God telling him
> to go to Rome ... Believing that he had heard, he set out ... Weeks and
> weeks later, he arrived there, having traveled most of the way on foot ... It
> was at a time of a festival in Rome. They were celebrating a triumph over
> the Goths. And he followed a crowd into the Coliseum, and then there
> in the midst of this great crowd, he saw the gladiators come forth, stand
> before the emperor [Honorius], and say, "We who are about to die salute
> you." And he realized they were going to fight to the death for the enter-
> tainment of the crowds. And he cried out, "In the name of Christ, stop!"
> And his voice was lost in the tumult there in the great Coliseum. And as the
> games began, he made his way down through the crowd and climbed over
> the wall and dropped to the floor of the arena. Suddenly, the crowds saw
> this scrawny little figure making his way out to the gladiators and saying,
> over and over again, "In the name of Christ, stop." And they thought it

was part of the entertainment, and at first they were amused ... when they realized it wasn't, they grew belligerent and angry. And as he was pleading with the gladiators, "In the name of Christ, stop," one of them plunged his sword into his body. And as he fell to the sand of the arena in death, his last words were, "In the name of Christ, stop." And suddenly, a strange thing happened. The gladiators stood looking at this tiny form lying in the sand. A silence fell over the Coliseum. And then, someplace up in the upper tiers, an individual made his way to an exit and left, and others began to follow. And in the dead silence, everyone left the Coliseum. That was the last battle to the death between gladiators in the Roman Coliseum. Never again did anyone kill or did men kill each other for the entertainment of the crowd. One tiny voice that could hardly be heard above the tumult. "In the name of Christ, stop." It is something we could be saying to each other throughout the world today.

Ronald Reagan's anecdote about Honorius' abolition of gladiatorial combats comes directly from the writings of Theodoret, a mid-fifth-century Syrian bishop. Here is Theodoret's original, shorter, version.

Honorius, who inherited the empire of Europe, put a stop to the gladiatorial combats which had long been held at Rome. The occasion of his doing so arose from the following circumstance. A certain man of the name of Telemachus had embraced the ascetic life. He had set out from the East and for this reason had repaired to Rome. There, when the abominable spectacle was being exhibited, he went himself into the stadium, and, stepping down into the arena, endeavored to stop the men who were wielding their weapons against one another. The spectators of the slaughter were indignant, and inspired by the mad fury of the demon who delights in those bloody deeds, stoned the peacemaker to death. When the admirable emperor was informed of this he numbered Telemachus in the array of victorious martyrs, and put an end to that impious spectacle.

(Theod. *HE.* 5.26)

Interesting as the two versions of the story may be, and convincing as they may seem, the fact is that there are no Honorian legal constitutions which decree the end of spectacles in the arena. If Honorius closed the games, as Theodoret originally claimed, it would be reasonable to expect to find an imperial law or two to mark this important milestone in Christianity's triumph over such a popular pagan custom. Yet, there is not a single legal pronouncement. While it is true that Honorius' Christian predecessors wrote laws which attempted to suppress gladiatorial combats, none of these were effective, such were the games' prevalence in Roman society. Gladiatorial fights did eventually end, though when and how this actually occurred is a matter of some debate. The story of the brave Asian monk is likely an urban legend, founded perhaps on some vaguely remembered, similar event (Bomgardner 2000, 205–6). As we have seen several times in this book, unsubstantiated stories sometimes have enough power to reach across the centuries, to be appropriated later for one purpose or another.

Honorius is commonly referred to as the 'emperor who closed the games,' supposedly inspired by Telemachus' martyrdom. In that case, we should look to other primary sources to see what they have to say on the matter. No contemporary source mentions it. Claudian is our main authority for Honorius' extravagant triumph through Rome in 404 but gives no account of any incident in the Coliseum, although, as noted earlier in Chapter 6, Honorius is supposed to have visited Saint Peter's tomb about the same time as the triumph, something which Claudian left out. Then again, if an unknown monk from the provinces was in fact killed in the Coliseum, it probably meant little to a pagan like Claudian. That said, that other great pagan writer, Zosimus, is also tight-lipped about Honorius' alleged closure of the ancient spectacle, an act that, if true, Zosimus would surely have had something to say about, if only to criticize a Christian emperor.

If Telemachus had intervened in a gladiatorial contest at the cost of his own life, the implication of such an action might not have been felt until much later. Since Theodoret wrote several decades after the event in question, it is conceivable that what was originally an innocuous episode acquired greater significance for Christians. Telemachus, also called Almachius, was canonized as a Christian saint, mainly due to Theodoret's few lines about him. The monk's feast day is January 1, which very neatly coincides with Honorius' sixth consulship in 404. It is curious that Theodoret's *Ecclesiastical History* places Telemachus' martyrdom between Honorius' accession in January 395 and John Chrysostom's appointment as Constantinople's archbishop in autumn 397. By this reckoning, if something indeed happened at Rome to convince Honorius to end human blood sports, it should therefore have been early on in his reign. But again, there are no laws prohibiting gladiatorial combats in the period 395–7 either. The nearest legal reference to gladiators that fits this timeframe is an incomplete law given at Rome in 399, which penalizes the procurement of gladiators as personal bodyguards by senators (*CTh.* 15.12.3. June 6, 399). In fact, people were still being sentenced to die by wild beasts in the arena (*damnatio ad bestias*) until at least 439 in Constantinople (*NTh.* 17.1. Oct 20, 439). The story of Telemachus the monk, therefore, highlights the danger of accepting historical sources at face value.

The soldier of Christ

Honorius' remarkable good fortune in surviving the numerous attempts by pretenders to depose him was credited by Christian authors to God's love for him, and vice versa on the emperor's part (*Soz. HE.* 9.11). For Honorius, respect for and belief in a divine order was fundamental for the spiritual and physical health of the state. Sozomen tells us that in order to 'insure the stability of imperial power, it is sufficient for an emperor to serve God with reverence, which was the course pursued by Honorius. Placidia, his sister ... likewise distinguished herself by real zeal in the maintenance of religion and of the churches' (Soz. *HE*. 9.16.1–2). Imperial propaganda promoted the idea that the imperial family's piety, devotion, and daily prayer were paramount for the empire's very survival. This is why late imperial art, from about 320 onwards, already martial in style, became so steeped in Christian symbolism. In the early fifth century, this blend of religion and militarism was an immensely important propagandist tool used by Honorius' government during the wave of violence inflicted upon the West by barbarian aggression and civil war. Figuratively at least, the emperor was supposed to be the eternal light of Rome, offering a psychological reassurance to his people. The imperial image, as portrayed in coinage, sculpture, and art, was the very embodiment of the state's strength and security. If the center held firm, then all was not lost, or so the thinking went.

Many ecclesiastical authors speak admiringly of the Catholic faith of emperors like Honorius and their families. Although Honorius was not the most military of Rome's Augusti, Christian writers certainly considered him to be a soldier of Christ, and described him thus. Furthermore, it was important that the Roman Catholic Church had the imperial household's patronage. Through his religious policies and endowments, Honorius enabled the Church to consolidate its power, and ensure that that institution continued to prosper long after the Western Roman Empire ceased to exist.

By the early sixth century, a schism had developed between the eastern and western Christian churches, and religious controversy, particularly on the subject of heresy, was widespread. A prominent cleric of this period was Severus, an ascetic monk and onetime patriarch of Antioch, who wrote many works – treatises, homilies, letters, and hymns against heretics. Seeking to instruct the rulers of his day, Severus looked to the past for inspiration. In a trio of hymns, Severus recalled the Catholic orthodoxy of Honorius, Theodosius I, and Gratian, and he placed these emperors on an equal footing with the biblical king David (Sev. Ant. 201–3; cf. Rapp 1998, 295). In his hymn for Honorius, Severus claimed that the emperor wore a concealed hair shirt and fasted regularly in order to achieve greater union with God. If this is indeed true, then this is an ascetic Honorius not otherwise recorded. Perhaps it may even explain the lack of children from Honorius and his two wives, for if the emperor had embraced the ascetic, celibate life, however noble that may have been thought of by clergymen, it was useless for the continuation of the Theodosian line.

> With David the divine king the religious Honorius said, "My soul hath gone out after thee and thy right hand hat helped me Lord," and since he thirsted to be admitted to inherit the kingdom of heaven, therefore the pride of the temporal kingdom was reckoned as nothing before him, but he longed for the life of the saints who are on mountains and in caves; and he humbled and trained his flesh by means of fasts, and under the purple

and the royal robe he wore a garment made of hair, while he practiced chastity and justice and said again like the great prophet David, "I am solitary or alone until I pass away, who also after he has taken his journey is with Christ our God, who greatly glorifies all those who love him."

(Sev. Ant. 201.6)

Sozomen relates an encounter between Honorius and his *magister equitum* Allobichus, or Alavicus, probably a Goth, which occurred in 409. The two men were taking part in a public ceremonial procession; Honorius was riding his horse, while Allobichus walked in front of him. Without warning the emperor, who suspected the *magister* of plotting against him, suddenly ordered Allobichus to be put to death on the spot. Honorius then dismounted from his horse, and loudly gave thanks to God for saving him from such a dangerous enemy (Soz. *HE*. 9.12.4–6; cf. Olymp. *Fr*. 15.1–2). All this transpired in front of a watching crowd – that ubiquitous entity found in so many ancient texts, what MacMullen calls an 'active participant in many moments when an emperor is overthrown or raised up, is loved or hated' (1988, 113). Honorius used the opportunity presented by Allobichus' treason to his advantage to publicly demonstrate his personal authority, and above all his Christian piety. In this way, Honorius could be seen to practice what his official propaganda so often preached – that he did indeed love and venerate God as his personal patron by praising the divine. Allobichus probably was a traitor who would have faced justice, but the way in which his humiliation and execution took place seems stage-managed, perhaps in order to give the emperor a chance to physically show his piety. Of course, the sight of an emperor acknowledging divine favor in front of his people was not unique to the late empire. Long before emperors were Christian, they frequently, and publicly, invoked the gods for assistance and thanked them if successful.

Laws of man, laws of God

Honorius' legal record on religion clearly show his steadfast commitment to the Catholic faith, particularly those laws he issued from Ravenna. Tony Honoré points out the frequency of the term Catholic among Honorius' laws, in contrast to those of the Roman East, and suggests that this spiritual focus in western imperial law was a response to the military disasters of the early 400s. 'Thirty of the sixty mentions in the *Codex Theodosianus* of the word *catholicus* ... come from the reign of Honorius. All but one are from the Ravenna period. The eleven texts that use the word orthodox (*orthodoxus*) are all eastern, so that, though *catholicus* is freely used in the east also, the divide between eastern and western Christianity begins to mark the language of legislation' (Honoré 1998, 229). Under Honorius, there was a marked increase in the physical destruction of pagan sites, images, and paraphernalia in the Roman West. His own father, as we saw, had appointed Maternus Cynegius to aggressively search out and destroy pagan idolatry across the eastern provinces, and was very effective in that role. Honorius followed his father's example in the West, for example, at Carthage in early 399, where pagans in the great North African city experienced the full brunt of sectarian hatred. Year after these events, Augustine relayed the story.

> As we know, in the most noted and eminent city, Carthage, in Africa, Gaudentius and Jovius, officers of the emperor Honorius ... overthrew the temples and broke the images of the false gods. And from that time to the present, during almost thirty years, who does not see how much the worship of the name of Christ has increased, especially after many of those became Christians who had been kept back from the faith by thinking that divination true, but saw when that same number of years was completed that it was empty and ridiculous?
>
> (Aug. *De civ. Dei*. 18.54)

By the early fifth century, it was obvious to at least some contemporary observers that Roman dominion in the West was no longer a given. Central imperial government was well aware of this uncomfortable reality. The emperor therefore was expected to exhibit leadership, but how could such an unsoldierly ruler like Honorius live up to his role if he did not lead armies into battle? Aside from propaganda, it was through his legislative voice that Honorius presented himself as a bastion of order in an increasingly disordered world. If any form of internal stability was to be sustained, religious and social dissent could not be tolerated. Short of widespread violent pogroms like those once pursued against Christians, all of which had utterly failed in their aims, the only path available to Honorius through which he could really implement his will was the rule of law. In this, Honorius was particularly adept. For example, he issued repeated legal pronouncements condemning and proscribing Donatism in North Africa. Honorius even went so far as to convene a council of bishops in Carthage in 411 in order to suppress the perceived threat the Donatist heresy posed to the Catholic Church. The upshot of the Council of Carthage was the exile of many Donatist bishops and the confiscation of their churches and lands. Thus, the Catholic Church's grip on North Africa was tightened.

After Stilicho's removal in 408, Honorius showed a much keener interest in drafting his religious and civil laws than he had previously. From late 408 until almost the end of his reign, Honorius played a greater role in writing his own legislation, particularly that concerning religious matters. After 408, the young emperor was now considerably freer to pursue the type of internal policies that fitted his personal religious ideology. In the latter part of his reign, from about 409 onward, Honorius' laws grew increasingly intolerant towards non-Catholic Christians. As he saw it, this group, comprising Jews, heretics, and pagans, impeded the progress of the state religion. The following legal excerpts represent a cross-section of Honorius' personal interest in the legislature after 408.

Emperors Honorius, and Theodosius Augustuses to Olympius, Master of Offices, and Valens, Count of the Household Troops. We prohibit those persons who are hostile to the Catholic sect to perform imperial service within the palace, so that no person who disagrees with Us in faith and in religion shall be associated with Us in any way.

(*CTh*. 16.5.42. Nov 14, 408)

[Emperors Honorius and Theodosius] to Jovius, Praetorian Prefect. A new crime of superstition in some way shall vindicate to itself the name of Caelicolists (sky-worshippers), hitherto unheard of. Unless such persons return to the worship of God and the veneration of Christianity within the limits of one year, they shall know that they also will be held subject to those laws by which We have commanded heretics to be restrained. For it is certain that if any doctrine differs from the faith of the Christians, it is contrary to Christian law. Certain persons, indeed, unmindful of their own lives and of Our law, dare to misuse this faith to such an extent that they compel certain Christians to assume the detestable and offensive name of Jews. Although those persons who have committed this crime have rightly been condemned by the laws (death by fire) of previous emperors, nevertheless, We are not displeased to admonish them frequently, in order that those persons who have been instructed in the Christian mysteries may not be forced to adopt a perversity that is Jewish and alien to the Roman Empire, after they have adopted Christianity … We direct that the authors of the deed … shall be subject to the penalty provided by previous laws since indeed it is more grievous than death and more cruel than murder if any person of the Christian faith should be polluted by Jewish disbelief … if any person should attempt to contravene this law, he shall know that he will be held guilty of the crime of high treason (punishable by death).

(*CTh*. 16.8.19. Apr 1, 409)

[Emperors Honorius and Theodosius] to Heraclianus, Count of Africa. The divine imperial response in accordance with which those persons of heretical superstition secretly resorted to their own rites shall be entirely annulled, and all enemies of Our holy faith shall know that if they should attempt further to convene publicly, in the accursed temerity of their crime, they will suffer the penalty both of proscription and of blood.

(*CTh*, 16.5.51. Aug 25, 410)

[Emperors Honorius and Theodosius] to Asclepiodotus, Praetorian Prefect … all other heretics shall know that all privileges which are forbidden them by the authority of the general sanctions shall be denied them by this constitution also. If any persons should attempt to contravene [this] they shall be punished.

(*CTh*. 16.5.59. Apr 9, 423)

It was not just religious reform that interested Honorius. Administrative corruption was rampant throughout the western – and eastern – provinces. Though he tried to rectify this problem through legal force, ultimately Honorius had no more success than earlier emperors (*CTh*. 1.16.14. Nov 25, 408). Nor was corruption confined to the civil service. It pervaded church institutions too. One of Honorius' remedies to this blight was to give bishops the power to expel delinquent priests from the Church. For this privilege, bishops were required to force miscreants to serve in local government. To prevent further fraud by defrocked clergy in their new civil positions, the imperial government threatened heavy monetary fines (*CTh*. 16.2.39; *Sirm*. 9. Nov 27, 408). Laws against clerical misdemeanor were repeated in 411 and again in 416, which indicates just how difficult it was for central government to solve the problem of corruption within the Catholic Church. Another such Honorian law prohibited clerics from abandoning wives and children that they already had prior to taking holy orders (*CTh*. 16.2.44. May 8, 422). The phenomenon of men renouncing their families in order to pursue a religious vocation seems to have been common enough to necessitate the drafting of such a law. The same constitution advocates that while such men should live with their families, they should nevertheless try to lead a form of ascetic life (Sessa 2011, 183). What this meant was that previously married men who became priests could remain wed, but under no circumstances were they allowed to have extra-marital partners. They should not, as the law states, 'be tarnished by the association of a so-called "sister"' (*CTh*. 16.2.44. May 8, 422).

Some of Honorius' legislation shows a compassionate side to his character. In 412, he tried to put an end to the odious practice of child exposure. This was where unwanted babies, infants, and young children were literally abandoned on the street, or on rubbish dumps, by their parents or guardians. For centuries, child exposure had been an acute social problem in the Roman world. In the wake of the recent barbarian and civil wars in the West, where so many children had either been orphaned or born as a consequence, Honorius felt compelled to alleviate the suffering of his most vulnerable subjects. He therefore decreed a law intended to curtail child exposure, though how effective Honorius' legal efforts actually were is very difficult to ascertain. Again, we see civil law emphasizing the role of bishops in their local communities.

> Emperors Honorius and Theodosius Augustuses to Melitius, Praetorian Prefect.
>
> We leave to owners and patrons no avenue of recovery if good will, the friend of compassion (*voluntas misercordiae amica*), has taken up children exposed in a measure to death, for no one can call his own child whom he scorned when it was perishing; provided only that the signature of a bishop as witness should immediately follow; and, for the sake of security, there can be absolutely no delay in obtaining this signature.
>
> (*CTh*. 5.9.2. March 19, 412)

While Honorius' legislation on Judaism was generally severe, he made some concessions, possibly in an effort to maintain a semblance of peace between citizens of different faiths. Three Honorian laws from 412 ensure that the Sabbath be recognized as a day when Jewish citizens could not be forced to do anything which might interfere with their religious observances. Furthermore, synagogues were off-limits to sectarian aggression from non-Jews since 'all persons must retain their own property in undisturbed right, without any claim of religion or worship' (*CTh*. 8.8.8. July 26, 412; 2.8.26. July 26, 412; 16.8.20. July 26, 412). Another law from the same timeframe, which was subsequently twice reissued, expressly forbade any violent acts against Jews because of their religion, and declared that Jewish homes and synagogues were inviolate. Yet this same law also declared that 'Jews shall also be admonished that they perchance shall not become insolent and, elated by their own security, commit any rash act in disrespect of the Christian religion' (*CTh*. 16.8.21. Aug 6, 412, 418, 420). Other restrictions were placed on the Jewish population. Jews were barred from joining the civil service or the military, though they were permitted to work in the legal profession (*CTh*. 16.8.24. Mar 10, 418; Humphries 1999, 101). The aforementioned anti-Semitic laws show us that the imperial government could, when it suited, make compromises with the Jewish community. Despite occasional displays of good will to his Jewish citizenry, Honorius also imposed unfair restrictions upon them. Thus, the emperor might be seen as reasonable by some, but unbending in his Christian values by others. What type of message did imperial condemnation of religious minorities send out to the wider public? It was a dangerous game, one which sometimes played out tragically, for example in 418, when the Jewish population of Minorca were violently compelled by their Christian neighbors to convert to the latter's faith.

The darkness of conversion

In February 418, over five hundred members of the Jewish population on the island of Minorca were forcibly converted to Christianity. This event is recorded by the island's bishop Severus in a lengthy letter to his fellow bishops. Jewish and Christian Romans had apparently lived together on Minorca in relative harmony until 418, when synagogues were burned and Jewish leaders forced into exile. Severus presents the mass conversion of his fellow islanders as having been directed by God, instead of accepting responsibility himself or for his accomplices. Events like the Minorca conversion occurred just over a century after Constantine I's promise of toleration for all religions. That promise faded over the fourth century, replaced with extreme bigotry.

Severus went to great lengths to assert that most of the converted did so of their own free will, and that God's intervention had been instrumental in the conversion. For those who refused to accept the Christian faith, Severus describes them as filled with 'fierceness and villainy,' an 'incurable sickness,' so much so that Minorca's capital, Magona (modern Mahon), 'seethed with so great a multitude of Jews, as if with vipers and scorpions, that Christ's church was being wounded by them daily' (Sev. Min. 3.5–6; 27.2). Such were the fruits of the legalization and imperial advocacy of Christianity, for as Severus himself concluded, it was right to 'take up Christ's zeal against the Jews … for the sake of their eternal salvation … perhaps the Lord wished to kindle this spark from the ends of the earth, so that the whole breadth of the earth might be ablaze with the flame of love in order to burn down the forest of unbelief' (Sev. Min. 31.2–4).

It is not at all surprising that an event like that at Minorca occurred if we consider how Constantine I had put his vision for the Roman state into play with repressive legislation against Jews, pagans, and heretics over his thirty-year reign. By the Honorian period, sectarian violence and religious bigotry were widespread in both parts of the Roman Empire. Consider, for instance, the anti-Semitism in the poetry of Prudentius, a frequent visitor to the courts of Theodosius and Honorius. If Prudentius' attitude is anything to go by, and reflects the mindset of late Roman Christian high society, small wonder then that provincial Christians felt emboldened to treat their Jewish neighbors how they wished.

> From place to place the homeless Jew wanders in ever-shifting exile, since the time when he was torn from the abode of his fathers and has been suffering the penalty for murder, and having stained his hands with the blood of Christ whom he denied, paying the price of sin.
>
> (Prudent. *Apoth.* 541–5)

Honorius is nowhere mentioned in relation to the cooption of Minorca's Jewish population into Catholicism. News of it may not have reached him, or if it did, he was preoccupied by two events: his peace settlement with the Visigoths in Gaul, and the episcopal elections in Rome.

The appointment of popes

From an early age, Honorius had entertained the advice of bishops like Ambrose of Milan, and counted some among his personal friends. When required to, however, Honorius was quite capable of punishing episcopal criminality with deposition and exile (*CTh.* 16.2.35. Feb 4, 405; Matthews 2000, 94–5). The Catholic episcopate had proved a match for more than one emperor before Honorius, as his father had come to realize when Ambrose threatened him into performing public penance. Early in his reign, Honorius had attempted to limit episcopal power to religious matters only, decreeing that only the civil authorities could have the final say in litigation cases. The purpose of this law was to curtail episcopal interference in the law courts (*CTh.* 16.11.1. Aug 20, 399; Dossey 2001, 99). Within a decade, however, things had changed somewhat. In December 408, the emperor granted episcopal courts the power of legal enforcement, though these ecclesiastical bodies still needed the support of the civil authorities.

> Emperors Arcadius, Honorius, and Theodosius Augustuses to Theodorus, Praetorian Prefect. The judgment of a bishop (*iudicium episcopale*) shall be valid for all persons who acquiesce in being heard by priests. For since private persons can hear those persons who have given their consent, even without the knowledge of the judge, We grant that this power shall be permitted to those persons whom We necessarily venerate, and We order that such reverence must be shown toward their adjudication as must be granted to your authority, from which it is not permitted to appeal. Also, in order that such cognizance (by a bishop) may not be without effect, execution of judgment shall be granted through a public office staff.
>
> (*CTh*. 1.27.2. Dec 13, 408)

When it came to episcopal elections, these could be notorious affairs, not least in terms of the violence that could occur between the factions supporting rival bishops. Such civil unrest presented problems for imperial governments in trying to keep the peace on the ground. Constantius II (337–61) had experienced this first-hand when he got involved in a succession dispute between two bishops at Rome, Liberius and Felix, in 355. Constantius preferred Liberius over Felix for the pontificate. The latter was aggrieved, and orchestrated a coup against the imperial favorite. In the end, Constantius had to forcibly eject Felix from the city before he could stir up any further trouble for Liberius or the emperor (Latham 2014).

In early 419, Honorius found himself embroiled in a similar situation to Constantius II over sixty years earlier. This time, it was between Eulalius and Boniface, both of who laid claim to the Holy See (Cristo 1977, 163–7; Norton 2007, 65). Correspondence between some of the principal actors in the 419 episcopal election drama is preserved in the *Collectio Avellana*, an assortment of edicts and letters of emperors, their senior officials, bishops, and popes, dating from the late fourth to the mid-sixth century. A useful primary source in lots of ways, the *Collectio Avellana* has nonetheless been termed problematic because of its various authors' biases (Blair-Dixon 2007, 59ff.). Yet, the same could be said for much of our primary evidence thus far.

On Saturday, December 27, 418, the day after the death of the unpopular Pope Zosimus, a Greek, a group of junior clergy, supported by a large number of laymen, seized and occupied the Lateran Basilica, the papal residence. There, Eulalius, former archdeacon to Zosimus, and also a Greek, was chosen by this group as the new pope. This is a far cry from the way modern Catholic pontiffs are appointed. As Stuart Cristo remarked, 'the exact detailed niceties of the procedure for electing popes have only gradually evolved during the many centuries of the existence of the papacy … in the fifth century the procedure was still quite indefinite and both parties could thus with right claim proper election and consecration' (1977, 165). Anyway, as Eulalius and his cohort congratulated themselves inside the Lateran on their apparent success, another man, Boniface, the dead pope's advisor, was elected pontiff by a majority of senior priests gathered at the titular Church of Theodora, on the old Salarian road that led from Rome to the Adriatic coast. By the evening of Sunday, December 29, 418, a crisis was in bloom and the city prefect Symmachus was rapidly called in to defuse the tensions. Symmachus was unable to bring the two factions to terms and so wrote to Honorius for help, asserting that in his opinion Eulalius was the rightful pope since he had been the first man chosen (*Coll. Avell.* Symm. *Ep.* 15.3). Four days later, Symmachus received a letter from Honorius in favor of Eulalius, for as far as the emperor knew, that man had been properly made pope. Honorius went on, promising amnesty to Boniface's faction for any illegality they may have engaged in, but the usurper pope, as Honorius thought Boniface to be, was ordered into exile (*Coll. Avell.* Hon. *Ep.* 15.3). Soon, however, two important churches in Rome which Honorius patronized, Saint Peter's Basilica and Saint Paul outside the Walls (San Paolo fuori le Mura), would experience scenes of angry, violent disorder.

Eulalius, happy he had the emperor's blessing, celebrated mass in Saint Peter's Basilica on January 6, while Boniface went to Saint Paul's to do the same. Symmachus sent a herald with Honorius' ultimatum to Boniface, who, in his anger, incited his supporters to beat the messenger. Boniface then marched on Rome at the head of his faction, almost reaching the inner precincts before Symmachus caught up with him and put him under house arrest.

With their pope incarcerated, Boniface's clerical supporters sent a delegation to Ravenna. They told Honorius that Eulalius was a fraud, and that Symmachus was mistaken in what he had told the emperor. Honorius was troubled by these revelations and revoked Eulalius' pontificate. The emperor wrote to the two aspirant popes demanding they come before him to explain themselves. He also requested that the other members of the Italian episcopate attend as well (*Coll. Avell.* I. Hon. *Ep.* 19.2–3). The subsequent meeting was unproductive, and so Honorius adjourned the matter until later that summer at Spoleto, where he would convene a synod representative of the bishops of all his remaining western dominion. By this point, as we have seen, Britain and some regions of Spain were no longer under Honorius' rule. The emperor wrote to bishops in Gaul and Africa, including Augustine of Hippo, ordering their compulsory attendance at the Spoleto conclave (*Coll. Avell.* I. Hon. Ep. 26.3). Honorius also appointed an interim bishop, Achilleus, to discharge papal duties at Rome, for Eulalius and Boniface had been told to leave the city until the final decision was made at Spoleto on who should be pope. Eulalius clearly felt himself to be the legitimate candidate. He called Honorius' bluff by reoccupying the Lateran Basilica. That way, Eulalius hoped, the emperor would be compelled to accept him as pope, and that would be that. It was the wrong move. Civil discord erupted in Rome between supporters of the two popes. The city prefect used the military to pacify the mob, and Honorius expelled Eulalius from Rome permanently. Boniface became pope with

Honorius' recognition on April 3, and held the office for four years, while Eulalius apparently received a lesser Italian see. In his second attempt at the papal throne, Eulalius is thought to have been given some level of support by Placidia and her husband Constantius – more about this marriage in the next chapter. Furthermore, as sister to the emperor, Placidia would have felt confident that her position might tip the scales in favor of Eulalius, and as Constantius had previously helped a friend become bishop of Arles, it was feasible that they might secure the Roman see for Eulalius (Prosp. Tiro. S.a. 412). Why exactly Placidia took Eulalius' side is not at all clear, however. She wrote directly to the North African bishops, appealing in particular to Augustine, and also to Paulinus of Nola, inviting them to attend the Spoleto synod (Cristo 1977, 165–6). The papal controversy of 418–19 is intriguing in that it shows just how deeply the religious world could impact upon secular government – even if the Church ultimately acquiesced to the emperor's authority. It is even more interesting to witness the emergence of Placidia, recently freed from Visigothic captivity, onto the political stage. A woman so often overlooked in her youth, she became an Augusta, dominating her son Valentinian III's administration until her death in 450.

Another important event took place in 418, not long before the papal election debacle, when Pope Zosimus was still alive. This was the excommunication and exile of Pelagius and his principal follower Caelestius from Rome. Pelagius was an ascetic theologian apparently of Romano-British extraction, who opposed the idea of predestination, arguing instead that humanity possessed free will. Essentially, Pelagius laid out what Christianity ought to be, rather than what Catholic doctrine said it was. Suffice to say he incurred considerable ire from leading luminaries of his day such as Augustine, Jerome, and their acolyte Orosius.

It seems that both Caelestius and Pelagius had legal training, for they represented themselves when brought in front of episcopal courts in 411 and 415 respectively (Humfress 2007, 193). Court sittings like these were the direct result of Honorius' gifting of legal power to bishops in 408. However, Pelagius and Caelestius each convincingly pleaded their cases and were acquitted. Augustine was incensed that they were not proclaimed heretics, and he pushed for Pelagianism to be outlawed. In a short time, Pelagius' teachings gained a not insignificant following, which inevitably brought it to the attention of the emperor. As such, Pelagius and those who adopted his views were excommunicated by the Council of Carthage in 418. He seems to have left the West for Jerusalem, where he probably spent his last days. Caelestius' fate is even less uncertain.

Pelagianism was considered a dangerous doctrine not only because it challenged core tenets of Catholicism, but also because it had the potential to inspire sedition. Pelagian belief achieved popularity among the overtaxed, downtrodden, lower classes of late Roman society. Pope Zosimus had even entertained some of Pelagius' ideas, but quickly recanted his opinions for fear of being accused of treason, as 'Pelagianism's emphasis on individual consciences could easily lead to a liberty of action which the regimented empire could only interpret as license' (Cristo 1977, 163). Laws against Pelagian doctrine were still being drafted after Honorius' death (*Sirm.* 6. July 9, 425), until finally it was declared a heresy in 431 by the Council of Ephesus. That notwithstanding, neither imperial nor canon law could prevent the dissemination of the Pelagian ideal, which lasted well into the sixth century. Even to this day, Pelagius' teaching divides opinion within the Christian faith (Bonner 1972; Keech 2012).

Those who flee to churches for sanctuary

It is interesting that, after the executions of leading figures such as Stilicho, Eucherius, Constantine III, and others between 408 and 411, we can discern changes to the law about how much authority the Church could have in providing sanctuary (*confugium*, *refugium*) to fugitives. The Council of Sardica in 343 had offered fugitives the Church's spiritual protection, though not necessarily physical refuge (NPNF2–14:7). Theodosius I and Valentinian II tried to formalize what categories of persons could legitimately claim church asylum, and the process was still ongoing when Honorius came to power (*CTh.* 9.44.1 July 6, 386; 9.45.1. Oct 18, 392; Ducloux 1994; Hallebeek 2004; Doyle 2014, 57ff.). We previously saw how badly the eastern chamberlain Eutropius had fared when he hid inside a church at Constantinople in 399, and how at Rome, in 408, senator Lampadius had removed himself to a church for fear of Stilicho's wrath. At different points in time, imperial law grappled with the question of church sanctuary, but we do get the sense from the historical narrative that it was morally suspect to breach sacred boundaries. In the preChristian world, contravention of temple sanctuary was considered a sacrilegious act, one which incurred the enmity of the gods, though whether vestiges of this idea translated to the Christian age is a matter of some contention (Ducloux 1994, 253; cf. Hallebeek 2004; Shoemaker 2011, 11ff.).

Ambiguous imperial legislature concerning church sanctuary aside, morally, violations of church property must surely have affronted some Christians. Such actions certainly bothered non-Christians like Ammianus Marcellinus (I acknowledge here that the historian's religion is questioned by some), who describes an incident involving a usurper who had taken refuge inside a church only to be dragged out and murdered by soldiers (Amm. Marc. *Hist.* 15.5.31). Even Stilicho was guilty of committing a similar act. At Milan in 396, a certain Cresconius, whom Stilicho had been pursuing, had hidden inside a church. Stilicho sent in his men, who pulled Cresconius out and imprisoned him, despite vehement opposition by the church's bishop. Yet, the same bishop later successfully petitioned Stilicho to surrender Cresconius (Paulin. *Amb.* 34.1–4). Cases such as these highlight the tenebrous nature of the powers that church sanctuary might possess. Even in instances where poor citizens sought church sanctuary, the situation is equally uncertain. Augustine tells of a North African tenant farmer who claimed church asylum to escape his oppressive landlord. However, the hapless farmer left the church environs to visit a friend's house for dinner and was caught and imprisoned by the landlord's agents along the way (Aug. *Ep.* 123; Shoemaker 2011, 23). Does this mean, then, that protection offered to fugitives by the Catholic Church only applied within the boundaries of its physical edifices?

The individuals listed above – Stilicho, Eucherius, Constantine, etc. – each sought church asylum to escape death from Honorius. As we know, he did not accept their claims, and thus they perished. Aside from the usurper Heraclianus at Carthage, who hid inside an old pagan temple and therefore could not really have expected safety, any immunity that church sanctuary might offer seems arbitrary. While persons of lesser status might find physical salvation within a church, usurpers and other *hostes publici* had no chance. Jews and other non-Christians definitely had no right to claim church sanctuary (*CTh.* 9.45.2. June 17, 397). Furthermore, if bishops interceded on a fugitive's behalf, as happened in Eucherius' case, the prelate could just be ignored. Despite Honorius' apparently unchristian disregard for the Catholic Church's protection of the desperate, he is not criticized for such deeds by ecclesiastical sources. This is perhaps because church sanctuary had not yet been legally defined when Honorius overruled whatever authority the Church thought it had over its own affairs. David Hunt states that bishops shared 'the authority for enforcing the procedures' of church sanctuary with the civil authorities (Hunt 1993, 151). This only seems to have applied in lesser cases, not when the emperor was bent on eliminating his rivals at any cost.

In April 409, Honorius wrote a constitution making it a crime of high treason to remove fugitives from churches against their will (*Cod. Just.* 1.12.2. Apr 1, 409; Shoemaker 2011, 39) In 419, he established a new set of rules for what the physical limits that guaranteed protection of a person in an ecclesiastical building should be, with restrictions, however. It should be noted that not all churches were large enough to act as a habitation for one or more persons.

> Emperors Honorius and Theodosius II, Pious Augustuses. It is fitting that humanity, which was known even before Our times, should temper justice. For when very many people flee from the violence of a cruel fortune and choose the protection of the defense of the churches, when they are confined therein, they suffer no less imprisonment than that which they have avoided. For at no time is an egress opened to them into the light of the vestibule. Therefore the sanctity of ecclesiastical reverence shall apply to the space of fifty paces beyond the doors of the church. If anyone should hold a person who goes forth from this place, he shall incur the criminal charge of sacrilege. For no compassion is granted to the fugitives if the free air is denied to them in their affliction. We grant to the bishop the right also to enter the courts of the prison on a mission of compassion, to heal the sick, to feed the poor, and to console the innocent; when he has investigated thoroughly and has learned the case of

each person, according to law he shall direct his intervention before the competent judge. For We know, and supplications have come to Us in regard to such cases in numerous audiences, that very many persons are frequently thrust into prison in order that they may be deprived of the freedom to approach the judge; and when a rather humble person once begins to suffer imprisonment before his case is known, he is compelled to suffer the penalty of outrage ...

(*Sirm.* 13. Nov 21, 419)

It was not until after Honorius' reign that the eastern empire declared that church sanctuary could be allowed for anybody who was in genuine fear for their life, though they had to be unarmed (*CTh.* 9.45.4. Mar 23, 431; 9.45.5. Mar 28, 432; Doyle 2014, 61–2).

It is very possible that Honorius' amendments to the civil law governing the status of church sanctuary occurred due to the episodes referred to above in which he himself had asserted direct control in order to have high-ranking fugitives killed. It may well be that the episcopate, so often slighted by the emperor or his representatives, negotiated these changes with Honorius. The law as to the extent of a church's sanctuary boundaries also give bishops the power to intervene in civil judicial cases, enter prisons, and dispense justice as they saw fit. If bishops were the ones pushing Honorius for change, it was a victory for the Church over the secular government.

The builder of churches

While staying at Ravenna in 405, Prudentius made a trip to Rome. The poet was impressed by the number of churches in the city:

Rome, thou ancient mother of temples, but now given up to Christ, Lawrence has led you to victory and triumph over barbarous worship.

(Prudent. *Peri.* II.1–4)

Saint Lawrence was a church deacon martyred in Rome during Valerian's Christian persecution in 258. After Constantine's embrace of Christianity, the cult of Lawrence became popular with emperors, none more so than Theodosius I. Lawrence was one of several martyrs adopted by the Theodosian family as their personal saints. Prudentius gives a dramatic account of Lawrence's martyrdom – he was literally grilled to death – during which he alludes to the coming of Christian emperors, specifically with Honorius in mind. Here, Prudentius posits a dying Lawrence outlining his future vision of a Christian Rome.

I forsee that one day there will be an emperor who will be the servant of God and will not suffer Rome to be in the service of vile, abominable rites, but will shut and bar her temples, block up their ivory doors, close their unholy entrances and make them fast with bolts of brass ... in this warfare Lawrence did not gird a sword on his side, but turned back the foe's steel against its wielder.

(Prudent. *Peri.* II.474–504)

Honorius later dedicated a church to Saint Lawrence in Ravenna, though apparently this was not his original intention, if we go by what Agnellus of Ravenna tells us in his list of the pontiffs of that city. The following excerpt from Agnellus is interesting, though it does have a touch of Procopius' favorite phrase 'people say.'

The church of the blessed martyr Laurence, located in Caesarea, was built by Lauricius, chamberlain of the emperor Honorius ... it was adorned with greatest care, with buildings of wonderful size. However, I will not remain silent about what I have heard from narrators about this just-mentioned church. The emperor Honorius ordered Lauricius to build him a palace in Caesarea. Having taken the money, he came to Caesarea and there built the just mentioned basilica of the blessed martyr. When it had been completely finished, he returned to his lord, to tell him that the hall he had commissioned was finished. And [Lauricius] found [Honorius] disturbed, and, sitting in the imperial costume, he began to ask the architect Lauricius in anger if the whole royal hall, which he had ordered him to make, had been completed in all its works. The envious and inveterate fraud of wicked men had assailed the ears of the emperor, saying that blessed Lauricius had not built an imperial dwelling but a church. Lauricius, responding, said that he had honorably built a great hall, with courts, and that he had placed below these high arches and many seats at the sides of the house. The anger of the emperor cooled. When, after a long journey, the emperor Honorius arrived at Caesarea, seeing the sublime buildings he was very pleased; but when he had entered within it, with a swift movement Lauricius fled behind the holy altar, in order to escape. When Honorius ordered him to be seized, he himself fell on his face flat on the ground, and went into a trance. A most precious gem which had been in the crown on his head was embedded in one of the stones. And raising up only his head, after his sight was restored to his clouded eyes, he saw, behind that altar of blessed Laurence which the most blessed bishop John had consecrated, the above-mentioned Lauricius standing there, and Laurence the athlete of Christ holding his hands over the neck of Lauricius. Then the emperor judged Lauricius to be more righteous than himself, and his anger was abandoned, and he began to venerate him as a father and considered him second only to himself among everyone in the palace.

(Agnellus 34–5)

It has been suggested that Agnellus, or rather whoever told him this tall tale, dreamt up the scene between Honorius and his architect after seeing mosaics of the emperor in the Church of Saint Lawrence (Deliyannis 2004, 71, 136–7). It seems highly unlikely that a high court official would have appropriated money in such an obvious way, less still that Honorius wanted another palace built outside his existing main palatial complex, which is where Caesarea was located. What we seem to have here is an original episode embellished for greater entertainment at some later date. Such is the unfortunate state of many of our so-called historical primary sources. However, the vision of Honorius is curious. Why make up a story of the emperor tripping over, and then losing but regaining his sight? Maybe it happened this way. I do not think so. If the Church of Saint Lawrence was finished very late in Honorius' reign, it may well have been the case that the emperor was already in the grip of the disease which eventually killed him, the so-called dropsy or swelling, now more commonly called edema, which has many forms – cerebral, pulmonary, peripheral, pedal, macular, and ymphedema. Symptoms of this wide-ranging medical condition include dizziness, nausea, drowsiness, fluid retention, and failing eyesight. I concur that this is purely my speculation, but the supposed vision of Honorius may contain a grain of truth, albeit a less supernatural one.

Unfortunately, there is no way of knowing what the mosaics of Honorius and Saint Lawrence actually looked like, as the church was pulled down in the sixteenth century (Deliyannis 2010, 62). As for other Honorian ecclesiastical foundations in Ravenna, these are attributed to the emperor's sister Placidia after her brother's death. It is probable, though, that as part of his court's move to Ravenna, Honorius oversaw the construction of churches and other sacred sites there, for example the Basilica of Ursus (Humphries 1999, 206). He took with him the relics of martyrs that he and his family held dear for their personal salvation, such as Gervasius and Protasius, patron saints of Milan and firm favorites of Bishop Ambrose (Aug. *De civ. Dei.* 22.8). Gervasius and Protasius were two brothers who had been executed for their faith in an early anti-Christian pogrom. Ambrose had dedicated the basilica at Milan to these two martyrs under the auspices of Theodosius. Honorius, therefore, would have wanted to carry their cult with him to his new northern capital. He need not necessarily have taken the saints' complete remains with him, and thereby deprive Milan of its sacred artifacts, just a token piece, since Christian relics tended to include bone fragments, personal items, or other objects. Ever since Empress Helena had brought pieces of the True Cross back from her pilgrimage to Jerusalem, it had become customary for the wealthy and powerful Christian élite to have expensive reliquaries, either containers or shrines, purpose made in which to house their precious relics. From late antiquity through to relatively recently, the relics trade became such a lucrative enterprise that is not at all unusual to find more than a few Christian saints who appear to have had several heads, hands, and feet!

Roma aeterna

Early in the 400s, Honorius tied himself and his family to the cult of Saint Peter when he built his crypt in the apostle's basilica, and, if Augustine is to be believed, integrated paying homage at the apostle's tomb into the imperial triumph in 404. Rituals like this replaced the custom of thanking the gods at the foot of Victory's statue in the Curia. Saint Peter's was not the only Christian site of worship to pique Honorius' interest in Rome, however. Some of these were pre-existing churches in need of repair, some were already under renovation or reconstruction, while others were entirely new creations of Honorius.

One of the best known of Honorius' ecclesiastical building initiatives in Rome is the Basilica of Saint Paul outside the Walls. This was originally a Constantinian foundation put up over the spot of the apostle's martyrdom along the Via Ostiensis, the road from the city to the port of Ostia. Its name derived from its location beyond the Aurelian Wall. In about 386, Theodosius, acting in conjunction with his western colleague Valentinian II, demolished the original church and began building an enormous new basilica at the site. Apparently Constantine's church was small and cramped, unlike the great holy edifices of Constantinople which Theodosius likely wished to emulate in the old western capital (*LP*. Xxxii). Honorius continued his father's work on Saint Paul's though it was not fully complete until late in the reign of Placidia's son, Valentinian III (425–55). Saint Paul outside the Walls was the last truly monumental imperial building project carried out at Rome in the last century of the western empire. In certain respects, the Theodosian family's reconstruction of Saint Paul's Basilica is reminiscent of the Flavian dynasty's erection of their own great flagship, the Coliseum – begun by Vespasian in 72, continued by his son Titus, and finished in 96 by his youngest son, Domitian. Just like the Flavians, Honorius' family ensured that they left an enduring visible legacy in the eternal city's physical landscape.

Another notable Honorian-era church is the Basilica of Saint Pudentiana (Santa Pudenziana). This was initially a smaller titular church dedicated to Pudentiana, a girl thought to have been martyred in the mid-second century. Her early shrine was built into an old bath complex, which served as the first papal residence in Rome until Constantine I's donation of the Lateran Palace to the papacy in 313. Today, Pudentiana is venerated in the city of Rome only. Theodosius initiated construction of her basilica and Honorius finished it. Its interior contains some of the most beautiful and vibrant Christian mosaics from the Honorian epoch. When entering Saint Pudentiana's, one is immediately drawn to an enormous mosaic scene in the church's apse, where a golden nimbate Christ sits on a richly decorated throne, his right hand raised in a gesture of speech (*adlocutio*), his left hand holding an open book inscribed 'Lord, protector of the Church of Pudenziana' (*Dominus conservator ecclesiae Pudentianae*). In effect, Christ is portrayed as the emperor was on coins and art. On each side, Christ is surrounded by the twelve apostles, who wear the purple-hemmed robes of the Roman aristocracy. These figures sit against a backdrop of a celestial Jerusalem, where, in the sky high above the city, floats a massive jeweled votive cross flanked by symbols of the four evangelists. A winged Victory and a male angel hover on the edges of the apse, each holding golden crowns, illustrative of the iconographic transition from pagan goddess to Christian angel. Ostensibly, the Saint Pudentiana mosaic represents the heavenly court of Christ, but its ceremonial layout, lux-uriant style, and triumphant iconography is more akin to an imperial court scene from Milan, Ravenna, or Constantinople. Though there is no record of Honorius ever visiting Rome again after 416, it is tempting to imagine him doing so before his death in 423. If he did, Honorius may well have been shown this mosaic either in its preparatory or finished state, for the emperor sponsored the construction of Saint Pudentiana. However, a succession of popes oversaw the project at different stages: Siricius (384–99), Anastasius I (399–401), Innocent I (399–417), Zosimus (417–18), and Boniface I (418–22). The last of these, Boniface, is thought to have been responsible for the Christ mosaic, perhaps intending it as a tribute to Honorius in recognition of the emperor's support during the rancorous 418 episcopal elections.

Honorius forever in Christ

We also find representations of Honorius outside the official sphere, though no less religiously themed. One of the most famous of these is the consular ivory diptych panel of Anicius Petronius Probus, western consul for 406 (Figure 8.1). Late Roman consular diptychs were compact writing tablets with very expensive carved ivory covers. The Probus Diptych was probably carved in Rome *c.* 405 or 406 and was meant as a luxury gift item. Consuls marked their office by having such pieces commissioned, sometimes as presents for notables, family, or friends, and whereas emperors 'commemorated their consulates with coins and medallions, subjects did so by distributing objects hardly less precious' (*CLRE* 87). For the diptych genre, it is an unusual piece in that it does not depict its honorand Probus, which was customary for such objects. Instead, it depicts Honorius on both of its leaves. Anicius Probus came from an ancient and very distinguished Roman family, which had supported Theodosius I in the West against usurpers and other enemies. So important was the family that two of Anicius Probus' brothers had already served as consuls in 395, a joint office that was immortalized through Claudian's pane-gyrical skills. The brothers' mother, Proba, was a firm Catholic who, in her compassion for the besieged starving population of Rome in 410, apparently had the city's Salarian gate opened to the Visigoths (Olymp. *Fr.* 11.3).

The Probus ivory is the first late Roman consular diptych that can be prop-erly dated, as it is a matter of record that Anicius Probus held the western con-sulship in 406, together with his eastern colleague Arcadius (*CLRE* 346–7). It is also the 'only securely identified representation of the emperor Honorius' outside of coinage (Kiilerich 1993, 65–7, 78–81, 136, 159). However, the dip-tych differs from coinage in the level of detail it offers us, something which was impossible to achieve on small coins. Both leaves of the Probus Diptych show Honorius as a bearded military commander (*imperator*). The twenty-two- or twenty-three-year-old emperor stands facing the viewer in more or less the same pose on either leaf, with some variations in appearance, dress, and iconography. For example, the right leaf has Honorius' *parazonium*

Figure 8.1 Ivory consular diptych of Anicius Petronius Probus, *c.* 406.
Source: © Museo del Tesoro della Cattedrale di Aosta, Italy.

(ceremonial sword) with an eagle-shaped hilt, a plainer one for the left leaf; he holds a scepter and shield in the right leaf, whereas on the other leaf he holds a Victoriola and a *labarum* inscribed IN-NOMINE-XPI(*Christi*)-VINCAS-SEMPER (In the name of Christ may you forever conquer).

The inscription D-N-HONORIO-SEMP-AVG (*Dominus Noster Honorius Semper Augustus*, Our Lord Honorius, Eternal Augustus) is the same on both leaves, and hangs over the emperor's nimbate head. It is the exact same inscription used on the emperor's coinage, and perhaps the diptych artist used one of these as his design template. Beneath Honorius' feet, on each leaf, is the inscription PROBVS-FAMVLVS-V-C-CONS-ORD (*Probus Famulus*

Vir Clarissimus Consul Ordinarius/Probus, Ordinary Consul, Most Highly Regarded Man, Servant?). It appears that Probus himself commissioned this, and probably other diptychs, to give as mementos to a chosen few. The word *famulus* is interesting, as it can mean a subject, a servant, or even a slave, though this last designation is the least likely use here. Lejdegård muses that even though the inscription at Honorius' feet suggests Probus' 'inferior status,' it also infers a special relationship with the emperor (Lejdegård 2002, 85–6; cf. Elsner 1998, 83–4; McEvoy 2013, 205–6).

Stylistically, the Probus Diptych is a blend of Christian and pagan mythological motifs, in what is otherwise termed 'Theodosian Classicism,' a very diverse blend of artistic styles from the fifth century BC to the second century AD. By Honorius' day, many traditional elements of so-called pagan art had been subsumed by the emergent Christian order to express itself visually. Therefore, we should be careful not to apply an exclusively Christian label to late Roman art of the kind found on the Probus Diptych. As Kiilerich says, 'style transgresses religious distinctions. From the point of view of style, one should not make too sharp a distinction between Christian and pagan art' (1993, 189–91). This is indeed a fair statement because, despite the best efforts of Christian imperial administrations, Honorius' included, pagans still existed within the Roman state, and they still practiced their ancestral rites, albeit under threat from a wide array of punishments.

As with other long-established customs – gladiatorial combats, religious festivals, and cults – late Roman art retained many polytheistic attributes. Indeed, we still see much of what we would consider pagan in modern Christian iconography, symbols, administration, titulature, language, art, and architecture. If, for example, one was to remove the images of Christ and the saints from an average pre-twenty-first-century Catholic church, very soon one would find oneself in a predominantly Classical or pagan setting.

As titular head of the western Roman state, Honorius represented the embodiment of political unity, military victory, and above all Christian triumph. The emperor's iconography in public and private art reflected this concept. Rome borrowed this idea of ruler cult from the East, via Hellenistic Greece. From Octavian Augustus on, the emperor's image was exalted in order to symbolize the very best of what Rome was supposed to be. When we look at Honorius' image in personal and official art, we see a continuation of the same type of propaganda used by every other emperor before him. The main difference in Honorius' case is, of course, that there is some Christian ideology added to the mix, but by the early fifth century that was a staple requisite for Christian Augusti. The imperial office positioned itself as God's representative on earth, just as much as the Roman papacy strove to represent itself. Martin Icks is right when he says that 'as leader of the Christian world, it was considered the emperor's task to protect the true faith and guard the unity of the church. By styling themselves as devout rulers ... Arcadius and Honorius could claim continued divine approval for their reign' (2014, 28). The concept behind the widely used imperial slogan *Victoria Augustorum* – that there could be no military, political, or social stability without an emperor – had to count for something in an age of waning western Roman hegemony, even if that victory was becoming more spiritual than temporal.

References

Blair-Dixon, Kate. 2007. "Memory and Authority in Sixth-Century Rome: The *Liber Pontificalis* and the *Collectio Avellana*." In *Religion, Dynasty and Patronage in Early Christian Rome, 300–900*. Edited by Kate Cooper and Julia Hillner: 59–76. Cambridge: Cambridge University Press.

Bomgardner, David L. 2000. *The Story of the Roman Amphitheatre*. London and New York: Routledge.

Bonner, Gerald. 1972. *Augustine and Modern Research on Pelagianism*. Wetteren: Villanova University Press.

Cristo, Stuart. 1977. "Some Notes on the Bonifacian-Eulalian Schism." *Aevum* 51: 163–7.

Deliyannis, Deborah M., trans. 2004. Agnellus of Ravenna. *The Book of Pontiffs of the Church of Ravenna*. Washington, D.C.: Catholic University of America Press.

Deliyannis, Deborah M. 2010. *Ravenna in Late Antiquity*. Cambridge: Cambridge University Press.

Dossey, Leslie. 2001. "Judicial Violence and the Ecclesiastical Courts in Late Antique North Africa." In *Law, Society, and Authority in Late Antiquity*. Edited by Ralph W. Mathisen: 98–114. Oxford: Oxford University Press.

Doyle, Christopher. 2014. *The Endgame of Treason: Rebellion and Usurpation in the Late Roman Empire, AD 395–411*. Unpublished thesis. Galway: National University of Ireland Galway. https://aran.library.nuigalway.ie/handle/10379/4631.

Ducloux, Anne. 1994. *Ad ecclesiam confugere: naissance du droit d'asile dans les église Ive–milieu du Ve s*. Paris: De Boccard.

Elsner, Jas. 1998. *Imperial Rome and Christian Triumph: The Art of the Roman Empire, AD 100–450*. Oxford: Oxford University Press.

Hallebeek, Jan. 2004. "Church Asylum in Late Antiquity: Concession by the Emperor or Competence of the Church?" In *Secundum Ius*: Opstellen aangeboden aan prof mr. P. L. Nève. Edited by E. C. Coppens: 163–82. Nijmegen: Gerard Noodt Instituut.

Honoré, Tony. 1998. *Law in the Crisis of Empire, AD 379–455*. Oxford: Oxford University Press.

Humfress, Caroline. 2007. *Orthodoxy and the Courts in Late Antiquity*. Oxford: Oxford University Press.

Humphries, Mark. 1999. *Communities of the Blessed: Social Environment and Religious Change in Northern Italy, AD 200–400*. Oxford Early Christian Studies. Oxford: Oxford University Press.

Hunt, David. 1993. "Christianizing the Roman Empire: The Evidence of the Code." In *The Theodosian Code: Studies in the Imperial Law of Late Antiquity*. Edited by Jill Harries and Ian Woods: 143–58. Ithaca, NY: Cornell University Press.

Icks, Martijn. 2014. "The Inadequate Heirs of Theodosius: Ancestry, Merit and Divine Blessing in the Representation of Arcadius and Honorius." *Millennium* 11.1: 69–100.

Keech, Dominic. 2012. *The Anti-Pelagian Christology of Augustine of Hippo*. Oxford Theological Monographs. Oxford: Oxford University Press.

Kiilerich, Bente. 1993. *Late Fourth Century Classicism in the Plastic Arts: Studies in the So-Called Theodosian Renaissance*. Odense: Odense University Press.
Latham, Jacob A. 2014. "Battling Bishops, the Roman Aristocracy, and the Contestation of Civic Space in Late Antique Rome." In *Religious Competition in the Third Century CE: Jews, Christians, and the Greco-Roman World*. Journal of Ancient Judaism Supplement 15. Edited by Nathaniel DesRosiers, Jordan D. Rosenblum, and Lily Vuong: 126–38. Göttingen: Vandenhoeck & Ruprecht.
Lejdegård, Hans. 2002. *Honorius and the City of Rome: Authority and Legitimacy in Late Antiquity*. Uppsala: Uppsala Universitet.
MacMullen, Ramsay. 1988. *Corruption and the Decline of Rome*. New Haven, CT and London: Yale University Press.
Matthews, John F. 2000. *Laying Down the Law: A Study of the Theodosian Code*. New Haven, CT: Yale University Press.
McEvoy, Meaghan. 2013. "The Mausoleum of Honorius: Late Roman Imperial Christianity and the City of Rome in the Fifth Century." In *Old Saint Peter's, Rome*. Edited by Rosamond McKitterick, John Osborne, Carol M. Richardson, and Joanna Story: 119–36. Cambridge: Cambridge University Press.
Norton, Peter. 2007. *Episcopal Elections 250–600: Hierarchy and Popular Will in Late Antiquity*. Oxford Classical Monographs. Oxford: Oxford University Press.
Rapp, Claudia. 1998. "Comparison, Paradigm, and the Case of Moses in Panegyric and Hagiography." In *The Propaganda of Power: The Role of Panegyric in Late Antiquity*. Mnemosyne Supplement 183. Edited by Mary Whitby: 277–98. Leiden: Brill.
Reagan, Ronald. "Remarks at the Annual National Prayer Breakfast." February 2, 1984. Online by Gerhard Peters and John T. Woolley. *The American Presidency Project (APP)*, www.presidency.ucsb.edu/ws/?pid=39211.
Salzman, Michele Renee. 2006. "Rethinking Pagan–Christian Violence." In *Violence in Late Antiquity*. Edited by Harold A. Drake et al.: 265–85. Surrey: Ashgate.
Sessa, Kristina. 2011. *The Formation of Papal Authority in Late Antique Italy: Roman Bishops and the Domestic Sphere*. New York: Cambridge University Press.
Shoemaker, Karl. 2011. *Sanctuary and Crime in the Middle Ages, 400–1500*. New York: Fordham University Press.

9   A kind of peace

> For ten years we have been cut down by the slaughtering swords of the Vandals
> and of the Goths! No forts set on rocks, no towns on lofty mountains, or
> cities protected by rivers, not all together have been able to overcome the wiles
> of the barbarians and their raging weapons … we have suffered the ultimate
> calamity …
>
> *Carmen de providentia Dei*, 34–8

In the years following their infamous sack of Rome, the Visigoths established
themselves in Gaul under Ataulf, supporting usurpers there and generally
causing trouble for the Honorian government. Ataulf tried to maintain economic and political stability in the regions he controlled by continuing to strike
coinage, although the currency continued to depict Honorius' name and image
(Figure 9.1). The Visigoths, like other barbarian conquerors in the late Roman
West, recognized the need to keep up imperial administrative methods, and they
used Roman bureaucrats, politicians, clergy, and artisans to help them for this
purpose. This practice of employing Roman talent to keep barbarian rulers in
power continued for a very long time after the end of the western empire.

In early 413, Honorius agreed a deal with Ataulf to send North African
grain to Gaul as part of a deal to retrieve his sister Placidia, still a Visigoth
hostage. Ataulf pledged to fight under Honorius' banner against the Vandals
in Spain. All was proceeding smoothly enough until the emperor was betrayed
by his *comes Africae* Heraclianus, who usurped power and attacked Honorius
in Italy. The grain shipments to Gaul were suspended and Ataulf, denied
his food subsidy, thought Honorius fickle. Consequently, their relationship
broke down.

In early 414, Ataulf married Placida in the recently seized Gallic town
of Narbo Martius (Narbonne). This Roman-barbarian union, technically
illegal under imperial law, sent a clear message to Ravenna that Ataulf was
not to be trifled with. The former usurper Priscus Attalus, still a 'guest' of the
barbarians, was reappointed by Ataulf as emperor, and even sang a few nup-
tial hymns at the wedding. This ceremony was supposed to have been extravagant, even if the wedding gifts were mainly loot from Rome (Olymp. *fr.* 24).
Placidia soon became pregnant and bore Ataulf a son, Theodosius, who died

Figure 9.1 Barbarous silver siliqua in the name of Honorius. Visigothic Gallic issue, *c*. 415. Obv. Honorius pearl-diademed, draped, and cuirassed. Legend: DN-HONORI-VS-PF-AVG (*Dominus Noster Honorius Pius Felix Augustus*/ Our Lord Honorius, pious and fortunate Augustus). Rev. Roma seated on cuirass, Victoriola in her right hand, inverted spear in her left. Legend: VICTOR[I]-A-AVGG[G] (*Victoria Augustorum*/Victory of the Augusti). Mintmark unintelligible.

Source: Reinhart, Münzen; cf. RIC X 3703.

shortly afterwards in Spain, where they had been forced to move in the face of a Roman military campaign. We are told that the little boy's parents were distraught, and they placed his body in a silver coffin that was interred in a Spanish church (Olymp. *fr.* 26). Many years later, Placidia reinterred her child's remains in his uncle's mausoleum at Saint Peter's Basilica (Johnson 1991). While some ancient (and modern) authors like to romanticize Placidia and Ataulf's relationship as courtly love or divine prophecy (Oros. 7.40.2; 43.7; Hyd. s.a. 414; Jord. *Get.* 31), we should be under no illusion as to Placidia's predicament. She was Ataulf's hostage, and though she might have had better living conditions than her fellow Roman prisoners, she probably had very little choice in deciding her immediate future for herself.

In early 414, hoping to get Placidia back through military force, Honorius sent his *magister* Constantius, who was also the western consul for that year, against the Visigoths. Philostorgius suggests that Constantius had an ulterior motive, that he wanted Placidia for himself as his wife (Philost. *HE.* 12.4–5). That she did marry Constantius later, and have two children with him, is true, but whether the *magister* had marriage in mind all along is unprovable (Olymp. *fr.* 33). At any rate, Constantius inflicted heavy losses on Ataulf in Gaul, forcing the Visigoths into Spain, where the little Theodosius was born, died, and was buried. As for the luckless Attalus, he was left behind by Ataulf as a token gesture for Honorius, whose punishment of the usurper is discussed below. Ataulf was assassinated soon after his infant son's death. Apparently, Ataulf's marriage to Placidia was not approved of by all members of the Visigothic élite, and her husband's dying wish was that she be returned unharmed to her family. Not long after Ataulf's murder, one of his successors, Vallia, sent Placidia back to her brother (Chron. Marcell. s.a. 414; cf. Oros. 7.43.1–15). It was Vallia who, after drastically reducing Vandal power in Spain, would negotiate a lasting land settlement for the Visigothic people with Honorius in 418 (Hyd. s.a. 417–18).

Also in 414, Honorius is thought to have visited Rome, perhaps to celebrate the defeat of the series of usurpers Constantine III, Jovinus, Sebastianus, and Heraclianus. The evidence for this particular visit is admittedly thin, but it is plausible that it took place. Certain modern scholars suggest that the 414 visit had a twofold purpose – to stage a military triumph and to repair damaged relations between the emperor and the Roman senate, some of whom felt Honorius had failed in his duty to protect them during Alaric's sieges of their city (Gillett 2001, 137–41; Lejdegård 2002, 57–9). Whatever may have transpired in Rome in 414, it is certain that Honorius held a triumph there in 416, the last such event recorded in Rome. On that occasion, Honorius exhibited a most valued prize – the usurper Priscus Attalus whom Constantius had seized after the former was abandoned by his Visigothic former allies.

In 415, Honorius' second wife, Thermantia, died at Rome from unknown causes. It had been seven years since her entire family's execution and her repudiation by Honorius. In that time, she had somehow survived the barbarian pillage of Rome while her sister-in-law Placidia and thousands of others had been enslaved or killed. It is ironic that the two sources that tell us of Thermantia's death are eastern: Zosimus, who says she died a virgin, and a seventh-century Byzantine chronicle that informs us that Thermantia's death was officially announced in Constantinople on July 30, 415 (Zos. 5.28.3; *Chron. Pasch.* s.a. 415). No contemporary western source mentions her death, which seems strange. Perhaps this was done to spare Honorius the embarrassment of having his subjects reminded that his divorced wife had been in Rome when Alaric took the city. It is particularly sad that neither of his wives, Maria and Thermantia, received much comment during, or indeed after, their short lives, in comparison to the achievements of other emperors' wives. It may well be that their father's disgrace extended to Thermantia and Maria as well, and thus all memory of the two sisters was suppressed.

A brief summary of Honorius' personal circumstances up to this late point in his reign might be considered. In 415, he was thirty years old. Over the course of his life, he had lost his parents, brother, wives, and foster parents (granted that was his own doing, but they were family nonetheless), and he had not been back to Constantinople, the city of his birth, since the age of ten. Honorius still endured on the western throne, but at what cost to his well-being? The personal tragedies, the political and military crises, and the numerous threats to his life – all of this must have put enormous pressure on him. Leadership can make for a lonely existence, and while Honorius may have grown used to isolation from a young age, over the last few years of his life he became even more isolated than ever. He had no children of his own, his sister was taken from him for several years, and even when she returned things were never the same between the two siblings again. To a man for whom family was most important, the solitude must have been onerous. If what our sources say about Honorius' deep devotion to the Catholic Church is accurate, it is small wonder that he sought solace in the divine.

Prostration and mercy

Attalus, as we have seen, had been kept as collateral by Alaric up until 410, and subsequently by Ataulf until 415, when he offered up the usurper to Honorius (Soz. *HE*. 9.8.10–11). Attalus' life among the barbarians must truly have been pathetic, and it was remarked that he was 'like a hollow statue of an emperor' (Oros. 7.42.9). Constantius brought Attalus in front of Honorius at Ravenna, where the emperor is supposed to have severed the fingers of Attalus' right hand, as Philostorgius' partially preserved and chronologically skewed text indicates.

> Ataulf, who had done many wicked deeds, was slain by one of his own men in a fit of anger. Thereupon the barbarians made their peace with Honorius, and having received provisions and part of Gaul for agriculture, they handed over to the emperor his sister and Attalus. Afterwards, Rome recovered from these many calamities and people settled there. The emperor visited it and encouraged its settlement with hand and tongue. And ascending a dais (platform), the first step of which he compelled Attalus to bestride ... [he] cut off two fingers of his right hand, one of which ... while the other is called the forefinger. And he banished him to the island of Lipara, inflicting no further penalty, but even providing the necessities of life ...
>
> (Philost. *HE*. 12.4–5)

After Ravenna, Honorius took his prisoner to Rome for a public triumph in 416. The wretched Attalus was made to walk in front of Honorius' chariot through Rome's streets to the city center where the emperor performed an ancient, symbolic ritual which involved placing a boot on the prostrate victim's neck (*calcatio colli*). Michael McCormick thinks that Honorius might have performed this act on horseback, since Philostorgius' account (above) suffers from several lacunae (McCormick 1990, 57–8). Perhaps, but it seems excessive for Honorius. That Attalus was mutilated seems certain, though it was not necessarily carried out by the emperor himself, as some have interpreted Philostorgius' passage to imply. Then again, Honorius had witnessed shocking brutality over the years, so it is possible that he had become desensitized to violence and perhaps fully participated in Attalus' ritual humiliation. Still, Philostorgius' account lacks the compassion shown by Honorius at other times.

In sparing Priscus Attalus, Honorius demonstrated clemency, an important imperial virtue. He could just as easily have had Attalus decapitated, and put his head on display, but maybe Honorius had seen enough of that for a while. From a public relations point of view, Attalus' exile showed Rome's senatorial assembly, of which he was a member, that the emperor was merciful, albeit to a point. Honorius' leniency might work to his advantage if he was to restore his standing with the senatorial élite.

Placidia and Constantius

Constantius entered his western consulship in January 417, and married Placidia at the same time as his inauguration. His star was indeed in the ascendant. She, according to the little we know of this marriage, was not enamored by him at all. He had persistently tried to get her to agree to marry him, but she rebuffed him every time. It could be that she actually disliked the man for having used famine as a weapon against her first husband Ataulf's people, despite her being their hostage. Does this mean that Placidia developed Stockholm Syndrome, and found affinity for the barbarians, or simply she was sick to death of being used as a pawn by powerful men? Oost thought so, and he was probably right that this was the likely scenario, especially considering that Placidia had lost her child, probably as a result of having to flee the armies of Constantius and her brother (1968, 141–2). Her religious views may also have played a part in her remarrying so soon after Ataulf's death. Placidia was just as much a prisoner among her own people as she had been with the Visigoths. Honorius forced her to marry Constantius. Her brother owed his *magister* a very great debt. It was Constantius who had come to his aid in the chaos following Stilicho's death, and when multiple wars streaked through the Roman West like fiery arrows.

So, on January 1, 417, Honorius gave his sister in marriage to Constantius. She was in her mid-twenties, while her new spouse was considerably older. We do not know how old Constantius was, but he had joined the army under Theodosius I, so the age difference was noticeable. If Constantius was attracted to Placidia for her looks or position is not known, neither do we really know how she found him physically. They had two children together, but that does not necessarily mean that there was mutual love involved. There was no poet to record their wedding night in detail like Claudian had for Honorius and Maria, but even if there had been, it would have been a manufactured reality. The few anecdotes there are about the couple's married life together are revealing as to the nature of their relationship. This excerpt from Olympiodorus is set during 421, when Constantius had became co-Augustus with Honorius.

> Libanius ... a consummate magician, able to achieve results even against barbarians without resort to weapons ... was given permission to make the attempt, but when his promise and his high repute came to the ears of the empress Placidia, the magician was put to death. For Placidia threatened

Constantius that she would break up their marriage if Libanius, a wizard and an unbeliever, remained amongst the living.

(Olymp. *fr*. 36)

A homeland for the barbarians

In 418, Honorius got down to realpolitik with the Visigothic leader Vallia. It must not have been an easy thing to do, but in the interests of peace and security, the emperor had no choice. Years of war exacerbated an already heightened sense of fear of barbarian peoples, but in 418, the truth was that the Visigoths were there to stay and the Roman world simply had to get used to that fact. Still, there was distaste for Roman-Gothic co-operation, particularly concerning the overreliance on barbarian *foederati* to supplement shortfalls in the imperial army. Honorius made overtures to anti-barbarian sentiment in the city of Rome by banning the wearing of trousers (*bracchae*), an apparel associated with barbarians, in 416 (*CTh*. 14.10.4. Dec 12, 416). Honorius' war on breeches was little more than a populist gesture designed to show that, despite his talks with the Visigoths, he nonetheless opposed the spread of foreign culture.

The distraction of anti-pants legislation aside, Honorius and Vallia's negotiation resulted in the granting of land to the Visigoths in Aquitania Secunda (Aquitaine), Gaul. After decades spent wandering a land where they were often treated with contempt, suspicion, and aggression, the Visigoths found themselves a niche in western Europe. Though it would take many more years before they eventually established their own kingdom in Spain, independent of Rome or anywhere else, the first concrete steps had been taken.

However good the Roman state's relationship was to be with the Visigoths after the Aquitanian settlement, there were other barbarian tribes operating inside Roman territory with whom similar cooperation was impossible. The Visigoth military therefore would be a necessary instrument of imperial power, that is, if they could be controlled. Honorius can hardly be faulted for conceding land to the Visigoths. He had inherited them from his father, and spent most of his reign trying to work out how best to deal with them. Rome could not simply kill its way through the issue, and compromise was the only realistic solution.

Honorius and Constantius Augusti

Constantius held his third consulship in 420, an accomplishment that not even Stilicho had achieved. By now, Placidia had borne Constantius two children: a girl, Iusta Grata Honoria, born in either late 417 or early 418, and a boy, Valentinian, born in July 419. Placidia and Constantius' son later succeeded Honorius as western Augustus in 425. In the preceding chapter on Honorius' religious endeavors, we saw how Constantius and Placidia took sides in the contested papal election in Rome. The city prefect Symmachus wrote to Constantius on this matter, and glowingly addressed him as 'Our

Most Illustrious, Exalted, Sacred, splendid and deserving eternal Lord, defender [of the Catholic faith]' (*Coll. Avell.* Const. *Ep.* 32). Bearing in mind this was in 419, two years before Constantius was elevated to share the throne with Honorius, it is clear that Constantius was destined for supreme power. Symmachus marked Constantius' third consulship with an inscription at Rome (*CIL* 6.1719). Here, Constantius was styled as the 'reviver of the state' (*reparatori rei publicae*), and the invincible father of the emperor (*parenti invictissimorum principum*). Such language was typically reserved for actual emperors, which suggests that it was accepted, among Roman élites at least, that Constantius was destined to rule the West. Symmachus' inscription acknowledged Constantius' pivotal role in defeating Rome's domestic and foreign enemies, and for having fathered an imperial heir. Actually, when Stilicho assumed guardianship of Honorius in 395, he had been styled *parens principum*, a phrase which O' Flynn calls a 'mysterious title that embodied his claim to supreme power' (1983, 16). Though the political situation in 420 differed from that of 395, Constantius' recognition as a de facto Augustus was due also to his marriage to Placidia and the birth of their children, especially their son. The glorification of Constantius does not necessarily mean something sinister was afoot against Honorius, however. Constantius' ascent to supreme power was practical. Whatever the reason, Honorius was unable to provide an heir, nor was he capable of commanding troops on campaign, for he had not been trained to do so, as Stilicho ought to have done for him. It is impossible to know who exactly made the decision to put Constantius on the throne – Honorius, Placidia, or Constantius himself – though it is likely that all three worked together to make it happen. By the late 410s, Honorius' health may have deteriorated so such a degree that he realized he had to ensure a smooth transition of power for his nephew Valentinian. Placidia, who, we are told, protested her arranged marriage to Constantius, demanded that her brother bestow the title of *nobilissmus puer* (most noble child) on her baby son. Honorius himself had been given this title in his infancy (Olymp. *fr.* 33). The reasoning behind Placidia's demand, and Constantius' subsequent acclamation, was to prevent a power struggle that might lead to civil war in the event of Honorius' death.

On February 8, 421, Honorius formally elevated his brother-in-law to the collegiate (AM 5913; Olymp. *frr.* 33, 37; Soz. *HE.* 9.16.2; McEvoy 2013, 213–15). Coinage for the new emperor depicted him in the customary fashion, but for once the militaristic nature of imperial ideology was not a propagandist gesture. Constantius was a very effective soldier, commander, and tactician (Figure 9.2). Theodosius II refused to accept this acclamation, or to allow Constantius' images to be put up in the eastern empire (Olymp. *fr.* 33.2).

Apparently, Constantius did not like his new role, for he found it too restrictive. He discovered for himself what Honorius' life was really like, perhaps gaining a new respect, or sympathy, for his former master.

> Constantius fell ill and regretted his elevation, that he no longer had the freedom to leave and go off wherever and in whatever manner he wished

Figure 9.2 Gold solidus of Constantius III. Ravenna mint, 421. Obv. Constantius pearl
and rosette-diademed, draped, and cuirassed. Legend: DN-CONSTAN-
TIVSPF-AVG (*Dominus Noster Constantius Pius Felix Augustus*/Our Lord
Constantius, pious and fortunate emperor). Rev. Constantius in armor and
cloak, standing, Victoriola in his left hand, *labarum* in his right, his left foot
trampling captive. Legend: VICTORI-A-AVGGG (*Victoria Augustorum*/
Victory of the Augusti). Field: R/V (Ravenna). Exergue: COMOB
(*Comitatus obryziacum*/pure gold mark).

Source: *RIC* X 1325.

and could not, because he was emperor, enjoy the pastimes which he had
been accustomed to enjoy.

(Olymp. *fr.* 33.2)

Constantius' reign was short. He died from pleurisy (inflammation of the lungs)
on September 2, 421, just seven months into his tenure (Olymp. *fr.* 33.2; Soc. *HE.*
7.24). It was alleged that he was preparing a military expedition for war against
Theodosius in the East because the latter had not recognized him (Philost. *HE.*
12.12). This proposed war against Honorius' nephew may have given rise to the
accusations made by Theophanes and Michael the Syrian (Rabo), who cried
foul, suggesting Constantius was murdered, though these are very late claims
from the ninth and thirteenth centuries (AM 5913; MS 77). Could Honorius,
or even Placidia, have been responsible for such a deed? We have seen their
direct involvement in high-profile killings in the past. Most other sources who
speak of Constantius' passing, however, just say that he died, possibly from
pleurisy, a infectious chest condition exacerbated by hard living. Constantius
was not a particularly young man, and considering how much fighting he had
been engaged in for over ten years, much of which was under adverse weather
conditions, it is not very surprising that his health had suffered. In the end, as
Olympiodorus says, 'death came upon him and freed him from his life and his

cares' (Olymp *fr*. 33.2). Though it became tradition that Constantius was buried at Ravenna or Milan, his remains were most likely interred in the Honorian mausoleum at Saint Peter's Basilica (Johnson 1991, 338).

Honorius' final years

As 421 drew to a close, Honorius was once more alone on the western throne. He set about re-establishing a working relationship with his nephew Theodosius II after the disagreement over Constantius' accession. With Constantius gone, cordiality could be restored. The coinage and legal pronouncements from late 421 onwards reflect both Honorius and Theodosius' efforts at repairing their ties. Honorius' coins emphasize harmony between Rome and Constantinople, while his military and religious numismatic iconography remained unchanged as ever (Figure 9.3).

Amid this renewed spirit of cooperation, Honorius and Theodosius jointly issued laws for the year 422 offer solutions to social and economic issues such as taxation, personal debt, and widows' property rights (*CTh*. 11.28.13. Feb 20; 8.8.10. July 11; 3.13.3. Nov 3, 422).

In 422, Honorius held the consulship for the thirteenth and final time. He was afforded the opportunity of marking this consular year by putting Maximus, the last of the usurpers who had opposed him, to death. Maximus

Figure 9.3 Gold solidus of Honorius. Ravenna mint, 421. Obv. Honorius pearl-diademed and helmeted, draped, and cuirassed, facing, holding spear in his right hand, a round shield with Chi-Rho in his left hand. Legend: DN-HONORI-VS-PF-AVG (*Dominus Noster Honorius Pius Felix Augustus/* Our Lord Honorius, pious and fortunate Augustus). Rev. Roma and Constantinopolis seated on cuirass in the form of an eagle, facing each other, both holding a wreath inscribed VOT/XXX/MVLT/XXXX between; palm branch below. Field: R/V (Ravenna). Exergue: COMOB (*Comitatus obryziacum/*pure gold mark).

Source: *RIC* X 1332.

(Figure 7.3) was a puppet emperor who had ruled from a small region in Spain from 409 to 411 (Oros. 7.42.4; Olymp. *fr.* 17). He was deposed in 411 and had been hiding with barbarians in Spain ever since. He rose up again in Spain in 420 to proclaim himself emperor but was captured when Honorius sent an expedition to reclaim Spain from the Vandals. Maximus was brought in chains to Ravenna, and executed during public games (Hyd. s.a. 420–2; *Chron. Gall.* 452 s.a. 422; *Ann. Rav.* s.a. 422; Chron. Marcell. s.a. 422). Some think that there were two usurpers named Maximus, but it is probably the case that it was the same man who usurped the *imperium* twice (*PLRE* II, 744–5).

Honorius' personal relationship with his sister Placidia seems to have fallen apart very quickly after her husband's death. Scurrilous rumor has it that Honorius became besotted with his sister, and was seen several times kissing her inappropriately (Olymp. *fr.* 38). Again, I wonder if Honorius was in the grip of illness, an unknown form of edema, would he have entertained incestuous designs? Would he have behaved in this way even if he was healthy? This story about the emperor's salaciousness – and his sister's too, for she was accused of immorality – is all too similar to tall tales about other Roman rulers, and other individuals as well. Remember Claudian's description of Gildo as the king of vice! Even our main source, Olympiodorus, says that it was gossip, yet he still chose to include it in his history. Olympiodorus also reveals that Placidia's close female advisors, Spadusa and Helpidia, with the aid of a male

Figure 9.4 Gold solidus of Galla Placidia. Aquileia mint, *c.* 425. Obv. Placidia pearl-diademed and draped, Chi-Rho on her right shoulder, *manus Dei* crowning her from above. Legend: DN-GALLA-PLA-CIDIA-PF-AVG (*Domina Nostra Galla Placidia Pia Felix Augusta*/Our Lady Galla Placidia, dutiful and wise Augusta). Rev. Victory standing, holding long cross in her right hand. Legend: / VOT XX MVLT XXX (*Votis Vicennalibus, Multis Tricennalibus*/ Prayers for the twentieth anniversary of reign, more offered for the approaching thirtieth anniversary). Field: A/Q (Aquileia). Exergue: COMOB (*Comitatus obryziacum*/pure gold mark).

Source: *RIC* X 1808.

servant, Leontius, poisoned her mind against her brother (Olymp. *fr.* 38). Oost thought that Spadusa was the wife of a court official named Felix, which is possible (1968, 170). Felix went on to become a *magister* in Placidia and Valentinian III's administration after Honorius' death. Felix even murdered Constantius' old friend Patroclus, the bishop of Arles. What a sordid hotbed of chicanery the late Roman palace was – a place where those responsible for looking after the imperial family continually conspired against their masters in order to further their own careers. Who, indeed, could an emperor and his family ever really trust? The upshot of this scandal saw Placidia taking her two children with her to Constantinople, where she was received by her nephew Theodosius II. We are told variously that she either fled in fear from her brother, or that he exiled her because of the infighting her entourage – Visigothic and Roman – were engaged in at his court (Olymp. *fr.* 38; Prosp. Tiro. s.a. 423). Placidia would never see her brother alive again. When she returned to Ravenna in 425, she first had to depose a usurper named Johannes before she could install her son Valentinian on the throne. It was through her regency over her son that Placidia became an Augusta of the Theodosian dynasty (Figures 9.4 and 9.5).

Figure 9.5 Gold solidus of Galla Placidia Augusta. Rome mint, *c.* 425–6. Obv. Placidia draped and diademed, her hair in a *Scheitelzopf* (elaborately plaited style), wearing earrings and necklace, Christogram on her right shoulder, crowned by the *manus Dei*. Legend: DN-GALLA-PLA-CIDIA-PF-AVG (*Domina Nostra Galla Placidia Pia Felix Augusta*/Our Lady Galla Placidia, pious and fortunate empress). Rev. Victory standing, long jeweled cross in her right hand, her left hand on her hip, star above. Legend: VOT XX MVLT XXX (*Votis Vicennalibus, Multis Tricennalibus*/ Prayers for the twentieth anniversary of reign, more offered for the approaching thirtieth anniversary). Field: R/M (Roma). Exergue: COMOB (*Comitatus obryziacum*/pure gold mark).

Source: *RIC* X 2007.

Last visit to Rome

The very last laws Honorius drafted from Ravenna were on August 6, 423, just days before his death. This body of legislation addressed senatorial criminality; curtailed the legal status of freedmen, probably those of barbarian origin; granted due process for accused persons; and forbade military executions at Rome without prefectal consent (*CTh.* 1.6.11; 2.1.12; 4.10.2; 9.1.19; 9.6.4. Aug 6, 423). Other than this small selection of legal evidence, we know nothing else about Honorius' final days or hours.

According to a Byzantine chronicler, 'after a comet had glowed on and off, the emperor Honorius met his appointed fate' (Chron. Marcell. s.a. 423). He was thirty-seven years old. Other sources are less dramatic (Olymp. *fr.* 39; Philost. *HE.* 12.13; Soc. *HE.* 7.22.20). True to form of our primary sources, there are different dates for Honorius' death, either August 15 or 27, 423. There is also some confusion as to whether it was Ravenna or Rome

Figure 9.6 Gold and sardonyx intaglio depicting the six-year-old Valentinian III's investiture at Rome in 425. The child emperor stands on a dais, between the spirits of his deceased relatives: his father Constantius III to his left, his uncle Honorius to his right. Constantius crowns his son with a laurel wreath, while Honorius has his hands placed on the boy's shoulders. Two male angels hover holding victory wreaths over the two senior emperors' heads. A Chi-Rho is directly above Valentinian's head, an Alpha and Omega on either side. The gem is inscribed *Flavius Romvlvs vestiarius fecit/* Flavius Romulus, clothes dealer, made this.

Source: © The State Hermitage Museum, Saint Petersburg, Russia.

where Honorius died. Overall, the death of Honorius was quiet, and received little comment, unlike his parents' funerals years before. It was primarily the Theodosian family who remembered and honored Honorius, even if most of the world did not care to (Figure 9.6). Valentinian III's legislation refers to his sainted uncle Honorius. In the matter of his funeral, all that we can be certain of is that at some point after his passing, Honorius' body would have lain in state. Then, his remains were taken by cortege to Saint Peter's Basilica, where he was interred in the purpose-built crypt deep beneath his beloved church (Johnson 1991, 335–6). Honorius' long reign was over.

Appraisal for the unloved

It is not easy to admire, or even like, Honorius. He spent almost his entire life on the western imperial throne, and what was there to show for it in the end? We might weigh his reign against the achievements of more hands-on Roman emperors; lambast him for the loss of Britain and other regions; or judge him for failing to produce children from two marriages. Through the ages, Honorius has been frequently dismissed as worthless on account of these judgments. However, to hold him responsible for the late Roman West's woes, without consideration of his personal situation, is to do him a disservice. I hope that the account of Honorius' life, as I have presented it, goes some way to rehabilitate his memory, and provide a glimpse behind the curtain of power, away from the pomp, ceremony, propaganda, and hyperbole.

Honorius was thrust into a post-civil war political situation aged just ten. He inherited immense problems from his father, not least of which was the Visigothic question. Theodosius died before his sons were really prepared for rule. In a way, their father set them up for failure through his continual appointment of guardians for them while he was away on campaign. Perhaps Theodosius hoped for something different than mud and blood for his sons, but the reality behind maintaining Roman power was war. In our own time, this is still much the same way power is projected. Theodosius did the best he could for Honorius, instructing family members – bound by kinship and marriage – to watch over his son. The emperor could not possibly have foreseen how Stilicho and Serena would interpret his wishes posthumously. If, as Stilicho claimed, he was carrying out his deceased master's directive, and had really wanted Honorius to succeed as an emperor, he should have fully trained the boy in the arts vital for civil and military leadership. Arguments have been made that Honorius was too unintelligent to be taught, but, in my opinion, these do not hold up to scrutiny. There were moments when Honorius showed personal courage, for example after the Ticinum massacre; or initiative, by removing Stilicho from the equation. Unfortunately, that is all these were – moments. Such were the results of close control over the child emperor.

And yet, Honorius remained the 'great survivor,' reigning for thirty years. This has been called an anomaly, the result of careful manipulation by those who sought to preserve their own station. When it suited Honorius, though, he proved quite adept at changing his own guard, so to speak. What perhaps we want is to see Honorius act as a military emperor. We want to see him get off the throne, don armor, jump on his horse, and dash into battle with sword drawn at the head of loyal troops. He wanted this as much himself, so Claudian told us. But that is the romantic ideal, not the reality. For so many people under Honorius' rule, theirs had been a struggle to survive the destruction of war, economic hardship, religious intolerance, and state oppression.

Depending on your point of view, one of Honorius' great achievements was his contribution to the rise of Catholic supremacy. His patronage of the Roman Church, his religiously inspired laws, and support for the papacy ensured that Catholicism grew stronger. Honorius' successors built on what he had done for the Church, as he himself had built on the foundations established by Constantine I. When it came to foreign policy, or rather internal policy now that the Visigoths were inside the Roman border, the settlement of those barbarians in Aquitaine was a remarkable accomplishment, even if it only achieved peace in the short term. Perhaps if Honorius could have compromised sooner with Alaric, in the late 390s, for instance, things may have been different, but Roman attitudes to barbarians would have had to have changed radically. It was only after the invasions of the 400s that a genuine compromise became possible.

Honorius' very long rule was the example for how later figurehead governments were run, especially those of emperors who were elevated to the purple as children. As powerful, and as sought after, as the imperial office was, however, it very often seems that the late Roman emperor was more like a hostage in his own court, as the excerpt on Aurelian below implies. Perhaps this is why soldier emperors such as Theodosius I preferred to spend so much time away from court. His sons were not so fortunate.

> Four or five men gather together and form one plan for deceiving the emperor, and then they tell him to what he must give his approval. Now the emperor, who is shut up in his palace, cannot know the truth. He is forced to know only what these men tell him, he appoints as judges those who should not be appointed, and removes from public office those whom he ought to retain. Why say more? As Diocletian himself used to say, the favor of even a good and wise and righteous emperor is often sold … nothing is harder than to be a good ruler.
>
> (SHA *Aur*. 43.1–5)

References

Gillett, Andrew. 2001. "Rome, Ravenna and the Last Western Emperors." *PBSR* 69: 131–67.

Johnson, Mark J. 1991. "On the Burial Places of the Theodosian Dynasty." *Byzantion* 61: 330–9.

Lejdegård, Hans. 2002. *Honorius and the City of Rome: Authority and Legitimacy in Late Antiquity*. Uppsala: Uppsala Universitet.

McCormick, Michael. 1990 (1986). *Eternal Victory: Triumphal Rulership in Late Antiquity, Byzantium and the Early Medieval West.* Cambridge: Cambridge University Press. Reprint.

McEvoy, Meaghan. 2013. *Child Emperor Rule in the Late Roman West, AD 367–455.* Oxford: Oxford University Press.

O' Flynn, John Michael. 1983. *Generalissimos of the Western Roman Empire.* Alberta: University of Alberta Press.

Oost, Stewart Irvin. 1968. *Galla Placidia Augusta: A Biographical Essay.* Chicago, IL and London: The University of Chicago Press.

Glossary of ancient terms

Literary terms

Carm.	*Carmen, Carmina*/poem(s)
Chron.	*Chronicon, Chronica*/chronicle(s)
Cod.	*Codex*/book
Ep. (Epp).	*Epistula, Epistulae*/letter(s)
Epit.	*Epitome*/summary
fr.	*fragmentum(a)*/fragment(s)
HE	*Historia Ecclesiastica*, Church History
Pan.	Panegyric/Praise poem
Praef.	*Prefatio*/Preface
Rel.	*Relationes*/motions, propositions
s.a.	*sub anno*/under the year, in the year

Late imperial terms

Adventus	Formal ceremonial entry of the emperor into a city, particularly after a military victory
Annona	Food supply from North Africa and Egypt designated for Rome, Constantinople, and other imperial cities
Augusta	Empress
Augustus	Senior member in the imperial *collegium*
Barbaricum	The world beyond Rome's frontiers
Caesar	Junior emperor; subordinate to the Augustus
Chi-Rho	First two Greek letters (X, P) of Christ's name
Clarissimus	Most Highly Regarded; rank held by all senators and their relatives
Collegium	Brotherhood of co-ruling emperors
Coloni	Tenant farmers for the most part
Comes	Count; a senior military/civilian administrative title

Comes sacrarum largitionum	Administrator of the imperial treasury
Consistorium	Imperial inner advisory council
Constitutio	Imperial law, decree, edict, or rescript
Curia	Curia Senatus/Senate House
Damnatio memoriae	Condemnation of memory of state enemies
Decurion	Member of municipal council
Dux	Duke; subordinate commander to the *magister militum*
Edict	Legal proclamation issued by the emperor
Foederati	Federated barbarian troops allied to Rome
Honestiores	Members of the privileged class, i.e. those with property and position
Hostis publicus	Enemy of the state
Humiliores	Members of the lower socio-economic class
Illustris	Most Illustrious; high-level administrative rank
Labarum	Military standard designed in the shape of a Chi-Rho
Magister equitum	Master of the Horse
Magister memoriae	Senior secretary responsible for issuing written replies to petitions made to the emperor
Magister militum	Master of the Army; highest-ranking general directly below the emperor's authority
Magister officiorum	Master of Offices; official with administrative responsibility for all imperial offices
Magister praesentalis	*Magister* commanding the army in the emperor's presence
Magister scriniorum	Master of the Imperial Bureau of Secretaries
Monetarius	Member of imperial minting guild
Nobilissimus	Most Noble/Esteemed; rank bestowed upon members of the imperial family and household, and the senate
Patrimonium	Imperial household; the private estates of the emperor
Praefectus praetorio	Praetorian prefect, senior administrative official subordinate to the emperor only. There were four prefectures – Italy, Gaul, Illyricum, and the Orient/East
Praepositus sacri cubiculi	Provost of the sacred imperial bedchamber/ chamberlain; an extremely important role. This official was responsible for the imperial family's personal security and their palace

Quaestor sacri palatii	Senior legal advisor to the emperor; responsible for drafting all forms of law
Rescript	Imperial legal *constitutio* issued in response to petition
Res privata	Imperial treasury; privy purse
Tribunus et notarius	Imperial notary/clerk
Tyrannus	Usurper/pretender; also a deposed emperor
Vicarius	Vicar; official in charge of dioceses

Numismatic terms and symbols

AVG	Augustus/Augusta; the number of G's indicates concurrent reigning Augusti; e.g. AVGGG represents three emperors
Barbarous	Barbarian imitations of Roman coins
Christogram	Monogram depicting the Chi-Rho; typically engraved upon a shield or a *labarum*
Clipped	Illegal practice of cutting pieces of metal from coins
COM	*Comitatus*; mint of the imperial court
COMOB	*Comitatus obryziacum*/Pure gold from the comitatensian mint
COS	Consul
Cuirassed	Chest armor/breastplate
DD NN	*Dominorum Nostrorum or Domini Nostri*/Our Lords
Diadem	Ornamental headband with pearls, rosettes, or laurel leaves; most emperors after Constantine I (306–37) are diademed
DN	*Dominus Noster, Domina Nostra*/Our Lord, Lady
Draped	Clothing other than armor, i.e. a cloak
Exergue	Space below the field of a coin's reverse side
Field	Flat area of a coin; usually between the legend and central design or type
Globus cruciger	Globe/*orbis* with cross representing God's earthly power
Labarum	Military standard with Christogram
Laureate	Wearing a laurel wreath
Legend	Inscription typically around a coin's edge
Manus Dei	Hand of God; depicted by a hand reaching from above
Mappa	Napkin dropped to signal the start of a circus race; a consular symbol
Miliarense	Large silver coin

Mintmark	Letters/symbols denoting which mint or *officina* produced the coin
Moneta Sacra	Sacred money of the imperial mint
Nimbate	A *nimbus*/halo about the emperor/empress's head
OB	*Obryziacum aurum*/fine or pure gold
Obv.	Obverse/front or head side of a coin
Officina	Imperial mint workshop
Orbis terrarum	A globe symbolizing supreme power
Paludamentum	Senior military commander's cloak
PF	*Pius Felix*/pious and fortunate
PS	*Pusulatum*/pure silver; a relative term since late imperial coins' silver content varied considerably
Rev.	Reverse/back of a coin
Semissis	Gold coin worth a half of a solidus
Siliqua	Silver coin
SM	*Sacra Moneta*/sacred money; official state currency
Solidus	Gold coin introduced by Constantine I
Striking/struck	The physical act of stamping coinage with a design
Tremissis	Gold coin worth a third of a solidus
Type	Central reverse design
Victoriola	Small Victory standing on globe
VOT	*vota*/vows or prayers made for the emperor's reign

General bibliography

Primary sources

Ancient authors and collections

Acta Conciliorum Oecumenicorum. Edited by E. Schwartz. Berlin: De Gruyter. 1914–40.

Agnellus of Ravenna. *The Book of Pontiffs of the Church of Ravenna*. Translated by D. M. Deliyannis. Washington, D.C.: Catholic University of America Press. 2004.

Ambrose of Milan. *Sancti Ambrosii oratio de obitu Theodosii*. Translated by Sr. Mary Dolorosa Mannix (Washington, D.C.: Catholic University of America Press. 1925. Other translations consulted are: Leo P. McCauley. "Funeral Oration on the Death of Emperor Theodosius." In *Funeral Orations: The Fathers of the Church* 22: 303–32. Catholic University of America Press. 1953. And "Oration on the Death of Theodosius I." In *Ambrose of Milan: Political Letters and Speeches*. 2nd edition. Edited by J. H. W. G. Liebeschuetz: 174–203. TTH 43. Liverpool: Liverpool University Press. 2010.

Ambrose of Milan. *Epistulae et acta CSEL* 82: 1968–96; NPNF2–10.

Ammianus Marcellinus. *Historia Rerum Gestarum/Historical Events*. 3 volumes. Translated by J. C. Rolfe. London and Cambridge, MA: Harvard University Press. 1935–9.

Annals of Ravenna. In *Medieval Studies in Honor of A. Kingsley Porter*. Edited by Wilhelm Köhler: 125–38. Cambridge, MA: Harvard University Press. 1939.

Ante-Nicene Fathers. Edited by Philip Schaff. Grand Rapids, MI: Christian Classics Ethereal Library. 1885.

Apophthegmata Patrum: Collectio alphabetica/The Sayings of the Desert Fathers: The Alphabetical Collection. Translated by Benedicta Ward. Cistercian Studies Series 59. Kalamazoo, MI: Cistercian. 1975.

Appian. *Roman History: Bella civilia/The Civil Wars*. Volume 3. Translated by Horace White. Cambridge, MA.: Harvard University Press. 1914.

Augustine of Hippo. All texts from *CSEL*.

Ausonius. *Works*. 2 volumes. Translated by Hugh G. Evelyn-White. London and New York: Heinemann. 1919–21.

Chronica Gallica/The Gallic Chronicle of 452. A new critical edition by Richard W. Burgess in *Society and Culture in Late Antique Gaul: Revisiting the Sources*. Edited by Ralph W. Mathisen and Danuta Shanzer: 52–84. Aldershot: Ashgate. 2001.

Chronicle of Marcellinus: A Translation and Commentary with a Reproduction of Mommsen's Edition of the Text. Translated by Brian Croke. Byzantina Australiensia 7. Sydney: Australian Association for Byzantine Studies. 1995.

Chronicon Paschale. *PG* 92.

Chrysostom, John. *Homilies on the Statues*. NPNF1–09: 455–728.

Claudius Claudianus. 2 volumes. Translated by Maurice Platnauer. London and New York: Harvard University Press. 1922; also *Panegyricus de sexto consulatu Honorii Augusti*. Edited and translated by Michael Dewar. Oxford: Oxford University Press. 1996.

Consularia Italica. MGH (AA) IX. Edited by Theodor Mommsen: 249–339. Berlin. 1892.

Carmen de providentia Dei; attributed to Prosper of Aquitaine. Edited and translated by Michael P. McHugh. Patristic Studies 98. Washington, D.C.: Catholic University of America Press. 1964.

Epitome de Caesaribus: A Booklet about the Style of Life and the Manners of the Imperatores Sometimes Attributed to Sextus Aurelius Victor. 2nd edition. Translated by Thomas M. Banchich. Canisius College Translated Texts 1. Buffalo, NY: Canisius College. 2009.

Eunapius of Sardis. *Historiarum fragmenta*. FCHLRE 2: 2–150.

Eutropius. *Breviarium Ab Urbe Condita of Eutropius*. Edited and translated by Harry W. Bird. TTH 14. Liverpool: Liverpool University Press. 1993.

Gennadius, Jerome and Gennadius: *Lives of Illustrious Men*. NPNF2–03.

Gesta Collationis Carthaginensis habitae inter Catholicos et Donatistas anno 411/Acts of the Council of Carthage 411. Volume 11, Col. 1344A. Edited by Jacques Paul Migne. 1844–65.

Gregory of Nyssa. *Oratio funebris in Flaccillam imperatricem/Funeral Oration for the Empress Flaccilla*. Edited by Andreas Spira: 475–90. Gregorii Nysseni Opera 9. Leiden: Brill. 1967.

Gregory of Nyssa. *Oratio consolatoria in Pulcheriam/Consolation for Pulcheria*. Edited by Andreas Spira: 441–57. Gregorii Nysseni Opera 9. Leiden: Brill. 1967.

Hydatius. *The Chronicle of Hydatius and the Consularia Constantinopolitana: Two Contemporary Accounts of the Final Years of the Roman Empire*. Edited and translated by Richard W. Burgess. Oxford: Clarendon Press. 1993.

Jerome. *Letters and select works*, NPNF2–06.

John the Lydian. *De Magistratibus Republicae Romanae Libri Tres/On Powers, or The Magistracies of the Roman State in Three Books*. Introduction, critical text, translation, commentary by Anastasius C. Bandy. Memoirs of the American Philosophical Society Series 149. Philadelphia, PA: American Philosophical Society. 1983.

Jordanes. *Romana et Getica*. MGH (AA) V/1. Edited by Theodor Mommsen: 1–52. Munich. 1882.

Lactantius. *De mortibus persecutorum/On the Deaths of the Persecutors*. ANF-07.

Libanius. *Selected Works*. 2 volumes. Translated by Albert F. Norman. London and Cambridge, MA: Harvard University Press. 1977–87.

Liber Pontificalis. The Book of Pontiffs: The Ancient Biographies of the First Ninety Roman Bishops to AD 715. 3rd edition. TTH 6. Edited and translated by Raymond Davis. Liverpool: Liverpool University Press. 2010.

Michael the Syrian. *The Syriac Chronicle of Michael Rabo (The Great): A Universal History from the Creation*. Translated by Matti Moosa. Teaneck, NJ: Beth Antioch Press. 2014.

Nicene and Post-Nicene Fathers. 2 series. Edited by Philip Schaff and Henry Wace. Edinburgh and Buffalo, NY: Christian Classics Ethereal Library. 1886–1900.

Notitia Dignitatum in Partibus Orientis et Occidentis/List of Offices for the Eastern and Western Parts. Edited by Otto Seeck. Berlin. 1867. Reprinted Frankfurt-am-Main. 1962.

Olympiodorus of Thebes. *Historiarum fragmenta*. FCHLRE 2: 152–220.

Orientius of Auch. *The Commonitorium of Orientius*. Translated by Sr. Mildred Dolores Tobin. Washington, D.C.: Catholic University of America Press. 1945.

Orosius. *Seven Books of History against the Pagans*. Translated by Andrew T. Fear. TTH 54. Liverpool: Liverpool University Press. 2010.

Palladius. *Dialogue Concerning the life of St. John Chrysostom*. Translated by Herbert Moore. London: Macmillan. 1921.

Panegyrici Latini. In Praise of Later Roman Emperors: Translation and commentary by C. E. V. Nixon and Barbara Saylor Rodgers, with the Latin text of R. A. B Mynors. Berkeley, CA and Oxford: University of California Press. 1994.

Paulinus of Milan. *Life of Saint Ambrose*. In Ramsey, Boniface. *Ambrose*: 196–218. London and New York: Routledge: 1997.

Paulus Diaconus. *Historia Romana*. Edited by Amedeo Crivellucci, Fonti per la Storia d'Italia 51. Rome. 1913.

Philostorgius. *Historia Ecclesiastica*. Translated by Philip R. Amidon. Writings from the Greco-Roman World 23. Atlanta, GA: Society of Biblical Literature. 2007.

Plutarch. *Life of Alexander. Plutarch's Lives*. Volume 2. Translated by John Dryden. London and Toronto: Dent. 1920.

Procopius. *De bello Vandalico*. Books 3–4. Volume 2. Translated by Henry B. Dewing. London: Harvard University Press. 1916.

Prosperi Tironis epitoma chronicon/Chronicle of Prosper Tiro. In *From Roman to Merovingian Gaul: A Reader*. Edited and translated by Alexander C. Murray: 61–76. Readings in Medieval Civilizations and Cultures 5. Peterborough, NY: Broadview Press. 2000.

Prudentius. *Apotheosis*. Translated by Henry J. Thomson. 2 volumes. London and Cambridge, MA: Harvard University Press. 1949.

Prudentius. *Contra Symmachum Book II: Introduction, Translation and Commentary*. Translated by Michael Peter Brown. Unpublished thesis. Newcastle upon Tyne University. 2003.

Psellus, Michael. *Chronographia*. Translated by Edgar Robert Ashton Sewter. Yale: Yale University Press. 1953.

Rufinus. *Historia Ecclesiastica*. NPNF2–02: 1086–1458.

Rutilius Namatianus. *De reditu suo/On his Return*. Translated by John Wight Duff and Arnold M. Duff. *Minor Latin Poets*: 753–829. London and Cambridge, MA: Harvard University Press. 1934.

Scriptores Historiae Augustae/Augustan History. Volume 3. Translated by David Magie. Cambridge, MA: Harvard University Press. 1932.

Severus of Antioch. *Hymns*. Edited and translated by Ernest W. Brooks, *PO* 6–7. Paris: Firmin-Didot. 1911.

Severus of Minorca. *Letter on the Conversion of the Jews*. Edited and translated by Scott Bradbury. *CPL* 576. Oxford: Clarendon Press. 1996.

Sidonius Apollinaris. *Poems and Letters*. Translated by William B. Anderson. London and Cambridge, MA: Harvard University Press. 1936–65.

Socrates Scholasticus. *Historia Ecclesiastica*. NPNF2–02: 23–451.

Sozomen. *Historia Ecclesiastica*. NPNF2–02: 521–959.

Symmachus. *Relationes*. NPNF2–10: 894–904.

Symmachus. *Epistulae, Q. Aurelii Symmachi que supersunt*. Edited by Otto Seeck. MGH (AA) VI. Berlin. 1883.

Tacitus. *Agricola and Germany*. Translated by Anthony R. Birley. Oxford: Oxford University Press. 1999.

Themistius. *The Private Orations of Themistius*. Transformation of the Classical Heritage 29. Translated by Robert J. Penella. Berkeley, CA: University of California Press. 2000.

Themistius. *Politics, Philosophy and Empire in the Fourth Century: Themistius' Select Orations*. Translated Texts for Historians 36. Translated with commentary by Peter Heather and David Moncur. Liverpool: Liverpool University Press. 2001.

Theodoret of Cyrus. *Ecclesiastical History, Dialogues, and Letters*. NPNF2–02: 71–812.

Theophanes. *The Chronicle of Theophanes Confessor: Byzantine and Near Eastern History, AD 284–813*. Edited and translated by Cyril Mango and Roger Scott, with the assistance of Geoffrey Greatrex. New York: Clarendon Press. 1997.

Vegetius. *Epitoma rei militaris/On Military Matters*. Edited by Michael D. Reeve. Oxford: Clarendon Press. 2004.

Virgil. *The Aeneid*. Translated by W. F. Jackson Knight. London: Penguin. 1958.

Zonaras. *The History of Zonaras from Alexander Severus to the Death of Theodosius the Great*. Translated by Thomas M. Banchich and Eugene N. Lane. London and New York: Routledge. 2009.

Zosimus. *New History*. Translated by Ronald T. Ridley. Byzantina Australiensia 2. Sydney: Australian Association for Byzantine Studies. 1982.

Epigraphic reference works

CIL Corpus Inscriptionum Latinarum. Berlin. 1893–.

ICUR Inscriptiones Christianae Urbis Romae Septimo Saeculo Antiquiores. 2 volumes. Edited by G. B. De Rossi. Rome. 1857–61.

IEph Inscriptiones Ephesi/Die Inschriften von Ephesos. Inschriften griechischer Städte aus Kleinasien 11–17. Edited by H. Wankel and R. Merkelbach et al. Cologne. 1979–84.

IG Inscriptiones Graecae. 49 volumes. Berlin. 1873–.

ILAfr. Inscriptions Latines d'Afrique. Edited by René Cagnat, Alfred Merlin, and Louis Chatelain. Paris. 1923.

ILS Inscriptiones Latinae Selectae. Edited by Hermann Dessau. Berlin. 1892–1916.

Legal reference works

Corpus Iuris Civilis (*CIC*). Edited by Theodor Mommsen. 3 volumes. Berlin. 1872–95.

Codex Iustinianus. *CIC*, Volume 2.

Codex Theodosianus (*CTh*). Edited by Theodor Mommsen. MGH (*AA*) XI. Berlin. 1894; *The Theodosian Code and Novels and the Sirmondian Constitutions*. Translated by Clyde Pharr, in collaboration with Theresa Sherrer Davidson and Mary Brown Pharr. Princeton, NJ: Princeton University Press. 1952.

Constitutiones Sirmondianae. Pharr: 477–86.

Institutiones. CIC, Volume 1.
Iustiniani Digesta. CIC, Volume 1.
Novellae. CIC, Volume 3.
Novellae Theodosianae. Pharr: 487–572.

Numismatic reference works

Bendall, Simon. *Byzantine Weights: An Introduction.* London: Lennox Gallery. 1996.
Catalogue of the Byzantine and Early Mediaeval Antiquities in the Dumbarton Oaks Collection, Volumes 1–2 by M. C. Ross. Washington, D.C. 1962–5; 2nd ed. of vol. 2 published 2005; Volume 3 by K. Weitzmann. 1972.
Classical Numismatic Group, Inc. Lancaster, PA and London. 1976–. www.cngcoins.com.
Cohen, Henry. *Description historique des monnaies frappées sous l'Empire romain.* 8 volumes. Paris. 1880–92. www.virtualcohen.com/henry-cohen-s-work.
Dumbarton Oaks Collection. Edited by Philip Grierson and Melinda Mays. *Catalogue of Late Roman Coins in the Dumbarton Oaks Collection and in the Whitmore Collection: From Arcadius and Honorius to the Accession of Anastasius.* Washington, D.C.: Dumbarton Oaks Research Library and Collection. 1992.
Late Roman Bronze Coinage, AD 324–498. Volume 1. Edited by R. A. G. Carson, P. V. Hill, and J. P. C. Kent. London: Spink. 1978.
Portable Antiquities Scheme. www.finds.org.uk.
Reinhart, Wilhelm. 1938. "Die Münzen des tolosanischen Reiches der Westgoten." *DJN* 1: 107–35.
Roman Imperial Coinage, Volume 9: *Valentinian I – Theodosius I.* Edited by J. W. E. Pearce. London: Spink. 1951.
Roman Imperial Coinage, Volume 10: *The Divided Empire and the Fall of the Western Parts, AD 395–491.* Edited by J. P. C. Kent. London: Spink. 1994.
Royal Numismatic Society of London. 1904–. http://numismatics.org.uk/.
Sylloge Nummorum Graecorum. Berlin. 1957–. www.sylloge-nummorum-graecorum.org/.

Secondary literature

Ando, Clifford. 2000. *Imperial Ideology and Provincial Loyalty in the Roman Empire.* Berkley, CA: University of California Press.
Bartholomew, Philip. 1982. "Fifth-Century Facts." *Britannia* 13: 261–70.
Birley, Anthony R. 2005. *The Roman Government of Britain.* Oxford: Oxford University Press.
Brown, Peter. 1978. *The Making of Late Antiquity.* Cambridge, MA and London: Harvard University Press.
Brown, Peter. 1995. *Authority and the Sacred: Aspects of the Christianization of the Roman World.* Cambridge: Cambridge University Press.
Brown, Peter. 2006. *The World of Late Antiquity AD 150–750*, 2nd edition. London: Thames and Hudson.
Burns, Thomas S. 1994. *Barbarians within the Gates of Rome: A Study of Roman Military Policy and the Barbarians, c. 375–425 AD.* Indiana, IN: Indiana University Press.

Bury, John B. 1923. *History of the Later Roman Empire: From the Death of Theodosius I to the Death of Justinian.* London: Macmillan & Co.

Cameron, Alan, and Long, Jacqueline. 1993. *Barbarians and Politics at the Court of Arcadius.* Berkley, CA: University of California Press.

Cameron, Averil. 2012. *The Mediterranean World in Late Antiquity, 395–700 AD.* 2nd edition. Routledge History of the Ancient World. London and New York: Routledge.

Cromwell, Richard S. 1998. *The Rise and Decline of the Late Roman Field Army.* Shippensburg, PA: White Mane.

Dignas, Beate, and Winter, Engelbert. 2007. *Rome and Persia in Late Antiquity: Neighbours and Rivals.* Cambridge: Cambridge University Press.

Elton, Hugh. 1996. *Warfare in Roman Europe, AD 350–425.* Oxford: Oxford University Press.

Frere, Sheppard. 1998. *Britannia: A History of Roman Britain.* 3rd edition. London: Routledge.

García-Gasco, Rosa, González Sánchez, Sergio, and Hernández de la Fuente, David (eds). 2013. *The Theodosian Age AD 379–455: Power, Place, Belief and Learning at the End of the Western Empire.* British Archaeological Reports (BAR): International Series.

Goffart, Walter. 1980. *Barbarians and Romans: The Techniques of Accommodation, AD 418–584.* Princeton, NJ: Princeton University Press.

Harl, Kenneth W. 1996. *Coinage in the Roman Economy, 300 BC to AD 700.* Baltimore, MD and London: The Johns Hopkins Press.

Harries, Jill. 1999. *Law and Empire in Late Antiquity.* Cambridge: Cambridge University Press.

Hodgkin, Thomas. 1880. *Italy and her Invaders.* Oxford: Clarendon Press.

Hodgkin, Thomas. 1889. *The Dynasty of Theodosius, or Eighty Years' Struggle with the Barbarians.* Oxford: Clarendon Press.

Honoré, Tony. 1998. *Law in the Crisis of Empire, AD 379–455.* Oxford: Oxford University Press.

Howgego, Christopher, Heuchert, Volker, and Burnett, Andrew. 2005. *Coinage and Identity in the Roman Provinces.* Oxford: Oxford University Press.

Humphries, Mark. 2008. "From Usurper to Emperor: The Politics of Legitimation in the Age of Constantine I." *JLA* 1: 85–100.

James, Edward. 2009. *Europe's Barbarians AD 200–600.* London: Pearson Longman.

Jones, Michael E. 1996. *The End of Roman Britain.* New York: Cornell University Press.

Kelly, Christopher. 2004. *Ruling the Later Roman Empire.* Cambridge, MA: Harvard University Press.

Lançon, Bertrand. 2000. *Rome in Late Antiquity: Everyday Life and Urban Change, AD 312–609.* Translated by Antonia Nevill. Edinburgh: Edinburgh University Press.

Liebeschuetz, J. H. W. G. 1991. *Barbarians and Bishops: Army, Church, and State in the Age of Arcadius and Chrysostom.* Oxford: Oxford University Press.

Lipps, Johannes, Machado, Carlos, and von Rummel, Philip (eds). 2013. *The Sack of Rome in 410 AD: The Event, its Context and its Impact.* Proceedings of the Conference held at the German Archaeological Institute in Rome, 04–06 November 2010. Deutsches Archäologisches Institut Rom: Palilia 28.

Lütkenhaus, Werner. 2012. "Observations on Zosimus' British Cities." *Britannia* 43: 268–70.

MacMullen, Ramsay. 1963. *Soldier and Civilian in the Later Roman Empire*. Cambridge: Cambridge University Press.

MacMullen, Ramsay. 1966. *Enemies of the Roman Order*. Cambridge: Cambridge University Press.

Matthews, John F. 1975. *Western Aristocracies and Imperial Court, AD 364–425*. Oxford: Clarendon Press.

Matthews, John F. 2000. *Laying Down the Law: A Study of the Theodosian Code*. New Haven, CT: Yale University Press.

Matthews, John F. 2007. *The Roman Empire of Ammianus*. New edition. Ann Arbor, MI: Michigan Classical Press.

Meyer, Elizabeth A. 2004. *Legitimacy and Law in the Roman World*. Cambridge: Cambridge University Press.

Millar, Fergus. 1977. *The Emperor in the Roman World, 31 BC–AD 337*. London: Duckworth Press.

Mitchell, Stephen. 2007. *A History of the Later Roman Empire, AD 284–641*. London: Blackwell Press.

O'Donnell, James J. 2005. *Augustine: A New Biography*. New York: HarperCollins.

Rousseau, Philip, and Raithel, Jutta (eds). 2009. *A Companion to Late Antiquity*. Blackwell Companions to the Ancient World. Ancient History. Malden, MA: Wiley-Blackwell.

Salzman, Michele Renée. 2017. "From a Classical to a Christian City: Civic Euergetism and Charity in Late Antique Rome." *Studies in Late Antiquity* 1.1: 65–85.

Salway, Peter. 1981. *Roman Britain*: Oxford: Oxford University Press.

Sarantis, Alexander and Christie, Neil (eds). 2013. *War and Warfare in Late Antiquity*. 2 volumes. *LAA* 8. Leiden and Boston: Brill.

Sauer, Eberhard W. 2003. *The Archaeology of Religious Hatred in the Roman and Early Medieval World*. Stroud: Tempus.

Sivan, Hagith S. 1985. "An Unedited Letter of the Emperor Honorius to the Spanish Soldiers." *ZPE* 61: 273–87.

Snyder, Christopher A. 1998. *An Age of Tyrants: Britain and the Britons, AD 400–600*. University Park, PA: Pennsylvania State University Press.

Varner, Eric. 2004. *Mutilation and Transformation: Damnatio Memoriae and Roman Imperial Portraiture*. Leiden: Brill.

Walton, Philippa J. 2012. *Rethinking Roman Britain: Coinage and Archaeology*. Collection Moneta 137. Wetteren: Moneta.

Wardman, Alan E. 1984. "Usurpers and Internal Conflicts in the Fourth Century AD." *Historia* 33: 220–37.

Wickham, Chris. 2005. *Framing the Early Middle Ages: Europe and the Mediterranean, 400–800*. Oxford: Oxford University Press.

Index

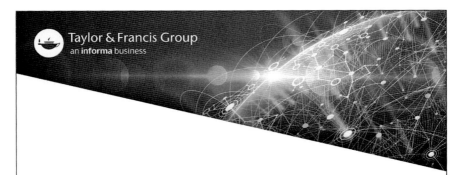